Online Education

Online Education

An Innovative Approach and Success in the Virtual Classroom

BOLA BAYODE, PH.D.

ISBN: 9780578655703

Library of Congress Control Number: 2020903963
Bright University Press, Charlotte, NC, USA
Printed in the USA

CONTENTS

PREFACE

Distance education has been an integral part of learning for many centuries. The learning method provides an opportunity for students who cannot achieve their academic goals through the traditional face-to-face environment to do so without the rigors of commuting to campus every day. Before the Internet became pervasive, schools primarily delivered lectures to students by correspondence. The explosion of web technologies in the early 1990s fundamentally changed the complexion of distance education and catapulted it to a new level. Educational institutions now have varieties of communication channels to connect with students, and they can receive lectures anytime and anywhere without waiting for the mailman.

Online course registrations have increased and continued to accelerate beyond the rate of overall higher education enrollments in recent years. The number of academic institutions that offer online programs has equally skyrocketed with no sign of abating anytime soon. As the number of students taking online education increase, debates have ensued over whether what online education can truly achieve has been exaggerated. At conferences and in publications, critics argue that schools may be sacrificing quality at the altar of convenience due to the lack of face-to-face interactions that exist in the virtual classroom. While the emotions that this debate provokes is not likely to subside any time soon, the incontestable fact is that online education is gaining ground every day and fast becoming a gold standard in higher education. In schools where online learning has not become part of their academic repertoires, professors use varieties of learning technologies to enhance teachings in the classroom.

As students at all levels look for flexibility and convenience, technology has become indispensable in meeting their educational needs. In organizations, technology is no longer a means to automate the work-process, but a tool for training and developing employees in today's highly competitive global environment. In the 21st Century, information and communications technology competence will become not only a prerequisite for learning and a gateway to prosperity but a catalyst for survival in the world that is increasingly becoming computerized.

Based on the current trajectory, observers believe that by the middle of this century, the majority of learning will take place online. Others who would not go that far acknowledged that the days of the traditional chalkboard instruction are waning as the teaching method is no longer sufficient in meeting the needs of today's students, especially those who grew up with computers. As education institutions embrace online education and governments at various levels see it as a solution to the overcrowding of classrooms, students must understand the intricacies of online learning as their academic success and achievements in future careers hinged on their knowledge of various web technologies that have become essential parts of today's pedagogies.

The author brings over two decades of practical experience in online education into the discussions and views shared in this book. Over the years, the author has taught and mentored thousands of students in the virtual classroom, which enables him to understand not only the challenges that students face in class but the strategies they can apply to succeed in an online course.

In this book, the author shares the best practices in online education that will benefit all categories of learners, from beginner students to advanced students. Apart from students, professors, school administrators, educators, researchers, and trainers will find arrays of information and resources embedded in this book useful in understanding online education and contemporary issues facing higher education. This book also contains valuable information that will enrich the knowledge of anyone interested in e-learning.

ORGANIZATION OF THIS BOOK

This book has twelve chapters that give a 360-degree view of online education. Each chapter begins with a set of objectives and an introduction and ends with a summary of the main points and discussion questions.

Chapter one provides the background to online education. In this chapter, we look at the nature of distance education and how the learning method has changed over the years. We also look at the history of the Internet, and the impact web technologies have on education.

Chapter two looks at the history of distance education and the roles that individuals played before academic institutions started offering correspondence courses. The section also looks at different generations of technologies and how they have impacted online education.

Chapter three delves into how different authors define online education. The chapter identifies different types of e-learning and the difference between online learning and traditional face-to-face instruction. The chapter also looks at some of the misconceptions about online education and how they conform to reality.

Chapter four focuses on online learning formats. The chapter discusses synchronous, asynchronous, and hybrid learning and identifies the advantages and disadvantages of each learning format.

Chapter five looks at how online education has grown in higher education and organizations. The chapter analyzes how the shortage of teachers, the global demand for higher education, the emergence of new economies, economic factors, and government policies contributes to the growth.

Chapter six discusses the emerging trends in online education and how blended learning, Massive Open Online Courses (MOOCs), social learning, gamification, simulation, personalized learning, adaptive learning, and mobile learning are recalibrating how students learn and how education institutions deliver their educational programs.

Chapter seven focuses on online learning technologies. The section looks at different learning management systems and the factors that institutions must consider before launching an online program. The chapter also discusses the functionalities of various course management systems and online classroom management.

Chapter eight outlines the benefits of online education. The chapter discusses the benefits of online learning to students, academic institutions, and other stakeholders. The section also looks at how organizations use e-learning technologies in their training programs.

Chapter nine discusses the challenges of online education and offers suggestions on how to overcome the obstacles.

Chapter ten discusses the strategies that students can apply to succeed in a virtual classroom. The chapter also identifies the questions that students should ask and answer before taking an online course.

Chapter eleven offers the best practices in online education. The section discusses the online classroom etiquette and the communication taboos in the virtual classroom.

Chapter twelve looks at the future of higher education. The chapter discusses how technology, globalization, internationalization, collaborations, and transnational education models will impact higher education and revolutionize the industry.

Each chapter contains a summary of the main points and discussion questions to stimulate understanding of the topics covered in this book.

The glossary contains definitions of key concepts and terminologies used in this book for quick review.

HOW TO USE THIS BOOK

The organization of this book makes it an excellent resource in a classroom setting, either as stand-alone course material or as a supplemental resource. This text is appropriate for undergraduate and graduate students at any stage of their study. Trainers can use this book for training, workshops, and conferences.

BOOK FORMAT

This book is available in paperbacks and digital formats.

For further inquiries, please contact onlineeducation@bright.university

1

ONLINE EDUCATION AND THE INTERNET

Learning Objectives: After studying this chapter, you should be able to:

1. Understand the elements of online education
2. Examine the nature of distance education
3. Discuss the origins of the Internet
4. Understand the impact of the Internet on education

INTRODUCTION

Distance education has metamorphosed since the learning technique became part of the instructional method over a century ago. Not only has its mode of delivery changed, but its terminology has evolved several times as well. The term has morphed from **home study** or **correspondence study** to **distance education.** In recent years, descriptions such as **online education, online learning, e-learning**, or **web-based learning** have become popular. Despite the evolution in terminology and the delivery method, the objective of distance education in meeting the needs of students who cannot take courses in a face-to-face environment has doggedly remained the same. Correspondingly, authors have interchangeably applied these terminologies to mean the same thing as it will be the case throughout this book.

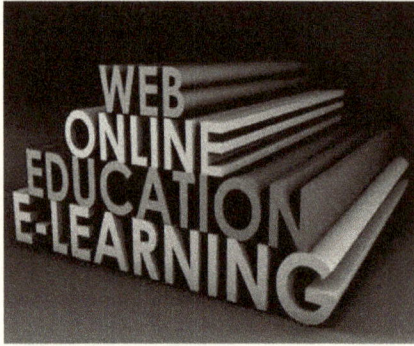

Chapter one provides the background to the major issues addressed in this book. In this chapter, we examine the nature of distance education and how it has altered the way students learn and transformed how education institutions deliver their academic programs. We also look at the origin of the Internet and the impact on education.

The Nature of Distance Education

Distance education has become a viable alternative to face-to-face learning, given the number of students who take their courses online and the number of educational institutions that offer online programs. In 2017, despite the decline in the overall post-secondary enrollments in the United States, the number of college students who took online classes grew. The number of students who took at least one class online grew from 31.1% in 2016 to 33.1% in 2017, and students who took blended courses (online and face-to-face courses) increased from 16.4% in 2016 to 17.6% in 2017. Among all institutions, public and private nonprofit colleges and universities experienced a two-percentage-point increase in the number of students who studied online, and schools that previously did not offer online program increased their online course enrollments.[1]

The **Center for Digital Education** (CDE) found that increased student interest is driving e-learning adoption. Although engagement vary between K-12 and higher education, 65% of tertiary institutions cited student demand and expectation as the primary factor for technology adoption, and other significant factors included instructor demand, improving student engagement, preparing students for the future and increasing student achievement.[2]

The **e-learning** market is expanding and rapidly growing as the worldwide market for online education reached $35.6 billion in 2011. The five-year **compound annual growth rate** (CAGR) estimated at around 7.6% puts the revenue in the sector at $51.5 billion by 2016 and the **learning management system** (LMS) market expected to grow by 23.17% between 2017 and 2018.[3] In 2018, the e-learning market was valued at $190 billion and predicted to increase at a **CAGR** of 7% from 2019 to 2025.[4]

The full adoption and recognition of technology for teaching and training has fast-tracked the development of learning management systems. Emerging technologies such as **augmented reality** (AR) and **virtual reality** (VR) devices, **artificial intelligence** (AI), **Big Data**, **machine learning**, and **wearable devices** will further expand the e-learning market. Access to e-learning materials will be instantaneous because cloud-based technologies will replace conventional learning systems and eliminates the need to download and install specific software applications before taking an online course.[5]

The Early Stage of Distance Education

Distance education has been around for many centuries. Although historians traced the genesis of distance education to the Roman Empire period, its wide adoption in the academic environment began about 200 years ago.

At the start of distance learning, students hardly had any interactions with their classmates and the opportunity to challenge the concepts taught in class. Students were primarily empty vessels into which professors poured knowledge. For decades, schools offered courses in shorthand, secretariat studies, accounting, commerce, law, and other vocational subjects. As distance education became popular, educational institutions extended course offerings to science, technology, humanities, and other disciplines. Today, distance learning has gone mainstream that education institutions deliver most courses online, from basic subjects that require little academic rigor, to advanced courses that involve complex analyses and higher-order thinking.

From the mid-1800s to the early 1900s, students received lectures primarily by **correspondence** (the mailing of course materials and receiving feedback through the post office) and used the same method to communicate with their schools. As society became advanced, educational institutions introduced the **radio, television, audio-tapes, cartridges, cassettes, videotapes**, and **CD-ROMs** to complement correspondence that had become deficient in meeting the needs of students. Suffices to say, these electronic devices provided some relief to students, but they did not go far enough to reduce their frustrations because the tools could only handle one-way communication at a given time. Students had to wait for several weeks before receiving their educational materials and the feedback they desperately needed from their professors.

In the early 1990s, there was a paradigmatic shift in distance education due to the exponential growth of the **Internet**. The new technology recalibrated not only the way students learn but how they communicate with their classmates and instructors.

Origins of the Internet

The **Internet** is a collection of loosely connected **networks** that are accessible by individual **computer hosts**, in a variety of ways, and available to anyone with a computer and a network connection anywhere in the world.[6] The history of the Internet began in the early 1960s due to the concerns that the **U.S. Department of Defense** (DoD) had about the possible effects of a nuclear attack on its computing facilities. On the 6th of December 1967, **DoD** awarded a contract to the **Advanced Research Projects Agency**

(ARPA) to study and design a computer network that could respond to the perceived threat of scientific and technological advantage the then **Soviet Union** exhibited when it launched the **Sputnik Satellite** to the orbit. **ARPA** hired the best brainpower in computing technology at the leading U.S. universities and research institutions and funded the project for many years.[7]

In an unrelated initiative but proved to be momentous, as **ARPA** was working on the **DOD** network project, a **RAND** (a contraction of **R**esearch and **D**evelopment) researcher, Paul Baran, was working on a classified U.S. Air Force contract. The project involved ways to strengthen the U.S telecommunication infrastructure so that it could survive a nuclear attack. **RAND** was also building telecommunication networks around the world that could send information through multiple channels instead of a central computer system, so the **Network** could function if parts of it were damaged or sabotaged by the enemy.[8]

In 1969, the researchers at the **ARPA** had a breakthrough when the **Advanced Research Projects Agency Network** (ARPANET) they developed connected four computers at Stanford University, University of California, Los Angeles (UCLA), University of California, Santa Barbara (UC-Santa Barbara), and the University of Utah. The network later became the framework for developing the **Internet**.[9]

ARPA achieved its primary objective within two years when the agency designed a system that could control the weapons systems and transferred files, but other uses for the network emerged in the early 1970s. In 1971, Raymond (Ray) Samuel Tomlinson, a researcher at **ARPA**, made improvements to the local inter-user mail program the **Send Message** (SNDMSG) command when he used the program to compose and send a message to himself and other users' mailboxes from another **ARPANET** computer.[10] In no time, many military and education research communities embraced the communication method, and other stakeholders used the networking system to transfer files and access computer remotely.[11]

Despite the success that **ARPA** achieved in connecting multiple computers, its mission of developing standardized **protocols** to guide **packet switching** and communication between several computers connected to a "galactic" network was unaccomplished. The connections of four machines at Stanford University, UCLA, UC-Santa Barbara, and the University of Utah was a milestone but did not constitute a "galactic" network. There was also a vast difference between the **Network Control Program** (NCP) that connected a national grid and the **NCP** that connect multiple networks globally. As a result, several working groups and organizations emerged in the 1980s and 1990s that pursued the galactic system task for interoperability between various networks and to resolve the standard issues. In 1986, the **Internet Engineering Task Force** (IETF) was established and took over responsibility for short-to-medium-term Internet engineering issues, previously handled by the **Internet Activities Board** (IAB).[12]

In 1998, the **Internet Corporation for Assigned Names and Numbers** (ICANN) which began as a public-private partnership started managing and coordinating the **Domain Name System** (DNS) to ensure that every web address is unique, and all users on the **Internet** can find all valid addresses when they search the web. By the mid-1990s, **ARPA** had achieved its mission as people from different countries connected to multiple computers on the Internet.[13]

The Internet in a Changing World

The **Internet** or the **World Wide Web** (WWW) has collapsed the communication walls that, for many generations, polarized people living in different parts of the world and opened a floodgate of opportunities for people to interact with ease, never fathomed in the history of human development. The United Nations specialized agency estimated that 3.9 billion, which is over 51% of the global population, would gain access to the Internet by the end of 2018.[14] In March 2019, over 4.3 billion people around the world had connected to the Internet.[15]

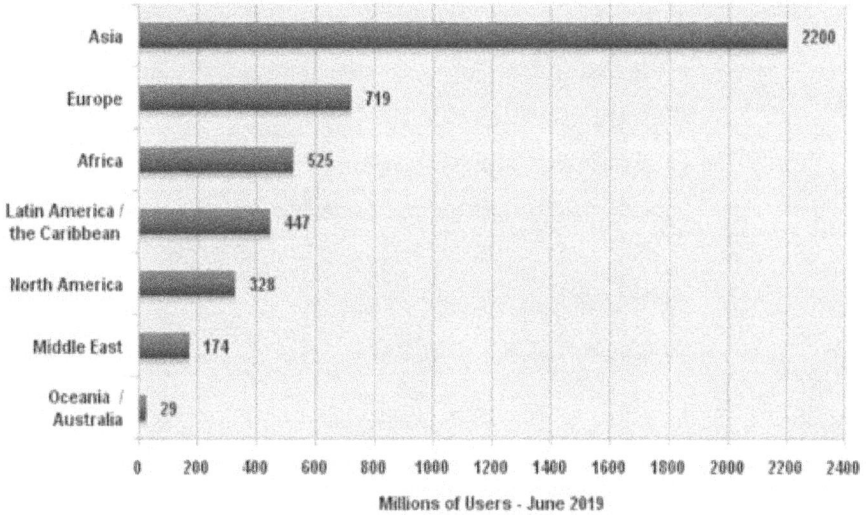

Figure: 1.1   Internet Users in the World by Geographic Regions

Source: Internet World Stats. Miniwatts Marketing Group (June 30, 2019).

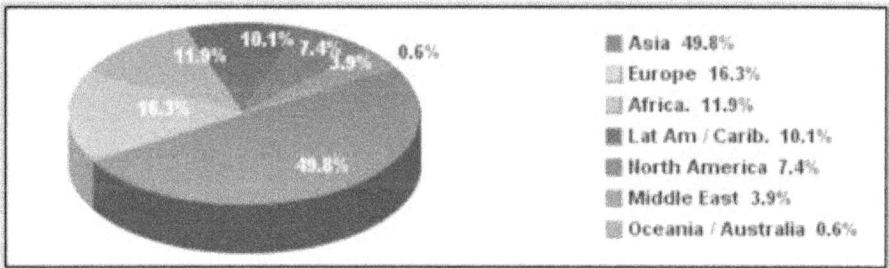

Figure: 1.2   Internet Users Distribution in the World by Regions

Source: Internet World Stats. Miniwatts Marketing Group (June 30, 2019).

Figure 1.1 shows the number of Internet users in each region, while figure 1.2 states the ratios of users in each area relative to the world population. In 2019, Asia had the highest number of people connected to the Internet at 49.8%. The Internet users in the region surpassed other regions because Asia had the world highest population led by China and India, with a population of 1.4 and 1.3 billion, respectively.[16]

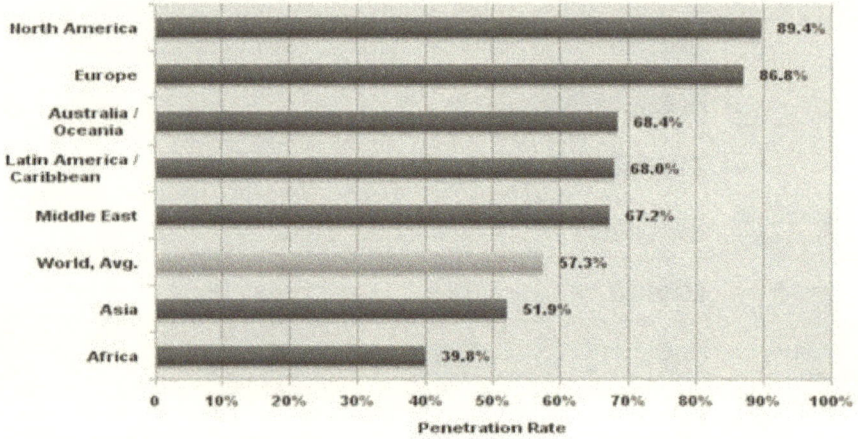

Figure: 1.3   Internet World Penetration Rates by Geographic Regions (June 2019)

Source: Internet World Stats. Miniwatts Marketing Group (June 30, 2019).

As figure 1.3 indicates, Asia had a penetration rate of 51.9%, which was lesser than North America, Europe, Australia, Latin America, or the Middle East. Africa had the lowest rate of 39.8% as of June 2019 compared with other regions.[17]

Overall, developing countries experienced Internet growth from 7.7% in 2005 to 45.3% at the end of 2018.[18] In just over ten years, Africa recorded the highest growth in internet connection from 2.1% in 2005 to 24% in 2018. The number of households with access to a computer also increased from 3.6% in 2005 to 9.2% in 2018 and 90% of people with Internet access use a 3G or higher speed network, while 96% of the global population now live within a range of a mobile system.[19]

The Internet and Education

The **Information and Communication Technologies** (ICTs) revolution has been driving knowledge acquisition and global economies for many decades. **ICT** has enhanced our cognitive capacities and communicative capabilities by transforming how we produce, store, retrieve, analyze big and small data, and changed our abilities to communicate textually,

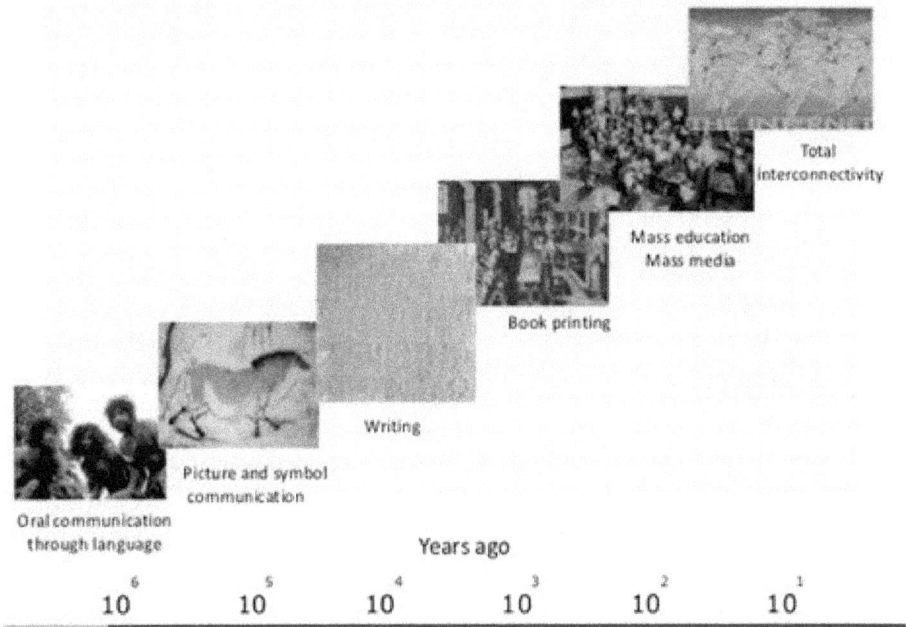

Figure: 1.4 Stages of Human Communication
Source: Rij & Warrington, 2011.

audio-visually, and graphically. The modern technology (starting with audiovisual broadcasting and the rise of computers) has changed how we communicate like those that began in the prehistoric times with the evolution of human speech (thousands of years ago), the creation of meaningful pictures (tens of thousands of years ago), symbols and writing (thousands of years ago), and book printing (hundreds of years ago).[20]

In retrospect, the education industry is the greatest beneficiary of the technology revolution that the world witnessed in the latter part of the 20th century. The **ICT** has transformed learning in ways that allow for real growth in numbers and various types of education providers, curriculum developers, modes of delivery, and pedagogical innovations.[21] Technology has significantly impacted the education industry, and with the availability of open-source content and Wikis, the roles of teachers are rapidly changing. Teachers are no longer the sole repository of content and knowledge but serve as guides, facilitators, and collaborators in students' educational experience in the classroom.[22]

The increased Internet penetration enables teachers to acquire the necessary skill, especially in areas where there is a shortage of professional training opportunities and use online resources to participate in professional discussions. For example, Polycom and CAPspace developed programs for training instructors, and social networking tools they can leverage in collaborating with their contemporaries around the world.[23] The Internet enables students to use cheaper digital learning materials in place of printed textbooks, which for the most part, scarce and generally expensive.[24] Students can attend institutions of their choice, no matter where they live, and education institutions can recruit students into their academic programs from any country.

Despite the high number of students taking online courses, 68.01% of students surveyed in the United States in 2017 did not enroll in online classes.[25] Online learning will transform as technology offers better interactive features. Artificial Intelligence and immersive technologies will replace current e-learning tools and change the roles of teachers in the virtual classroom.

Summary of Main Points

- Distance education has evolved over the years, and its terminology changed several times as well. The term has changed from home study or correspondence study to distance education. Recently, web-based learning, online learning, e-learning, and other descriptions have become popular.
- The number of students who take online courses and the number of educational institutions that offer online programs continue to increase each year, and the e-learning market continues to expand.
- The history of the Internet began in the early 1960s. The technology exploded in the early 1990s with a significant impact on education.
- The number of people with an Internet connection and the penetration rates is increasing as more than half of the world population has Internet access, and 96% of the global population now live within a range of a mobile system.

- Online education will continue to grow. Artificial intelligence and immersive technologies will change the role of teachers in the classroom.

Discussion Questions

1. Distance education has evolved over the years. Discuss the early stage of distance learning and how the Internet has transformed the learning technique.
2. The Internet has changed the education industry. From your research and experience, discuss how it has changed the industry. Identify and discuss some of the ills of the Internet to society.
3. Observers believe the future of higher education is online. Do you agree or disagree with the statement? Support your position with credible sources and evaluate based on your personal experience or from what you read in the news.
4. The Internet is the tool-of-choice that education institutions use in facilitating online education. Identify and discuss other learning technologies and how those technologies will impact online learning in the future.

2

THE HISTORY OF DISTANCE EDUCATION

Learning Objectives: After studying this chapter, you should be able to:

1. Understand distance education in the past
2. Examine distance education today
3. Discuss generations of online education technologies

INTRODUCTION

In this chapter, we look at the history of distance education and the roles that individuals played before academic institutions embraced the learning technique. We also examine how different technology impacted distance learning from the time education institutions used correspondence for distance education to when the Internet became the primary delivery method.

Distance Education in the Past

The history of distance education can be traced back to 1728 when Caleb Phillips advertised in the **Boston Gazette**, seeking students to take short-hand lessons via **correspondence** that he would send to them weekly and instructed like students who lived in Boston.[1] In 1836, Josiah Holbrook launched the **lyceum movement** in Connecticut, in the U.S. and used the organization to promote learning for males and females of all ages on the belief that everyone in the society should have access to education.[2]

In the 1840's Isaac Pitman, a British educator, started teaching shorthand through Great Britain's Penny Post. Pitman would send an assignment to students by mail and used the same medium to send them more work and feedback. His symbolic writing was popular among secretaries, journalists, and individuals who did a great deal of note-taking and writing.[3]

In 1873, Anna Ticknor launched the **Anna Ticknor Society** in the United States with a mission to eradicating illiteracy from society. Her organization offered home studies to the underprivileged class, especially women, who did not have access to education. The Boston-based volunteer society provided correspondence instructions to over ten thousand of its members over a twenty-four-year period.[4]

The Industrial Revolution that began in the mid 18th century in Europe and America transported the two societies from the agrarian economy to an industrial economy. On the same token, it intensified the need for workers with the required skills to operate the specially-designed machinery used for mass production of iron and textile materials.[5] In the mid-1800s, schools began offering correspondence courses to individuals who wanted to study but could not quit their jobs or afford the high cost of traditional education.

In 1858, the University of London launched its **external study programs** for students who lived outside London and students from abroad.[6] In 1874, Wesleyan University in Illinois became the first institution in the United States to offer distance education, and the University of Wisconsin was the first to use the term *distance education* in its school catalog published in 1892.[7]

Between 1903 and 1918, distance education budded under President Charles Van Hise at the University of Wisconsin. During the period, the institution enrolled over thirty-five thousand Wisconsin residents in its distance education program and generated over $800,000 in tuition fees.[8] In 1890, Thomas Foster founded the Colliery Engineer School of Mines and offered courses in mine safety to railroad and ironworkers. The school later changed its name to **International Correspondence School** (ICS), and by 1923 the school had enrolled over 2.5 million students in various courses.[9]

In the early 1900s, distance education accelerated in the United States. From 1918 to 1946, the U.S. government granted over 200 radio licenses to educational institutions across the country to broadcast lectures to students. Between 1922 and 1923, the **Federal Communications Commission** (FCC) issued radio licenses to the University of Salt Lake City, the University of Wisconsin, the University of Minnesota, and Pennsylvania State College.[10] However, there was a lack of interest from educators and the public due to the poor quality of teaching. Also, commercial broadcasters opposed radio instruction because they contended that radio should be limited to its primary role of news broadcasting and advertising.[11]

Despite the opposition, radio instruction continued to expand and paved the way for television instruction in the 1940s. Television instruction received the endorsement of students due to its interface capability and capacity for broader transmission. However, students must live within the coverage area and available at a specific time of the day to receive lectures.

Table: 2.1   Generations of Distance Education Technologies

	First Generation	Second Generation	Third Generation	Fourth Generation
Primary Feature	Predominantly one technology	Multiple technologies without computers	Multiple technologies, including computers and computer networking	Multiple technologies, including the beginning of high-bandwidth computer technologies
Time Frame	1850 to 1960	1960 to 1985	1985 to 1995	1995 to 2005 (estimated)
Media	• Print (1890s) • Radio (1930s) • Television (1950s and 1960s)	• Audio cassettes • Television • Videocassettes • Fax • Print	• Electronic mail, chat sessions, and bulletin boards using computers and computer networks • Computer programs and resources packaged on disks, CDs, and the Internet • Audio conferencing • Seminar and large-room videoconferencing via terrestrial, satellite, cable, and phone technologies • Fax • Print	• Electronic mail, chat sessions, and bulletin boards using computers and computer networks plus high-bandwidth transmission for individualized, customized, and live video interactive learning experiences • Computer programs and resources packaged on disks, CDs, and the Internet • Audio conferencing

(Continued)

Table: 2.1 (Continued)

	First Generation	Second Generation	Third Generation	Fourth Generation
Communication Features	• Primarily one-way communication • Interaction between faculty and student by telephone and mail • Occasionally supplemented by onsite facilitators and student mentors	• Primarily one-way communication • Interaction between faculty and student by telephone, fax, and mail • Occasionally supplemented by face-to-face meetings	• Significant broadband communication from faculty to you via print, computer programs, and videoconferencing • Two-way interactive capabilities enabling asynchronous and synchronous communication between faculty and you and among students • Internet good for text, graphics, and video snippets	• Desktop videoconferencing via terrestrial, satellite, cable, and phone technologies • Fax • Print • Two-way interactive real-time capabilities of audio and video • Asynchronous and synchronous communication between faculty and you and among students • Full thirty frame-per-second digital video transmission with databases of content resources available via the Internet and World Wide Web • Lengthy digital video programming available on demand

Source: Sheron and Boettcher, 1997.

Table 2.1 shows that from the 1850s to 1960s, education institutions primarily used correspondence to deliver lectures. Later, radio and television became parts of the distance learning method. Between the 1960s and 1980s, schools introduced audio, video, cartridges, and CDs and used them with correspondence. Also, communication between students and instructors was one-way through the postal system. From 1985, the mode of delivery of distance education changed due to the growth of the Internet and higher communication bandwidth that enabled data to travel faster.

Distance Education Today

From the 1960s to the mid-1980s, education institutions introduced several electronic tools to make distance learning more attractive. The effort failed to achieve the intended purpose because the available tools could only handle one-way communication at a time. Mostly, students communicated by correspondence and had to wait for several weeks before receiving feedback from their schools.

From the late 1980s to the early 1990s, the rapid growth of the **Internet** changed the fortune of distance education. The new technology has a two-way communication capability that enables students and instructors to communicate simultaneously. Likewise, the technology allows education institutions to integrate multimedia and interactive features such as e-mails, live chats, bulletin boards, discussion boards, whiteboards, videos, and web cameras into distance education, which gives students different learning experiences in the virtual classroom.

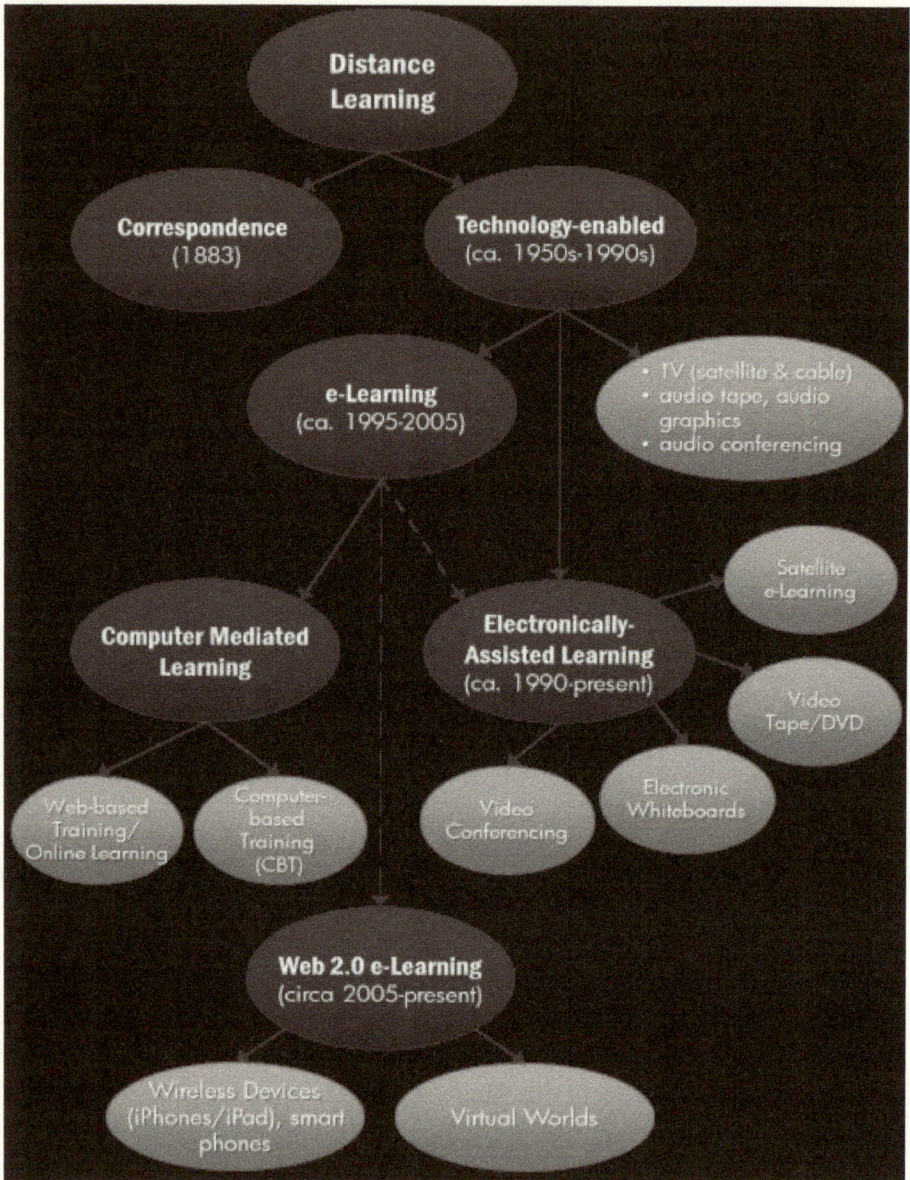

Figure: 2.1 The Family Tree of Distance Learning

Source: Holden and Westfall, 2009.

Figure 2.1 shows the chronology of online learning technologies and their intersections.

Summary of Main Points

- The history of distance education dates back to 1728 when Caleb Philips first offered distance learning in shorthand. In the 1840s, Isaac Pitman offered shorthand through Penny Post in Britain.
- In 1873, Anna Ticknor launched the Ana Ticknor Society in the United States. In 1858, the University of London began offering distance education to students both at home and abroad, followed by educational institutions in the United States.
- Between the 1900s and 1950s, distance education witnessed a slow but steady growth through radio and television instructions. In the 1960s and 1970s, education institutions integrated audiocassettes, videocassettes, cartridges, and CD-ROMs with correspondence.
- In the early 1990s, distance education radically transformed due to the explosion of the Internet. The new technology has multimedia and two-way communications capabilities.

Discussion Questions

1. Discuss the role that individuals played in the early days of distance education. How has the role changed over the years?
2. Discuss some of the most notable events in the history of distance education. What impact did these events have on the growth of distance education?
3. Compare and contrast correspondence instruction and web-based or online instruction. Discuss the advantages that one has over the other.
4. Provide the chronology of distance learning technologies. Which of these technologies has impacted distance education the most, and how?
5. How much would you agree that technology has been the most potent for online education growth? Provide a rationale for your answer.

3

ONLINE EDUCATION DEFINITIONS AND TAXONOMIES

Learning Objectives: After studying this chapter, you should be able to:

1. Define online education and terminologies
2. Discuss E-learning types
3. Understand the categories of online learning
4. Describe the characteristics of distance learning
5. Understand the misconceptions about online education

INTRODUCTION

Over the years, distance education has evolved, and each generation has interpreted the instructional technique based on convenience and historical relevance. As this chapter establishes, traditional education and distance education are different stylistically, though both share symbiotic relationships. Likewise, the two learning techniques have become so entwined that authors recommend that e-learning be called a "digital strategy."[1]

Despite the overlapping areas between online education and conventional learning, there are elements of online learning that do not exist in face-to-face learning and vice-versa, even if those differences are tangential and occur at a theoretical level. In this chapter, we examine the misconceptions about online education and how the myths conform to reality.

Distance Education Definitions

In the past, writers viewed distance education through the lenses of the postal system. In recent years, the focus of characterization has shifted to electronic technologies and the Internet. Notwithstanding the time in history, there has always been a consensus among scholars on what distance learning means through publications in textbooks and peer-reviewed journals.

In 1986, **Homberg** defined distance education as "the various forms of study at all levels which are not under the continuous, immediate supervision of tutors present with their students in lecture rooms or on the same premises, but which, nevertheless, benefit from the planning, guidance, and tuition of a tutorial organization."[2] In 1987, the **American Journal of Distance Education** (AJDE) defined distance education as "institutionally based formal education where the learning group is separated and where (education institutions) use interactive communications systems…to connect instructors, learners, and resources."[3]

Homberg and AJDE looked at distance education from different perspectives. However, it would be misleading to contrast the two because, in 1986 and 1987, the Internet was already available, but schools used the technology mainly for research and hardly for learning. In 2001, **Sankaran** and **Bui** defined distance education as "the process of instruction and learning via virtual classrooms where teachers and students are separated in space and sometimes in time."[4] The authors and **AJDE** took a technology-based

Table: **3.1**   Allen and Seaman, 2017.

Item	Definition
Distance education	Education that uses one or more technologies to deliver instruction to students who are separated from the instructor and to support regular and substantive interaction between the students and the instructor synchronously or asynchronously. Technologies used for instruction may include the following: Internet; one-way and two-way transmissions through open broadcasts, closed circuit, cable, microwave, broadband lines, fiber optics, satellite or wireless communication devices; audio conferencing; and video cassette. DVDs, and CD-ROMS, if the cassette, DVDs, and CD-ROMS are used in a course in conjunction with the technologies listed above.
Distance education course	A course in which the instructional content is delivered exclusively via distance education. Requirements for coming to campus for orientation, testing, or academic support services do not exclude a course from being classified as distance education.
Distance education program	A program for which all the required coursework for program completion is able to be completed via distance education courses.

approach in their definitions because, in 1987, though at a rudimentary level, education institutions had begun offering online learning over the Internet.

The **Integrated Postsecondary Education Data System** (IPEDS) developed the most comprehensive definition of online education so far (see table 3.1).[5] Broadly, distance education encompasses programs delivered to students at a remote location, including their homes either **synchronously** (real-time) or **asynchronously** (delayed time). There is **hybrid** or **blended** (technology with face-to-face) learning that requires students and teachers to meet once, or periodically, in a physical setting for lectures, laboratories, or examinations, so long as the time spent in the physical environment does not exceed 25% of the total course time.[6]

Online Education Terminologies

Online education has different terms that overlap and used broadly by authors. There are over 20 different terminologies commonly used to describe online learning, as follows:

> Internet-mediated teaching, technology-enhanced learning, web-based education, online education, computer-mediated communication (CMC), telematics environments, e-learning, virtual classrooms, I-Campus, electronic communication, information and communication technologies (ICT), cyberspace learning environments, computer-driven interactive communication, open and distance learning (ODL), distributed learning, blended courses, electronic course materials, hybrid courses, digital education, mobile learning, and technology-enhanced learning.[7]

As extensive as these terminologies, they do not capture all aspects of online learning. The broader category of distance education includes earlier technologies such as correspondence courses, educational television, and video conferencing.[8] As online education transitions from web technologies to cloud computing and the delivery moves from desktops to mobile devices, authors will introduce new terminologies.

TYPES OF E-LEARNING

E-learning or **electronic learning** is "the use of Internet technologies to deliver a broad array of solutions that enhance knowledge and performance."[9] There are **academic**, **corporate**, and **informal** e-learning; however, academic e-learning and corporate e-learning overlap depending on the curriculum and the educational objective.

Academic E-Learning

Academic e-learning includes educational programs delivered by schools to students online, and it's a significant part of the learning process from elementary school to higher education institutions. For decades, academic institutions such as schools, colleges, universities, and training centers have been using electronic technologies for teaching students. In recent years, the pervasiveness of web technologies has accelerated academic e-learning and take it to a new level from K-12 to higher institutions.

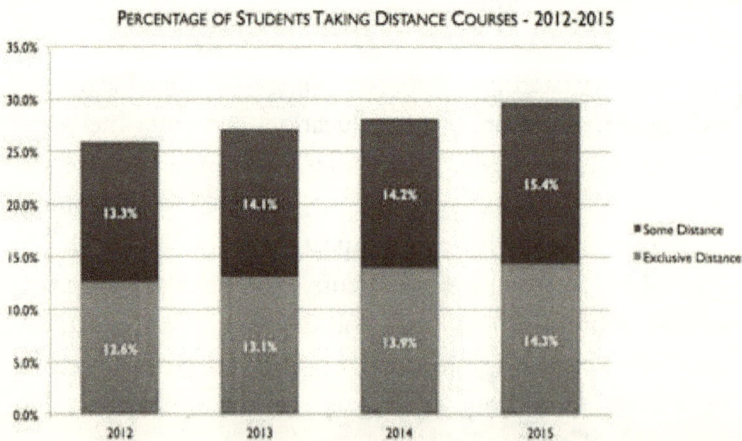

Figure: 3.1

Source: Allen, E., and Seaman, J. (2017)

In the Fall of 2014, 2,910 of the 4,806 higher-education institutions in the United States or 61% of the total universe of institutions in the country reported enrollments of students in an online program.[10] The University of Maryland, George Washington University, Clemson University, Georgetown University, and Boston University are among thousands of public and private universities in the United States that offer academic e-learning. Students can now take an entire degree program at Stanford University, Harvard University, Columbia University, and Emory University online.

In Great Britain, the University of London, the University of Liverpool, Lancaster University, the University of Ulster, and dozens of other universities combine online education with their campus-based programs. A survey of higher-education institutions showed that over two-thirds of big institutions offer online courses.[11]

At the K-12 level, academic e-learning is expanding as elementary and high school students can complete entire studies online. Enrollments in online K-12 schools are also growing at a steady pace of about 6% per year.[12] In the 2013-14 academic year, 75% of all school districts across America offered online or blended courses, and 30 states had statewide full-fledged online schools.[13] In 2019, approximately 310,000 K-12 students in the United States enrolled in online schools, and state-supported virtual schools (with supplemental online course programs) operates in 23 states and serve about 420,000 students with almost a million online course enrollments.[14]

Corporate E-Learning

Corporate e-learning enables employees to gain specific skills and acquire the knowledge to undertake tasks and perform them in the workplace. For decades, corporate training has been the standard practice for most organizations. With the prevalence of the Internet, online training has become indispensable for companies because it's convenient, cheaper, affordable, and efficient. Multinational

companies such as Coca-Cola, HSBC, Pfizer, UBS, and Tellabs primarily use e-learning in training their employees around the world.[15]

In recent years, academic education and organizational training have converged as companies and educational institutions collaborate in offering training programs, and education institutions accept training courses as credits into degree programs. In the United States, the McDonald's employee management training curriculum carries the **American Council on Education** (ACE) accreditation in which students can transfer credits to a two or four-year program in college or university. Over 1,800 colleges in the United States accept McDonald's **ACE** credit recommendations, and a restaurant General Manager who has completed the curriculum has 18-24 transferable credits from the restaurant management training to a degree program.[16]

Chiron Group, **Siemens**, **Groninger**, and **PFAFF** collaborate with Central Piedmont Community College (CPCC) through which high school students in North Carolina attend a paid apprenticeship program while working on their **Associate in Applied Science** (AAS) degree in Mechatronics Engineering Technology. Students can earn **AAS** at Glendale Community College, Arizona, while completing an occupational program at a **General Motors** (GM) location. The **GM Automotive Service Educational Program** (ASEP) teaches students across the United States and Canada exclusively on current **GM** vehicles with a paid dealership internship and four semesters of classroom and laboratory instructions. Graduates qualify for an entry-level technician position at a **GM** dealership repair center anywhere in the country, and **Fiat-Chrysler MOPAR College Automotive Program** (CAP) leads to the award of **AAS** degree after students have completed the required internship program.[17]

Informal E-Learning

Informal e-learning is an online instruction offered for free or for a fee by individuals and organizations. Informal e-learning does not require official registration or proof of completion, or award of a certificate; anyone can take informal e-learning if the person has a computer and Internet access. Individuals and organizations can offer short-courses on their websites or through social and professional networking sites such as YouTube,

Facebook, Twitter, and LinkedIn. For instance, **Home Depot**, a leading building tool and materials store in the United States, has dozens of videos on YouTube that teach customers how to complete relatively simple **do-it-yourself** (DIY) projects on a wide range of products sold by the company. The **Bank of America** (BOA) through **Khan Academy** provides free personal finance courses to customers and offers free tools and information on **BetterMoneyHabits.com** that helps customers understand how to make a smart and better financial decision.[18]

Categorization of Online Education

The percentage of time students spent receiving lectures determines whether a program is an online education, face-to-face, or blended learning. Online learning entails having 80% of the course content online, while blended learning requires 30% to 80% of the course contents delivered online.[19] The face-to-face program requires no technology either in writing or orally. The less technology used in the classroom, the more an academic program fits into the traditional education system. Conversely, the more technology used in class, the more the course conforms to online education.

Table: 3.2   Online Program versus Traditional Program

Proportion of Content Delivered Online	Course Type	Typical Description
0%	Traditional	Course with no online technology used in content delivery either in writing or orally.
1% to 29%	Web Facilitated	A course that uses web-based technology to facilitate what is essentially a face-to-face course. May use a course management system (CMS) or web pages to post the syllabus and assignments.
30% to 79%	Blended/Hybrid	The course combines technology instructions with face-to-face learning. A substantial proportion of the content is delivered online, typically uses online discussions, and usually has a reduced number of face-to-face meetings.
80+%	Online	A course where most or all the content is delivered online. Typically have no face-to-face meetings.

Source: Allen, E. and Seaman, J. (2015)

Table 3.2 highlights the difference between traditional, online, and blended education based on the percentage of content delivered online vis-a-vis the material taught in a face-to-face classroom.

Characteristics of Online Education

The following attributes separate online education from traditional education.

1. The instructional structure physically separates teachers from students.
2. A combination of media, such as television, audio-tapes, video-tapes, video conferencing, audio conferencing, e-mail, phone, fax, Internet, computer software, and print, may be deployed as communication tools.
3. Knowledge and content are available from many sources, not just the teacher.
4. Schools can deliver the courses at any time and any place. But direct interaction is possible between teacher and student, student and student, and groups of students.[20]
5. Computer-mediated classrooms: faculty and students engage with each other through keyboards and monitors, relying heavily on the written word rather than face-to-face exchange.
6. Separation in time between communications: teachers and students depend on asynchronous modes of communication, such as e-mail exchanges.
7. Availability of services online: student services, such as advising, counseling, mentoring, and library services, are integrated with the online teaching and learning environment.[21]
8. There is the personalization of learning experience regarding the individual interests, achievement level, life circumstances, and goals of each student.
9. Students can access courses from anywhere and at any pace, based on the individual needs of each student.
10. Online education closely resembles how we work remotely in collaboration with multiple and diverse stakeholders.
11. The courseware allows for learning to be captured, researched, and archived for continual enhancement and expansion.[22]

MISCONCEPTIONS ABOUT ONLINE EDUCATION

Online Learning Requires Less Time and Effort

There is a belief that students spend less time and effort learning online compared to the face-to-face classroom. To the contrary, studies show that students spent more time on tasks in the virtual classroom than in the face-to-face environment.[23]

Depending on the course objectives, students could spend six hours or more each week listening to lectures, working on assignments, participating in class discussions, and completing other course activities in the virtual classroom.

Similarly, instructors spend quality time teaching, preparing class notes, participating in class discussions, grading, and providing feedback to students in the virtual classroom. Although the online environment offers flexibility and convenience that do not exist in a face-to-face setting, that doesn't mean that students spend less time and effort learning online.

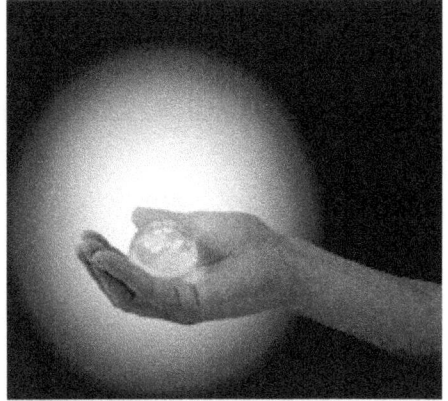

Online Students Have Less Workload than Campus-Based Students

Another misconception about online education is that campus-based students have more workload than online students. Contrary to the assumption, online students and campus-based students carry the same workload if they are in the same program. Most education institutions that offer online education offer face-to-face courses, and use the same syllabus regardless of the environment where students take courses.

Accrediting agencies also address academic rigor, student support, faculty credentials, and administrative issues with education institutions during accreditation review exercises. At national, regional, and professional levels, accrediting agencies use the same sets of standards to review and authenticate the quality of online and campus-based programs.[24] In some instances, schools must comply with specific accreditation guidelines, including online programs, to maintain their accreditations. In the virtual classroom, students complete some course activities that they may not have to complete if they take face-to-face courses. For example, online students must participate in weekly class discussions. If a student fails to participate in class discussion, the student faces an uphill battle to pass a course because the task may account for up to 20% of the overall course grade. In the face-to-face environment, instructors expect students to contribute to class discussions, but they won't penalize students that choose not to participate in class discussions.

In an online course, students must research the discussion topics before sharing them in the discussion forum. The myriads of tasks that students perform in an online class and the responsibility imposed on them invalidate the argument that online students carry less workload than their peers who take face-to-face courses.

Online Instruction is Less Effective than Face-to-face Instruction

Another fable about online education is that online instruction is less rigorous than face-to-face teachings. Studies show that a well-delivered online class is as effective as face-to-face courses because instructors ensure that lectures are intensive, and they consider in advance any potential confusion that students might have and proactively provide helpful tips to help them succeed in class.

Research on student achievement and performance when using online learning technologies versus face-to-face instruction has been overwhelmingly positive. **The North Central Regional Education Laboratory** (NCREL) reported that, on average, students perform equally well or better in an online course than a face-to-face course.[25] In a study of MBA students who took an **information management system** (IMS) course at the campus and online environment, the average performance of students in both settings was 74%. Although the students who took the online version faced some challenges (being their first online class), the adversity they faced in class did not reflect negatively on their grades more than their classmates who took the course at the campus.[26]

Ninety percent of students who used online instructional resources were happy with the experience, and more than 83% of them stated they would recommend online education to other students.[27] In 2009, the United States Department of Education conducted a meta-study on the effectiveness of online learning versus face-to-face learning. The study showed that students who took all or part of their courses online performed better, on average than those who attended campus-based classes and the learning outcomes of students who took online courses exceeded those of their counterparts who received only face-to-face instruction.[28] The conclusion of the meta-study demonstrates that instructional methods have little effect on academic performance but how students can comprehend and internalize the concepts taught in class.

The Quality of Face-to-Face Learning Exceed Online Instruction

One of the most hotly debated issues in academia and perhaps more ferocious in the larger society is the quality of degrees earned online versus the degree earned in the face-to-face environment. The superiority debates have become redundant because most traditional educational institutions run online programs with their face-to-face education, and different schools use different criteria to define quality.

In 2002, only 48.4% of **chief academic officers** (CAOs) had a favorable view of online education or believed that the learning method was essential to the strategic goals of their institutions. By 2011, the number of **CAOs** or institutions that thought that online education was crucial to their strategic goals reached an all-time high of 65.5%.[29] Fast forward to 2015, 71.4% of academic leaders rated online learning outcomes as the same or superior to face-to-face learning.[30]

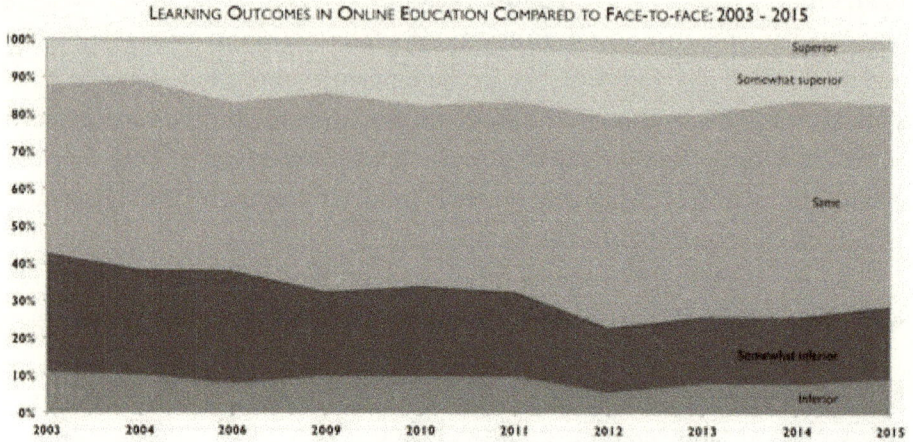

LEARNING OUTCOMES IN ONLINE EDUCATION COMPARED TO FACE-TO-FACE: 2003 - 2015

Figure: 3.2

Source: Allen, E., and Seaman, J. (2017)

As picture 3.2 shows, from 2003 to 2015, at least 57.2 % of **CAOs** believed that online learning outcome was the same, somewhat superior or superior to face-to-face learning. In 2015, 78% of students thought that the academic quality of their online courses was "better" or "about the same" as their experiences in traditional classrooms. Although the general acceptance of degrees earned in online programs can vary by industry, the **U.S. News** notes that in the field of education, online master's degrees are so typical that employers don't think of them much at all. Those in hiring positions who have been to school recently have either taken a blended or fully online course and know that the classes can be just as rigorous as campus-based classes.[31]

In 2006, a survey of 107 employers representing various industries across the United States showed that 85% of employers believed that online degrees were more acceptable than in 2001, and as far back as 2006, 86% of organizations in the country would hire an applicant who received an online degree.[32]

Summary of Main Points

- Distance education has evolved over the years, and each generation has interpreted the instructional technique based on convenience and historical relevance.
- There are over 20 different terminologies commonly used interchangeably to describe online learning.
- The three-common e-learning types are academic e-learning, corporate e-learning, and informal e-learning. Educational e-learning and corporate e-learning overlap, depending on where learning takes place.
- There is a misconception that online students have less workload than campus-based students. Studies show that online students carry the same workload as campus-based students because institutions use the same syllabi for online and campus-based courses.
- There is a fallacy that students spend less time and effort learning online. Studies show that online students spend quality time in completing tasks in the virtual classroom than students in a face-to-face class.
- There is a misconception that online instructions are not as robust as face-to-face instructions. Studies show that well-delivered online education can be as effective as face-to-face instructions.
- There is a misconception that the quality of degrees earned in the traditional face-to-face environment is superior to degrees earned in the online environment. Students noted that their online experience was "better" or "about the same" as their experience in the traditional classrooms.

Discussion Questions

1. What is the difference between online education and traditional education? Do you agree that online learning is less stressful than face-to-face learning? Provide a rationale for your position.
2. Identify and discuss the three types of e-learning and ways educational institutions can leverage each learning type in their academic programs.

3. Despite the long history of distance education, there are misconceptions about the learning technique. Identify and discuss the misunderstandings and research studies that debunked the misconceptions.

4. Before reading this chapter, what misconceptions did you have about online learning, and how has your reading in this chapter changed your opinion about those fallacies?

5. There is an assumption that online education is of a lower quality compared with face-to-face learning. How far do you agree with the hypothesis? Defend your position and recommend ways to improve the quality of online education.

4

ONLINE EDUCATION FORMATS

Learning Objectives: After studying this chapter, you should be able to:

1. Describe the synchronous learning
2. Understand the advantages and disadvantages of synchronous learning
3. Describe the asynchronous learning
4. Understand the advantages and disadvantages of asynchronous learning
5. Describe the hybrid learning
6. Understand the advantages and disadvantages of hybrid learning

INTRODUCTION

The online education formats are synchronous, asynchronous, and blended or hybrid. A school can choose synchronous or asynchronous or combine the two formats based on its educational objectives and what the institution considers to be best for students. In this chapter, we outline the difference between the three learning formats and discuss their advantages and disadvantages.

SYNCHRONOUS LEARNING FORMAT

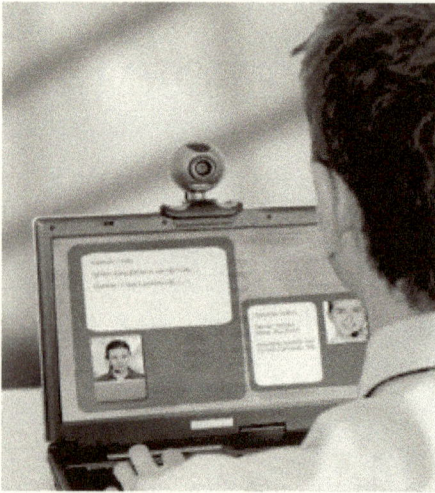

A synchronous learning format is a real-time event in which students and instructors log into class at the same time and participate in course activities. In the synchronous environment, you must have a computer with audio or video capability to take a course. The synchronous environment resembles the traditional classroom except that you use technology for instruction. In a synchronous course, if your class starts at 6 pm on Thursday, you must log to the virtual classroom at that time and participate in the learning activities.

Advantages of Synchronous Learning

1. The synchronous format enables you to exchange information in real-time and receive feedback immediately.
2. The synchronous format reduces the feeling of isolation because you interact live with classmates and instructors.
3. In the synchronous learning environment, you can attend lectures at home, office, or any location if you have a computer and Internet access.
4. In the synchronous environment, there are interactive tools such as discussion boards, whiteboards, videos, and chats that you can use to communicate and share information.

5. The synchronous technologies enable instructors to record and archive lectures for future use.
6. The synchronous format provides a dialectic learning atmosphere and a high degree of interactivity because you can hear, talk, and possibly see the instructors and classmates during a lecture.
7. The synchronous instructional technologies support just-in-time learning because instructors can live stream and share new information as it becomes available.
8. The synchronous format reduces attrition because instructors control the class pace and systematically guide students to complete required course activities.

Disadvantages of Synchronous Learning

Despite the advantages of synchronous learning, the instructional format has some drawbacks:

1. A computer glitch could cause you to miss a live lecture.
2. The spontaneity of the synchronous environment gives you little time to think through your ideas before sharing them in class.
3. The live nature of the synchronous environment forces you to go at the speed of classmates, no matter your preferred learning styles.
4. In the synchronous class, you won't be able to contribute much to discussion unless you can type fast because most conversations are by chatting.
5. During a live lecture, natural events, such as storm, fire, or flood, can interfere with technology. Also, human actions such as visitors, phone calls, and children can distract from learning.
6. The obligation to attend lectures at a specific time of the week could impact other areas of your life if you combine work with learning.
7. A synchronous format could be expensive because you may need special software to use some programs in a live course.
8. A synchronous class mimics a face-to-face classroom setting. As a result, if you're a shy person and not comfortable in a group setting, you would have the same feeling in a live course.

ASYNCHRONOUS LEARNING FORMAT

The asynchronous format involves using course management systems, pre-recorded videos, e-mails, CD-ROMs, or correspondence for learning. Unlike the synchronous class, you can participate in course activities at your convenience but use communication tools such as emails, chats, online discussion forums, and bulletin boards to communicate.

The asynchronous format is on-demand learning with more control over the learning time, process, and content. Most e-learning systems are designed for the asynchronous environment because they are easy to develop and inexpensive to maintain.[1]

Advantages of Asynchronous Learning

1. The asynchronous format is convenient, no matter your learning style or preference, because you decide when to attend lectures and when to complete course activities.
2. In an asynchronous environment, you spend less time online because you can download and print course materials and read them offline.
3. The delayed interaction of the asynchronous class enables you to think through your comments before sharing them, which reduces the tendency of making provocative comments that you might later need to retract.
4. The asynchronous format allows you to take the class with you whenever you go as long as you have a computer and Internet access.
5. In an asynchronous learning environment, the classroom door never closes! You have access to lectures and educational materials, twenty-four hours a day, seven days a week.

Disadvantages of Asynchronous Learning

1. In today's fast-paced environment, what is breaking news a minute ago could become old news a second later. The asynchronous format elongates the time between when you request information and when you receive feedback.

2. The asynchronous format enables students to participate in class activities at different times, causing different students to receive contradictory information at different times.

3. In a sizeable asynchronous class, a post can get buried in the threaded discussions, making conversations challenging to follow, and students responding to messages meant for their classmates.

4. In some asynchronous courses, you only interact with the course content, amplifying the feeling of isolation.

5. The asynchronous format causes procrastination because of the flexibility to complete course activities at one's convenience.

BLENDED LEARNING FORMAT

Blended learning is when education institutions combine face-to-face instructions with technology, so long students spent less than 79% of the time learning online. A 2009 **U.S. Department of Education** study showed that blended learning is more effective than face-to-face instructions or online learning. Blended learning improves comprehension and test scores for 84% of students that use the learning format and reduces in-class time by as much as one-half giving instructors more time to focus on topics that are problematic for students.[1]

Campus Technology found that 55% of higher education faculty in the United States used blended learning in all or some of their courses.[2]

Studies by the **Bill & Melinda Gates Foundation** show that high-quality blended courses help at-risk students master content twice as fast as they would with only one learning format and increase their performance rates by one-third.[3] Different schools use blended learning for different reasons.

Columbia University provides the following reasons for combining online education with face-to-face learning:

> The power of combining traditional (face-to-face) and non-traditional elements (online) enables us to give students an experience that goes well beyond what they could obtain in a classroom. A difficult concept, for example, becomes clearer when it is viewed side-by-side with a simulation or interactive map. A student's experience of a powerful lecture is enriched by the opportunity not only to hear but to see its subject matter represented visually in video and animation.[4]

Advantages of Blended Learning

1. Blended learning enables online students to experience campus-life, making students a part of the academic community and reducing isolation a bane of online education.
2. The blended format allows schools to use technology and students to demonstrate practical knowledge in a face-to-face environment.
3. The hybrid enables you to leverage face-to-face communication and electronic communications simultaneously.
4. The hybrid format offers skilled competency opportunities because of exposure to different learning and communication technologies.
5. Blended format reduces traffic congestions and overcrowding of lecture rooms, saving schools money they can invest in other projects.

Disadvantages of Blended Learning

1. Blended learning could be expensive because you spend money at both ends of the learning spectrum. Plane tickets, feeding, and lodging for a one-week residency could cost thousands of dollars, coupled with the cost of computers, Internet service, and other technologies.

2. The hybrid format is inconvenient if you combine work with learning because you must take time off work to attend lectures at the campus.

3. Blended format fuses two learning approaches that are incompatible with each other. Face-to-face and technology have different characteristics. You can confuse what to do online with what to complete in a face-to-face environment.

Summary of Main Points

- Online education formats are synchronous, asynchronous, and hybrid.
- Synchronous learning allows real-time interactions and students to receive the same information in class.
- In the synchronous environment, communication is easy to manage because of the live nature.
- Computer glitches can cause you to miss lectures because of the live nature of the synchronous environment.
- In the synchronous environment, you have limited time to think through your responses before sharing them in class.
- The asynchronous format delays the flow of information because students and instructors participate in class activities at different times.
- In an asynchronous environment, you can download lecture materials when you have access to the Internet and use them later.
- The asynchronous environment allows you to think through your comments before sharing them in class.
- The asynchronous format enables workers who work outside the home to study while on the road.
- Asynchronous discussion is challenging to manage because students can respond to messages meant for their classmates undercutting the forum discussion objectives.
- The hybrid format provides the opportunity to have face-to-face and online interactions.

- The hybrid format reduces traffic congestion and lessens the pressure on the campus facility when schools combine online learning with face-to-face instruction.
- The hybrid format could be expensive because you spend money on technology and incur costs to attend the face-to-face section.
- The mixing of two instructional methods that are at variance with each other can confuse learners.

Discussion Questions

1. What is synchronous learning? Discuss the advantages the learning format has over other types of learning formats.
2. Synchronous learning provides higher learning outcomes than asynchronous or hybrid. To what extent do you agree or disagree with this assertion?
3. What is asynchronous learning? Identify and discuss the advantages of asynchronous learning and the benefits to various stakeholders within the academic community.
4. Identify and discuss the disadvantages of synchronous learning and why a school should use the learning format over asynchronous learning.
5. What do you understand about hybrid or blended learning? Evaluate the advantages of this learning format and the advantages and disadvantages it has over synchronous and asynchronous learning.

5

THE GROWTH OF ONLINE EDUCATION

Learning Objectives: After studying this chapter, you should be able to:

1. Understand how teacher shortages contribute to online education growth
2. Explain how an increase in demand for higher education boost online education
3. Examine the space problem in higher education
4. Discuss the emerging economies and educational needs
5. Understand how economic factors drive online learning
6. Discuss how government policies impact online education
7. Explain the growth of online learning in higher education
8. Describe the growth of online learning in organizations

INTRODUCTION

Online education has surpassed expectations given the number of students who take online courses and the number of institutions that offer online programs. The revolution that has taken place in the online education sector could be the tip of the iceberg of how the pedagogy will expand in the future.

In this chapter, we look at how the shortage of teachers and the emergence of new economies impact online education. Also, we discuss how the economic recession and government policies, as well as the increased demand for higher education, affect online learning.

The Second Wave of Online Education

In the late 1800s, distance education soared in the United States. During the period, many adults who wanted to pursue higher-education programs in the U.S could not do so due to work commitments and lack of financial resources.[1] Between 1881 and 1900, Wesleyan University enrolled up to 1,900 students in its **independent-study program**. Despite the purpose distance learning program was serving at the time, in 1906, the Executive Board of Wesleyan University and educators in the United States recommended its termination because they felt the instruction lacked a high standard of excellence.[2]

Despite the vote of no confidence passed on distance learning, the instructional method continued to grow in the United States. In the late 1960s, many Americans who wanted better opportunities relocated to different parts of the country in search of new careers and to gain new skills. The phenomenon increased the demands for informal and non-traditional learning coupled with the skyrocketing cost of traditional education and widespread dissatisfaction with the traditional educational institutions in the country.[3]

In the mid-1960s, the United Kingdom formed a **Commission** with the remit of increasing higher education opportunities for working adults. Subsequently, the British government established the **Open University** (OU) in 1969, which domestically and internationally enrolled more than one hundred thousand adult students and produced about twenty thousand baccalaureate graduates every year. The **OU** proved to be successful, as it ranked near the top of British universities in both research and teaching but cost 40% less than the average tuition fees of the traditional universities. Observers adjudged the initiative as one of the most successful education policies ever developed in Great Britain.[4] The immediate success of the university became the catalyst for the acceleration of distance education programs in the United States. In 1968, the **Division of Correspondence Study**, which later changed its name to the **Division of Independent Study**, brought some improvements to distance learning by integrating videotape, programmed instruction, television, telephone, and other multimedia into teaching and learning.[5] The development of chip technologies and microelectronics, which emerged in the mid-1960s and became prominent in the early 1970s, added new impetus to distance education, especially how students communicated with each other and their professors.[6]

From the 1980s to the early 1990s, a confluence of events occurred that fundamentally changed the landscape of distance education in the United States. The economic recession at the end of the **Cold War** and the growth of the Internet led to the rapid adoption of web technologies in training by businesses and industries, colleges, and universities.[7] By December 2000, more than 3,000 higher-education institutions in the United States were offering **web-based** classes, and thousands of private e-learning companies, individual corporations, and industry organizations that produced coursework and educational materials had emerged.[8] In 2009, 66% of institutions in the country reported an increase in demand for new online courses and programs, and the overall need for existing online courses and programs reached 73%.[9]

FACTORS FOR THE GROWTH OF ONLINE EDUCATION

Decreasing Number of Teachers in the Classroom

Teacher shortages and personal decisions of parents have contributed to the growth of online education in recent years. Studies show that almost half of all new teachers in the United States leave the profession within five years. In 2010, the **National Center for Education Statistics** (NCES) forecasted that public schools in the United States would need to hire about 330,000 to 364,000 teachers a year between 2011 and 2017 to bridge the shortage gap. Although the continuous exodus of teachers from the classroom is a national problem, the crisis is more endemic and critical in rural areas, which enrolls about 23% of all students in the United States. Most schools in rural communities find it difficult to attract teachers with content knowledge in science subjects and often struggle to replace qualified teachers in other disciplines as many of the old teachers enter the retirement age.[10]

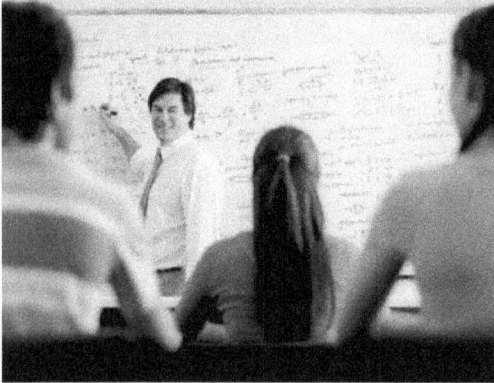

To reduce the effects of teacher shortages in the classroom, many school districts in the United States offer online learning. A conservative estimate (that includes online home-schooled children) showed that, as of 2011, at least 455,000 PreK-12 (Kindergarten to High School) children in the U.S. attended all their classes online. While this number is a mere 0.74% of the total of school children in the U.S., this is a paradigm shift in the education landscape in the country because of the propensity for more states to allow fulltime PreK-12 students to attend online schools as the number of teachers declined. An estimated 8.2% or 4.75 million U.S. PreK-12 students would take all their classes online by 2016. While all domestic school systems are unique, the U.S. stands out because it has the largest population of online PreK-12 students, so far in the world. The large (and growing) number of children attending online primary and secondary schools fulltime in the U.S. is a trend found nowhere else in the world.[11]

In China, the mass migration of people from rural communities to urban cities has drastically reduced the number of teachers in rural areas. The incident prompted the Chinese government to introduce online learning technologies in teaching science subjects in rural areas.[12] China now has three of the world's mega-universities in which over 100,000 students mostly use distance learning methods. The **Chinese Ministry of Education** is actively promoting distance education and hopes other countries around the world will adopt its innovative learning approach.[13]

Increased Global Demand for Higher Education

Over the past few decades, the world population has grown astronomically, and there is no sign that the growth will abate anytime soon.

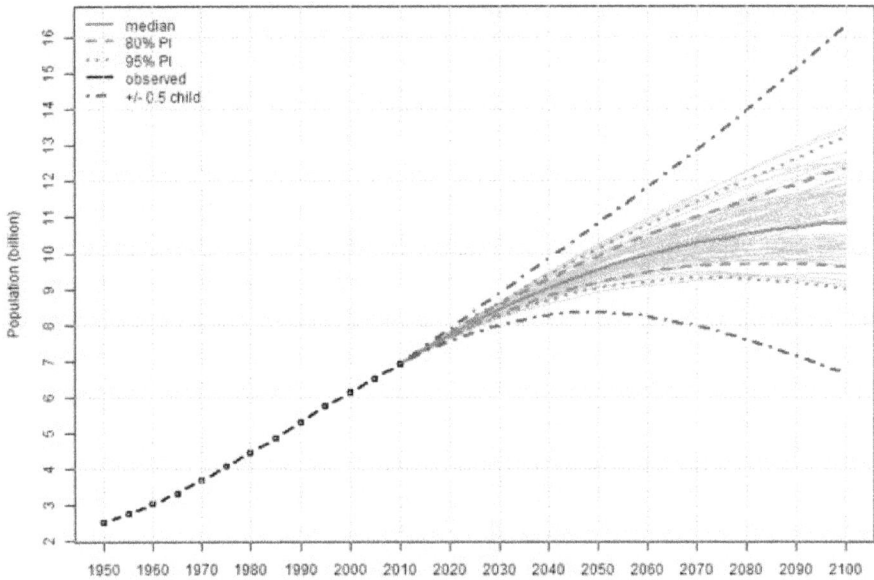

Figure: 5.1   World Population Probabilistic Growth

Source: United Nations, 2014.

Demographically, just four countries– India, China, U.S., and Indonesia will account for over half of the world's 18–22 population by 2020 and a quarter would come from Pakistan, Nigeria, Brazil, Bangladesh, Ethiopia, Philippines, Mexico, Egypt, and Vietnam. The forecast shows that the 18–22 years old in Nigeria, India, Ethiopia, Philippines, and Pakistan will grow by 3.9 million, 2.9 million, 1.9 million, 1.2 million and 0.9 million respectively over the next decade.[14]

Currently, there are over 7 billion people in the world, and the forecast indicates that the growth will continue in the future (see figure 5.1). As the world population grows, the number of primary and secondary students that will be seeking a higher education will increase. In Africa, Latin America and the Caribbean, the Middle East, and Eastern and Central Europe, the demand for higher education continues to exceed supply despite massive improvements in enrolment numbers over the years. In the 21st century, life-long learning will become crucial as competition for jobs requiring training beyond secondary school intensifies.[15]

In 2007, approximately 150.6 million students enrolled in tertiary institutions globally, an increase of 53% over the number recorded in 2000.[16] In 2011, the average percentage of students entering higher education institutions worldwide exceeded 30% of the cohorts. In developed countries such as the United States and Western Europe, higher education growth has saturated at about 85 to 90% of college-bound students. In other regions, higher education is growing, with the fastest increase in Central and East Asia.[17] In 2013, an estimated 167 million students (all ages) from around the world enrolled in higher education institutions. By 2025, 267 million students will be seeking such opportunities.[18]

As figure 5.2 demonstrates, every region experienced higher education enrollments between 2000 and 2007 with the most dramatic gains in upper-middle and upper-income countries while Sub-Saharan Africa achieved the lowest increase in gross tertiary enrolments.[19]

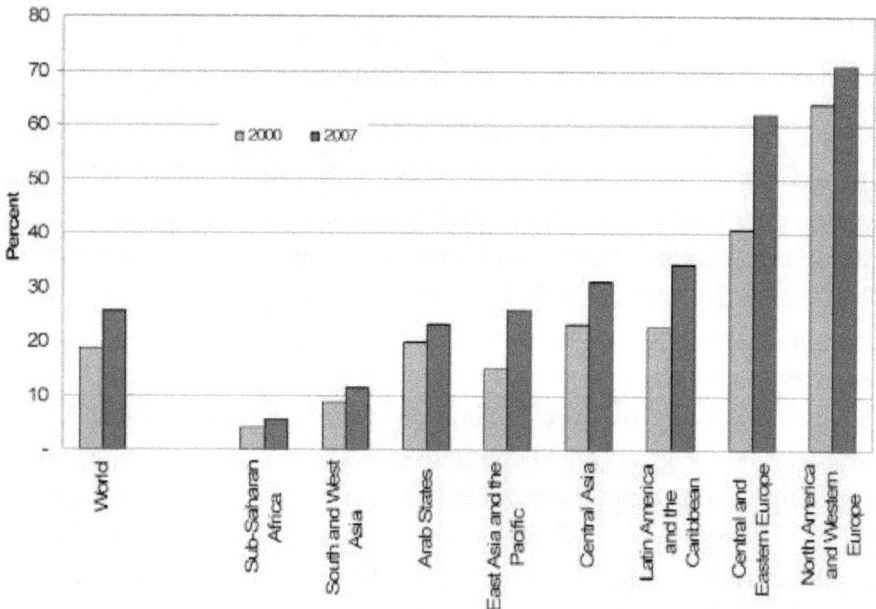

Figure: 5.2   Tertiary Gross Enrolment Ratio by Geographical Region, 2000 and 2007

Source: Altbatch., Reisberg, and Rumbley (2009).

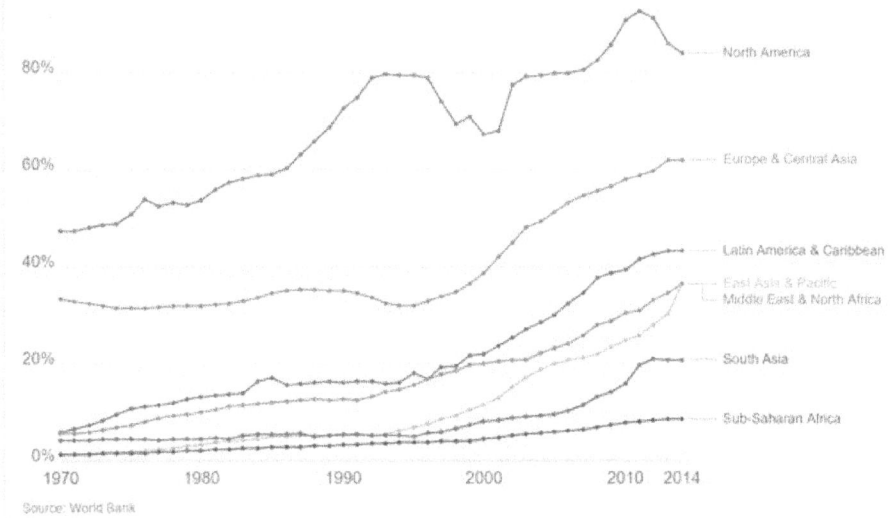

Figure: 5.3 Enrollment in tertiary education

Source: Max Roser and Esteban Ortiz-Ospina (2018)

From figure 5.3, from 1970 to 2014, on the average, tertiary education growth occurred in the upper-middle and upper-income countries, and since 2010, enrollment consistently remained above 60% in Europe and Central Asia and above 80% in North America. Congruently, admissions have increased in other regions, including Africa, that lagged in previous decades. As the Africa population surges from 1.3 billion in 2020 to 2.4 billion in 2050, higher education opportunities will decline given the current ratio of higher education demand versus available space.[20]

For instance, the **National Universities Commission** (NUC), which regulates university education in Nigeria, noted that between 2012 and 2017, less than 20% of applicants to Nigerian universities gained admission, leaving 6.3 million qualified students without admission prospects with approximately 90,000 Nigerians studying abroad. In Ghana, the universities accommodate around 20% of applicants and given quality issues in the private education sector, the demand for study abroad is increasing. The **United Nations Educational, Scientific, and Cultural Organization** (UNESCO) estimated that 12,560 Ghanaians studied abroad in 2017, an increase of 40% from 8,965 in 2012. A conservative estimate showed that about 7,000 of the students studied in China alone. Kenya will have a population of 5.7 million college-aged students by 2024. The cohort holds the promise of meeting Kenya's goal of becoming a middle-income country by 2030 but the country's education system does not equip students with skills the country needs. Kenya's higher education system has expanded in recent years due to the emergence of several private universities and polytechnics, but low quality and funding issues have truncated the educational effort. **UNESCO** estimates that 14,000 Kenyans study abroad, and the United States, Australia, the United Kingdom, and South Africa are their largest host countries.[21]

Higher Education and the Space Conundrum

At the risk of oversimplification, the financial pressure that countries face encumbers them in providing social services, including education. Distance education offers opportunities in meeting the enrollment demand in countries that are struggling to expand higher education admissions. In India, the government could not increase enrollments from 40% to 65% due to financial constraints and teacher shortages.[22] Subsequently, the Indian government aggressively pursued distance education programs, and today the country has at least 11 open universities for those interested in taking professional courses and other educational programs. Also, over 50 distance learning organizations that cater to the needs of higher education operate in the country.[23]

In the United States, college enrollment grew 50% from about 10 million in the late 1980s to almost 15 million in 2010 because of the tendency of high school graduates to attend college after graduation.[24] In 2005, the Chancellor of the California State University predicted that the system could see a 10% annual increase in the student population that would require the state to build a mid-size campus every year for ten years.[25] The university introduced online learning in coping with the high enrollment number. In Maryland, the Regents of the University System of Maryland approved online education programs in its thirteen colleges and encouraged students to take at least 12 credits of their courses in the virtual classroom.[26]

In 2014, the Council of Higher Education in South Africa published a white paper that required higher education institutions to offer online courses. In South Africa, 23 universities in the country now offer some form of distance learning to expand higher education at low cost.[27] While the situation in each country is different, online learning will be vital in Africa in both chance and affordability as the number of university-age students doubles from 200 million to 400 million by 2045.[28]

The Emerging Economies and Educational Needs

Research shows a strong correlation between **gross domestic product** (GDP) and **purchasing power parity** (PPP) and tertiary enrolment, particularly in countries where the annual household income is more than USD 10,000. Some countries like China and India that performed strongly in the 2000s are forecast to grow significantly wealthier in the coming decades. These nations are followed closely by Angola, Vietnam, Bangladesh, Sri Lanka, Indonesia, Nigeria, Pakistan, Malaysia, and Brazil, although these countries will most likely have an annual household income below USD 10,000 in 2020 and beyond.[29]

Since the 1960s, countries like Hong Kong, Singapore, South Korea, and Taiwan have maintained steady economic growth. Although there are encouraging signs that these countries will maintain the economic momentum in the future, the growth they achieved over the years has created unintended consequences as their expenditures and demand for social programs, including education, have risen sharply. It is not surprising that Asia had the highest growth rate in higher education demand at 17.3%, followed by Eastern Europe at 16.9%, Africa at 15.2%, and Latin America at 14.6%.[30]

The United States, the United Kingdom, Australia, and Canada have made substantial financial investments by bringing technology into the classroom. While these countries can still use technology to expand educational opportunities for their citizens, the greater need for web-based education are developing economies where demand for higher education exceeds the available space.[31]

In the emerging economies, educational transformation is taking place, but governments can't keep up with the educational needs of their people.[32] For the most part, students compete for limited spaces in universities, while admission to the top-ranked institutions has become exclusive right of the privileged few.[33] In 2012, India, China, South Korea, and Malaysia were ranked second, third, fourth, and fifth after the United States in the top eight countries that offered online education.[34] In South Korea, the government, through the Korea Education and Research Information Service and 16 **Metropolitan and Provincial Offices of Education** (MPOE), use e-learning technologies to connect 6,147 online teachers, 1.6 million students, and 2,692 parent tutors for an estimated cost savings of $40 billion per year. The government has also created a national online tutoring system that helps students prepare for examinations.[35] The use of digital textbooks with a tablet-based, multimedia learning environment piloted by the South Korean government, has shown signs of success, as the learning management systems significantly improved student-to-student and student-to-teacher interactions in the classroom.[36]

Economic Factors

In recent years, two phenomena have influenced and dominated the financing of higher education. First, higher education is increasingly essential to economies, individuals, and societies striving for democracy and social justice. Second, the cost of higher education is rising at a pace beyond which most countries' public revenue streams can absorb.[37]

In 2008, the financial inferno that engulfed the world scorched from North America to Europe, Sub-Saharan Africa to the Asia-Pacific, and the Middle East. The financial predicament stunted economic growth and heightened financial anxieties in many countries.[38] In the United States, several financial institutions collapsed, with many manufacturing and service organizations either closed or laid-off thousands of employees. Also, the price of crude oil spiraled out of control, reaching a record high of $148 per barrel in the world market. Before 2008, although some countries were already fragile economically with high inflation and low **GDP**, the financial crisis delivered the final blow and exacerbated their anemic economic situation.

In the late 1980s, the United States government reduced its procurement of military hardware as the perceived threats of the Cold War subsided. However, the aftershocks of the decade-long War continued to reverberate across the country, resulting in massive layoffs of scientists, engineers, mid-level managers, and other highly skilled professionals.

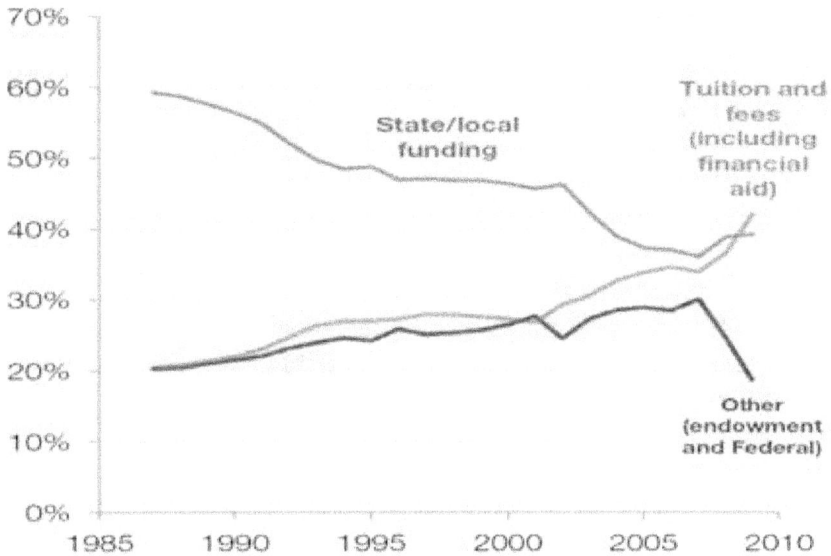

**Figure: 5.4   Share of Revenue at Public Four-Year Institutions
in the United States**

Source: The Economics of Higher Education (December 2012)

Consequently, many states experienced a decrease in tax revenues and struggled to finance social programs, including education.[39] Between 2006 and 2008, states that had budget surpluses experienced budget deficits of between 2% to 4% by 2009 and 2010. In 2011, several states ran deficits between 5% and 7%.[40]

From figure 5.4, in 2007, the federal government contributed about 30% to education funding while the local governments and the states shouldered about 35% of the cost, respectively. By 2015, the role had reversed as the states and the local governments each contributed 45% of the expenditure, while the federal government provided a paltry of 10%. Overall, the federal government spending on education decreased from $44.6 billion in 2011 to $38.2 billion in 2015, while tuition and financial aids to students increased.[41] Today, a generation of young Americans bear the brunt of decades of run-away college costs, and many college graduates are entering the workforce

**Average Tuition,
Public 4-Year**

	2000	2011
In-State	$4,248	$7,077
Out-of-State	$11,094	$16,340

■ In-State ■ Out-of-State

Figure: 5.5   The Economics of Higher Education (December 2012)

with staggering student loans that are inhibiting them from buying homes, cars and start families.[42]

In 2000, the average tuition for in-state students at a public four-year college in the United States was $4,248 and $11,094 for out-of-state students. By 2011, the average fees for in-state students had almost doubled at $7,077 and out-of-state to $16,340 (see figure 5.5).[43] In the survey by the **Pew Research Center**, 84% of college graduates disclosed that college education was a good investment, but 75% of them acknowledged that the cost was too high.[44] As costs weigh heavily on the decision of candidates for choosing a school, education institutions offer online education, not because of their sudden fascination with interactive technology but a strategic imperative in coping with the budget shortfalls and reducing the costs of education.

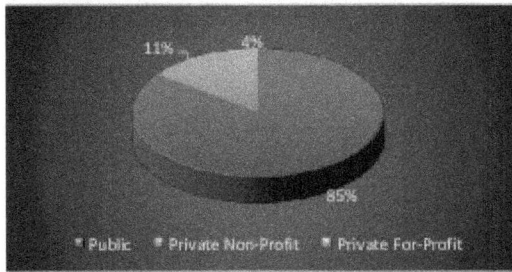

Figure: 5.6 Distance Education Enrollments by Sector: 2014

"Some But Not All Distance Education Courses"

Poulin, R., and Straut, T. (2016).

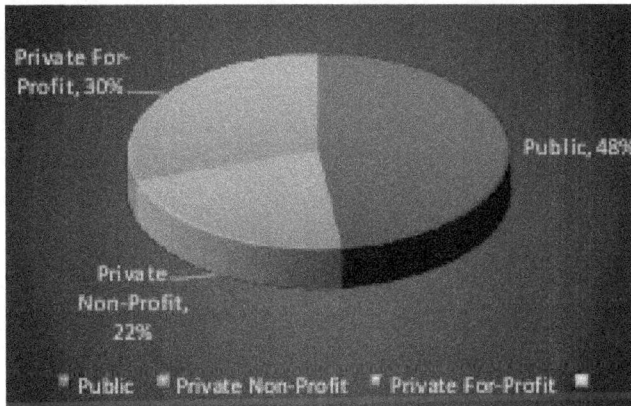

Figure: 5.7 Distance Education Enrollments by Sector: 2014

"Exclusively Distance Education Courses"

Poulin, R., and Straut, T. (2016)

In 2014, over two-third of public institutions in the United States enrolled students in some or fully online courses, and a robust number of students exclusively took online classes at private non-profit and private for-profit education institutions (see figures 5.6 and 5.7). In 2015, 72.7% of all undergraduate and 38.7% of all graduate students in public institutions in the United States took online courses. The percentage of students taking at least one distance education course grew by 3.9%, and more than one in four students (28%) now takes at least one distance education course. Kathleen S. Ives, the CEO and Executive Director, Online Learning

Consortium, asserted that online education growth in the United States is no longer a fad, but a trend… "distance education enrollments in the face of declining overall higher education enrollments suggest an important shift in the American higher education landscape, with contemporary learners leaning to online options."[45]

Government Educational Policies

A country's educational policy is a significant factor in adopting e-learning, and the process begins with the government establishing procedures and a country-wide rollout of technology infrastructures.[46] As the expansion of higher education based on traditional education models saturates, countries look for a cost-effective way to accommodate the increasing numbers of nontraditional and lifelong students seeking higher education opportunities.[47]

In 1998, the Republic of Ireland established the **National Centre for Technology in Education** (NCTE) for the Schools IT 2000 initiative. The Technology Integration Initiative supports schools in developing ICT infrastructures and assists students in getting online. The Irish government offers grants for schools to purchase computers and provide Internet access for students. **NCTE** established approximately ninety pilot projects in several "lead" schools and worked collaboratively with education centers, businesses, industry, third-level institutions, and the community.[48] In August 1999, the U.S. Department of Education provided $10 million to colleges, universities, companies, and nonprofit organizations to help adults have access to distance learning opportunities.[49]

In 2009, Mexico launched the **National Online University** that enrolled over 35,000 students in two weeks.[50] In September 2012, the Malaysian government announced the National Education Blueprint that covers years 2013-2025, which "will equip 10,000 public schools nationwide with 4G Internet access and a virtual learning platform. In early 2012, the Japanese government passed the **Distance Education Universities Law** that authorized online programs in 54 universities and 11 junior colleges. In October 2012, the Ministry of Education in Angola launched **E-net** commonly referred to as **Escola Internet** in partnership with the domestic telecom **Unitel** and China-based **Huawei**, to provide Internet access in all secondary schools in the country.[51]

Chile was the first country in Latin America and the third in the world after the United States and the United Kingdom, to roll out Think.com (ThinkQuest.org), an innovative, educational, web-based program sponsored by the **Oracle Foundation**, placing Chilean educational facilities at the cutting edge of world-class, state-of-the-art technology.[52] **Oracle Foundation** with over eighty partners globally, provides schools, students, and teachers with the resources that enable them to collaborate and share ideas from any location.[53]

In 2002, the Pakistani government launched a virtual university that offers computer science and **information technology** (IT) degree programs over the television and online to allow the best of its **IT** faculty involved in knowledge transfer without relocating them.[54] The Pakistani government expects the virtual university to accelerate the workforce development that will enable the country to advance in the field of information technology like India, its rival neighboring country.[55]

In 2001, the **Sloan Foundation** made 116 grants and committed twenty-six million dollars specifically to developing online courses and programs over the next several years in the United States.[56] From 1992 to 2009, Sloan Foundation provided $75 million in support of the **Asynchronous Learning Networks** (ALNs) so students could have access to high-quality higher education resources and training materials anytime and anyplace.[57] The **World Bank** sponsors online educational programs in Africa and other developing countries, and the **United States Distance Learning Association** (USDLA) organizes lectures and conferences for professionals in the distance learning industry attended by education practitioners in the United States and other countries.

In the United States, some states are moving away from the "seat time" standards that require students to be in classrooms for a certain amount of time before earning a degree to mastery-based standards that recognize achievement when a student has mastered the material, no matter how many hours the student sits in a class. In the state of Alabama, schools can apply for waivers from the Alabama State Department of Education's Innovation Zone/Flexibility Initiative from the "seat time" standard to a mastery-based model. Also, students taking online, self-paced courses (including MOOCs) can receive credit for job training and skills.[58]

Despite significant inroads that many nations have made in the online education sector, some countries have not expanded e-learning beyond the pedestrian level. Countries like the United States, Australia, and the United Kingdom have attained preeminence in resource allocation and technological advancement to support online programs. Some countries in Eastern Europe have yet to determine the role of online education in the future of their educational systems.[59]

In Africa, most nations lack the infrastructural resources and human knowledge for effective implementation of online education programs while school administrators and teachers lack the experience to integrate online instructional technology into their curriculum. Internet service is also out of reach for most of the population, and when available, the cost is exorbitantly high. For example, the price of Internet connection for subscribers in Sierra Leone is 118% of the annual **per capita income** (PCI), while the same service is only 1% for subscribers in Australia.[60]

Despite the challenge that some countries face, online education will continue to grow. India and South Africa are heavy importers and users of distance learning programs, while China, Thailand, and Japan are developing distance learning technologies to support higher-education programs in their countries.[61] The Republic of Ireland is one of the largest developers of e-learning software programs in the world that countries like the United States use for online education.

Growth of Online Education in Higher Education

Given the current trajectory, the actual growth rate of online education could be higher than the reports show. In the United States, the overall higher education enrollment fell by 2% from 2012 to 2014. However, distance education enrollment grew by 7% for students taking "at least one" distance learning course and rose by 9% for students taking "exclusively" distance learning courses.[62] The annual growth rate of online enrollments continues to grow beyond the percentage of overall higher-education admissions.[63]

Online course enrollments are accelerating because of the growing number of students who seek flexible formats for courses, certificates, and degree programs to support career placement, advancement, and transition to a new career and those that wish to pursue advanced studies.[64] For fourteen years consecutively, **Babson Survey Research Group** that tracked online education in the United States reported that the number of students taking at least one distance course increased steadily.[65] Education institutions with distance education programs remained confident, with 77.1% agreeing in 2015 that online education was vital to their long-term strategy.[66]

In 2002, about 16.6 million students enrolled in degree-granting post-secondary institutions in the United States, with 1.6 million of them taking at least one online course.[67] Eduventures, a Boston-based provider of market research for the education industry, reported that the number of students who enrolled in online higher-education programs in 2004 grew by almost 34%.[68] In 2012, the number of students who took at least one online course was 7.1 million compared with 1.6 million who took the course in 2002.[69] In 2014, a total of 5.8 million students took distance education courses with 2.8 million took all their classes at a distance, and about 3 million took some of their courses online.[70] In the United States, almost all higher-education institutions now offer one form of online education, and "if the trend continues, it will be just a matter of time before distance education becomes the dominant form of teaching and learning."[71]

Table: 5.1 Total and Online Enrollment in Degree-Granting Postsecondary Institutions–Fall 2002 through Fall 2012

Year	Total Enrollment	Annual Growth Rate Total Enrollment	Students Taking at Least One Online Course	Online Enrollment Increase over Previous Year	Annual Growth Rate Online Enrollment	Online Enrollment as a Percent of Total Enrollment
Fall 2002	16,611,710	NA	1,602,970	NA	NA	9.6%
Fall 2003	16,911,481	1.8%	1,971,397	368,427	23.0%	11.7%
Fall 2004	17,272,043	2.1%	2,329,783	358,386	18.2%	13.5%
Fall 2005	17,487,481	1.2%	3,180,050	850,267	36.5%	18.2%
Fall 2006	17,758,872	1.6%	3,488,381	308,331	9.7%	19.6%
Fall 2007	18,248,133	2.8%	3,938,111	449,730	12.9%	21.6%
Fall 2008	18,698,630	4.7%	4,606,353	668,242	16.9%	24.1%
Fall 2009	19,036,860	6.9%	5,579,022	972,669	21.1%	27.3%
Fall 2010	21,016,126	2.9%	6,142,280	563,258	10.1%	29.2%
Fall 2011	20,994,113	-0.1%	6,714,792	572,512	9.3%	32.0%
Fall 2012	21,253,086	1.2%	7,126,549	411,757	6.1%	33.5%

Source: Allen, E., and Seaman, J. (2015)

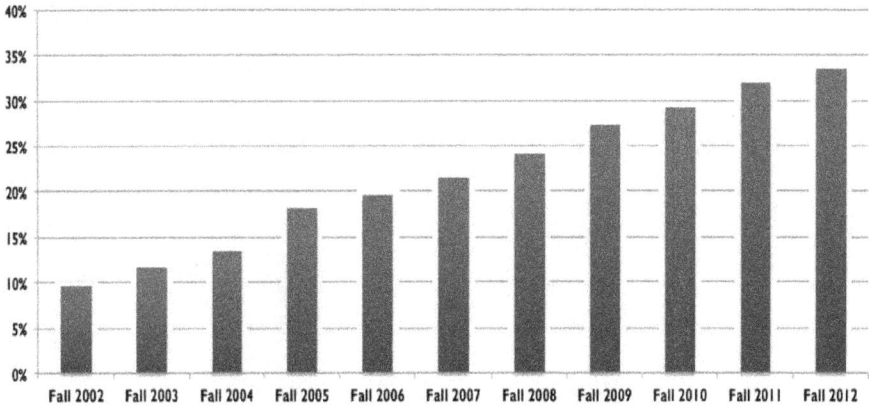

Figure: 5.8   Online Enrollment as a Percent of Total Enrollment-Fall 2002 through Fall 2012

Source: Allen, E., and Seaman, J. (2015)

In the fall of 2002, only 9.6% of higher education students took at least one online course (see table 5.1 and figure 5.8). In the same year, only 66.1% of public institutions, and 34.6% of private institutions believed that online education was strategically crucial to the future of their institutions. By 2006, the percentage among public institutions had increased to 74.1%, while the rate for private institutions had improved to 50%.[72]

PERCENTAGE OF STUDENTS TAKING DISTANCE COURSES - 2012-2015

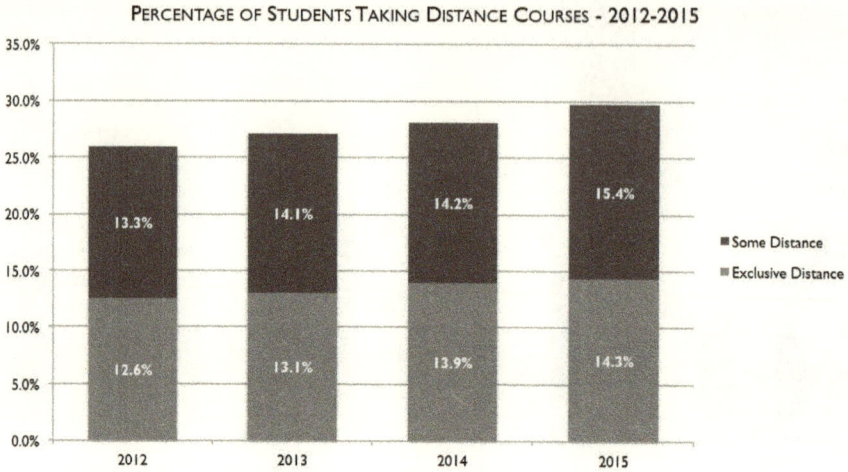

Figure: 5.9

Source: Allen, E., and Seaman, J. (2016)

As figure 5.9 shows, the number of students who received "exclusively" their courses online from 2012 to 2015 increased each year, and in 2015, 29.7% of all higher education students took at least one online course.

DISTANCE EDUCATION ENROLLMENTS

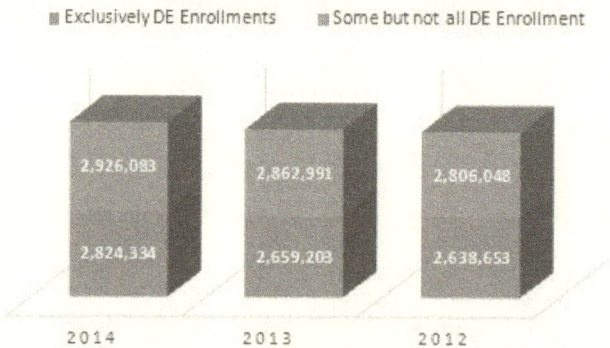

Figure: 5.10

Source: Allen, E., and Seaman, J. (2016)

In the United States, 2.8 million students took some of their courses online in 2012, while 2.6 million exclusively took their classes online. In 2014, the number of students that partially took their courses online had reached 2.9 million, while those who solely took their courses online was 2.8 million (see figure 5.10). Evidence of an increase in online education enrollment is also showing in Latin American countries, the Middle East, and Sub-Sahara African countries. In China, the United Kingdom, South Korea, India, Australia, and Western Europe, online education enrollments continue to grow as many higher institutions offer a fully online program or blended program.

Growth of Online Education in Organizations

Given the popularity that online education attracts in academics, one could mistakingly conclude that the growth that has taken place so far in the sector is exclusive to the education sector. Contrarily, corporate organizations, government agencies, and non-profits organizations have a long track record of using online learning technologies and resources for training. In 1999, 20% of corporate training was conducted online, with a projection of a 40% increase by 2003.[86] By the end of 2003, the number of **Global 2000** companies that had used some form of e-learning for training reached almost 90%.[73]

In 2002, organizations spent over $5.5 billion on **web-based training** (WBT) because investment in employee training has become inevitable, given the discrepancy between the output of public education and the demand by corporations for specialized skills and knowledge.[74] In 2003, companies spent approximately $11 billion on online education and training with a projection of eighteen billion dollars by 2005.[75]

In the United States, from the **National Restaurant Association** to the **American Medical Association**, and the **Red Cross** distance learning help workers to obtain and maintain certifications in their regulated industries, and for the professional development of members, bridging the learning gaps within the educational system in the country.[76] **BEST** organizations that reported increased usage of formal learning by 50% while **Global 500** (G500) organizations offered 42% of their training hours online.[77]

The United States Military is one of the primary users of online education in the world.[78] The Military provides over 2.3 million hours of distance learning each year to military personnel serving in the remote areas of the world so they could have the same educational opportunities as their counterparts at home and the U.S. general population.[79] The course materials are divided into different modules and learned sequentially with the chance for the servicemen to apply the knowledge gained in class to their jobs in combat.[80] The U.S military measures accountability and quality of instruction by the number of reduced military casualties and military efficiencies in a conflict environment.[81]

E-learning enables employees to acquire knowledge without disrupting their workflow.[82] Globalization has changed the production system and transformed the work environment with employees sometimes separated by thousands of miles, and often operating from different countries. IBM saved about eighty million dollars in one year in travel and housing expenses by administering online training to employees.[83] In 2001, Dow Chemical offered six hundred online training programs to employees. Through the program, Dow employees completed fourteen thousand courses in one week![84]

Summary of Main Points

- In the United States, the second wave of distance education started in the late 1800s when many adults who wanted to pursue higher-education programs could not do so due to work commitments and lack of financial resources.
- The British government established the Open University (OU) in 1969, which proved to be one of the best educational policies formulated by the British government with a ripple effect in other countries.
- The decreasing number of teachers in the classroom, especially in the rural areas is boosting interest in online education in the United States, China, and other countries.

- Online education is growing due to the global demand for higher education and an increase in the number of primary and secondary school students.
- The emergence of new economies has increased the government spending on social programs, including education, which the revenue streams of many countries cannot absorb.
- Economic factors are boosting online course enrollments due to the high cost of higher education as students and schools look for alternative ways to reduce costs. Also, governments support technology-based education in the face of dwindling revenues.
- Countries initiate educational policies to increase access to education as the expansion of higher education based on traditional education models stagnate.

Discussion Questions

1. Evaluate how online education has grown in the past twenty years. Discuss the factors responsible for the growth.
2. Discuss how modern technology has impacted online education and the effects on students. Which technology has changed online learning the most? Provide a rationale for your answer.
3. Based on your reading in this chapter, which factor has impacted online education the most? Support your answer with appropriate examples.
4. Identify and discuss at least three factors that have impacted online learning. Based on your understanding, how do you see those factors shaping online education in the future?
5. Discuss the benefits of online education to organizations. How can organizations use online learning to improve productivity?

6

THE EMERGING TRENDS IN ONLINE EDUCATION

Learning Objectives: After studying this chapter, you should be able to:

1. Understand blended learning
2. Explain residencies
3. Understand Massive Open Online Courses (MOOCs)
4. Discuss social media use in education
5. Explain the effect of gamification in learning
6. Discuss how simulation enhances learning
7. Explain the personalized learning approach
8. Describe the adaptive learning system
9. Understand mobile learning in education

INTRODUCTION

Technology has transformed distance learning significantly, but it's not the only phenomenon that has altered the learning approach. In this chapter, we discuss how blended learning, Massive Open Online Courses (MOOCs), social learning, gamification, simulation, personalized learning, adaptive learning, and mobile learning is changing how students learn and how education institutions deliver their educational programs.

THE NEW PARADIGM IN ONLINE EDUCATION

Blended Learning

Blended learning is when students complete parts of course activities online and some at the campus, or students take a mix of online courses with face-to-face courses. In the United States, 84% of higher education institutions and 41% of K-12 schools now offer blended, and fully online courses and 88% of education leaders from kindergarten to higher institutions either agree or strongly agree that blended learning has significantly increased at their institution over the past five years.[1]

An education institution offers blended learning based on its educational objectives and academic priorities. At Cornell University, the University of Illinois and Stanford University faculty post their lectures online and then use the class time for application, problem-solving, and assessment.[2]

At San Jose University, electrical engineering students can watch revamped **edX** lecture videos at home and attend classes twice a week to discuss topics and complete other course activities.[3] The University of Illinois offers 80-blended programs that target three essential areas of study of the undergraduate program in general education, business education, and health professional education in the graduate program.[4] In California, online students attend a portion of their

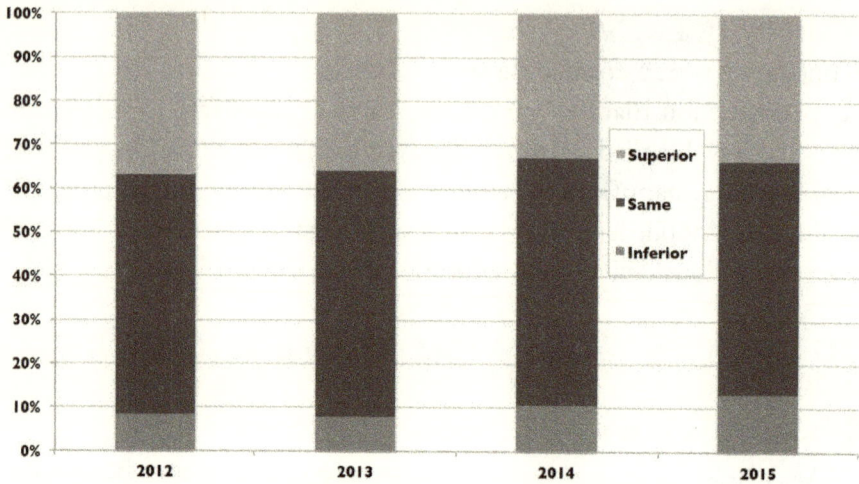

Figure: 6.1 Learning Outcomes in Blended/Hybrid Course Compared to Face-to-Face: 2012 - 2015

I. E. Allen and J. Seaman (2016)

classes in a face-to-face classroom as part of the state's requirements for online programs.[5]

As figure 6.1 depicts, an overwhelming majority of educational leaders rate blended learning as equal or superior to face-to-face learning. Most schools offer blended learning because it cultivates deeper thinking and promotes active learning among students. Research showed that students who took a blended course improved their test scores and achieved a median midterm test scores of 10 points than their classmates who took the campus-based version.[6]

Residency

A residency allows students taking online courses to have face-to-face interactions with their classmates, faculty, staff, and school administrators at a physical location. Residency programs vary from one institution to another, but schools ensure that the sessions are intense and meet the needs of students.

In the United States, the University of Phoenix, Argosy University, Nova Southeastern University, and other educational institutions combine residency programs with their online programs. Walden University offers a residency across major cities in the United States, Europe, and South America that students in various disciplines attend all year round.[7] Traditional education institutions such as Georgetown University, Emory University, Purdue University integrate residencies with their online education. In the United Kingdom, the University of London requires external students to attend campus at a designated time of the year, though students can fulfill the residency requirements at a local school, college, or University in their countries of abode. External students attending the University of Kent spend up to six weeks on campus each year before graduation.[8]

At Indiana University's Kelley School of Business, students in the online MBA program participate in a mandatory, one-week residency before classes begin. The initial orientation visit at the campus helps ground the students and prepares them for the rigors of the online environment. Likewise, it provides an opportunity for students to build connections and maintain strong relationships with the university's academic community. Kennesaw State University found that online students who attended a face-to-face orientation were less likely to drop out of school. A follow-up study that looked at alternative methods of retaining students, such as frequent phone calls by instructors were not as beneficial in student retention as a brief campus residency. Master students in agribusiness at Kansas State University visit the campus twice a year to reduce a feeling of isolation and opportunity for the students to meet and work on problems together.[9]

At Pennsylvania State University, although no formal residency required for online students, the institution offers a variety of in-person and online activities to help students develop a sense of campus community. The students attend the Penn State's annual All-University Day, appear at the football games, and World Campus tailgate party, as well as participate in graduation open houses. The World Campus uses the **Second Life** virtual world to live-stream a "huddle with the faculty," during which professors introduce themselves and answer students' questions.[10]

Massive Open Online Courses (MOOCs)

Massive Open Online Courses or **MOOCs** is the learning delivered to hundreds and sometimes thousands of students either for free or for a fee with little or no interactions with a professor. MOOCs began in 1999 when the **Massachusetts Institute of Technology** (MIT) launched its **OpenCourseWare** program by allowing faculty to make samples of their lectures available online to the public free of charge. By 2013, **MIT** had put more than 2,000 courses online, and more than 125 million students from around the world have logged on to the **courseware** since 2001.[11]

However, other leading universities in the United States, such as Yale University, Harvard University, Carnegie Mellon University, Duke University, to mention a few, have initiated MOOCs since **MIT** launched its MOOCs in 1999. In the United Kingdom, the University of London, through **Coursera** and other major higher education institutions in partnerships with the **British Open University**, has launched the MOOCs program as well.

Coursera, edX, Udacity, FutureLearn, Desire2Learn (D2L), **Udemy**, and **Khan Academy** are the leading MOOC providers, but many local educational organizations exist around the world that partner with educational institutions in offering MOOCs. The universities that were already offering MOOCs gave the following six primary reasons for launching the program:

1. Extending the reach of the institution and access to education;
2. Building and maintaining a brand;
3. Improving economics by lowering costs or increasing revenues;
4. Improving educational outcomes for both MOOC participants and on-campus students;
5. Innovation in teaching and learning;
6. Research on teaching and learning.[12]

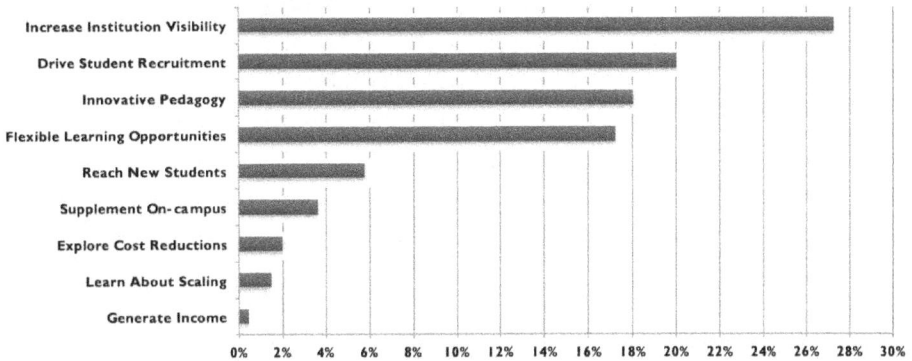

Figure: 6.2 Primary Objective for Institution's MOOC: 2013

Allen, I. E & Seaman, J. (2014)

As figure 6.2 demonstrates, there are other motivations education institutions offer MOOCs apart from the six main primary reasons. Against the rising profile of MOOCs in recent years, debates have ensued whether the learning approach pollutes the quality of higher education because less than 20% of students enrolled in MOOCs completed their classes, and students may have problems converting the courses into college credits. Also, MOOCs are college-level courses, and a high number of students who take the courses are ill-prepared for college-level work. From 2012 to 2013, the proportion of academic leaders that believed that the credentials for MOOCs completion would confuse higher education increased from 55% to 64%.[13]

In February 2013, the **American Council on Education** (ACE) approved five MOOC courses in the field of mathematics and science for college credit at the University of California, Irvine, Duke University, and the University of Pennsylvania. Students who meet all requirements and complete one of the five pre-approved courses in Pre-Calculus, Introduction to Genetics and Evolution, Bioelectricity, Calculus, and Algebra can present the result to these universities for credit consideration or prerequisites for undergraduate programs.[14] While the **ACE** accreditation of MOOCs is ground-breaking, the transferability of credits could be problematic because schools establish policies and determine the criteria for accepting courses to a degree program.

In the United States, schools must register with the appropriate Board of Education and pay the required fees to recruit students and for the certificates issued to students to be valid. In the state of California, community colleges and state universities and other colleges must carefully navigate around vague regulatory and administrative requirements of **Western Association of Schools and Colleges** (WASC), and the **Accrediting Commission for Community and Junior Colleges** (ACCJC). The two accreditation agencies demand that all students, whether on-campus or online, receive "equivalent student services" and schools must have "regular effective contact," with them both of which are hard to satisfy because schools often use different criteria to interpret the regulations.[15]

MOOCs and Opportunity for Higher Education

Despite the row over MOOCs, the learning approach could be the antidote to the intractable problems facing higher education. Over the past few decades, the population of students seeking higher education admissions has skyrocketed without corresponding space to accommodate them. Many countries are also facing teacher shortages while governments at the local, state, and national levels have difficulties funding education, limiting the chance of students seeking education opportunities in fulfilling their academic dreams. In the state of California, thousands of students in the state university are on the waiting list in taking basic and introductory algebra classes, preventing them from graduating from a four-year degree program on time. Recently, the State Senate introduced a bill that mandates public colleges and universities to give credit for online courses to alleviate the challenges that students face due to space problem.[16]

As the future of higher education hangs in the balance, MOOCs offer tremendous prospects in creating an entirely new education model and opportunity in reaching a broader market that universities couldn't serve due to physical limitations. Also, MOOCs offer a unique business opportunity for education institutions to unbundle learning and customize educational offerings for students.[17] Mostly, MOOC platforms pursue two primary learning objectives concurrently: (1) offering highly scalable forms of learning to large numbers of learners, and (2) offering blended learning to campus-based students.[18]

In October 2016, **MIT** launched a program in supply chain management whereby students take the first semester's worth of courses for the one-year professional program through **edX**. The classes are available for free, but students who complete five courses and pay $150 in identity-verification fees for a course can earn a credential known as **MicroMasters,** making them eligible to take a comprehensive final exam. Students who receive a passing grade can complete the master's degree on campus. In December 2017, **MIT** announced a second program in data, economics, and development policy that students didn't have to come to school until after two years into their degree programs. The **MicroMasters**, which brings dozens of new degree-seeking students to campus, has recalibrated the discussion on how **MIT** delivers graduate-level education and provides clues on how the institution will admit students going forward. A 2014 report predicted that **MIT** could graduate the first batch of bachelor's degrees online sooner than expected because MOOCs give students more flexibility and reduces the time they spend on campus. Students also found the opportunity to take MOOCs significantly less stressful than face-to-face courses.[19]

In the United States, public universities face financial difficulties, while students and parents are at their wit's end because of the increasing tuition costs and escalating debt profiles amidst stagnant graduation rates and volatile employment markets.[20] In 2008/2009, the average tuition, including room and board per year at a public four-year university was $16,460 and $38,720 at a private nonprofit university. In 2018/2019, the average tuition was $21,370 for a public four-year university and $48,510 for a private education institution.[21]

Organization for Economic Co-operation and Development (OECD) reported that between 2000 and 2010, the average tuition per student per year in **OECD** countries (currently, 35 members mostly from developed and developing countries) increased from $9,086 to $13,528 per year, an increase of almost 50% within ten years.[22] As the **return on investment** (ROI) of a university degree comes under intense scrutiny and cost weigh heavily on the decision of students for choosing a school, MOOCs offer a real solution to the rising costs of higher education.

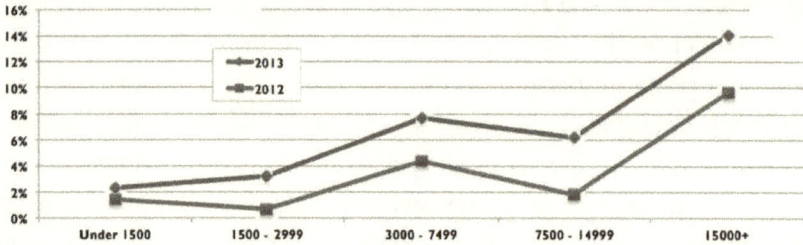

Figure: 6.3   Institutions with MOOC by Size of Institution: 2012 and 2013

I.E., Allen and J. Seaman (2014)

As figure 6.3 establishes, big institutions with 15,000 student enrollments were more likely to offer MOOCs, while smaller institutions with less than 3,000 enrolled students were the least likely. The bigger an institution, the quicker the institution can amass resources in developing a new program, while smaller institutions proceed gradually due to financial constraints and lack of required human resources. In sum, between 2012 and 2013, the percentage of higher education institutions that offered MOOCs increased from 2.6% to 5.0% and rose from 8.0% in 2014 to 11.3% in 2015.[23]

In February 2013, Wesleyan University partnered with Coursera to offers six MOOCs.[24] In August 2013, the **University System of Georgia** (USG), which comprises four research universities, four comprehensive universities, ten state universities, 13 state colleges, the Georgia Archives, and the Georgia Public Library Service, introduced MOOCs to allow students earn additional credits toward **USG** degrees.[25] The **USG** currently hosts more than 60,000 courses in the **Desire2learn** (D2L) learning platform and receiving more than 50 million hits per day. The USG's chief academic officer noted that "a key measure of success for an online learning initiative is its demonstrated ability to help increase student learning and graduation rates...from a student's perspective, partnerships with organizations such as **Desire2Learn** provide the University System with more options to help students succeed academically."[26]

In May 2013, **Coursera** partnered with ten state university systems and public university flagships in the United States that include the State University of New York (SUNY), the Tennessee Board of Regents and

University of Tennessee Systems, University of Colorado System, University of Houston System, University of Kentucky, University of Nebraska, University of New Mexico, West Virginia University and University System of Georgia in offering MOOCs. **SUNY** alone enrolls over 460,000 students and continues to expand its existing database of online courses.[27] Elke Leeds, Assistant Vice President of Technology Enhanced Learning at Kennesaw State University, stated: "…Education institutions strategically design MOOCs to increase access, shorten degree completion time, and reduce costs while reinforcing the relationship between higher education and the citizenry." The MOOC initiative has grown from seven to more than 30 certificate, bachelors, masters, and doctoral programs within a short period.[28]

In 2013, the Georgia Institute of Technology College of Computing announced its first professional MOOC Master of Science degree in computer science in collaboration with **Udacity**, a MOOC provider, and **AT&T**, the top communication company in the United States. The three organizations partnered to address the U.S. growing shortage of qualified workers in **science**, **technology**, **engineering**, and **mathematics** (STEM) fields and expanding access to quality education at affordable rates.[29] The prospect of one of the U.S. top universities offering a low-cost degree in computer science has generated significant interest within the academic community. As a respected institution, Georgia Tech has a direct connection to a **Fortune 100** corporation that will use the computer degree to fill its vacancies pipeline. Some educators argue the leap from individual noncredit courses to full degree programs is a paradigm shift in the evolution of MOOCs and a real change in higher education as the computer program will cost $6,600, substantially less than the $45,000 that the program cost on-campus.[30]

In 2015, **edX** collaborated with Arizona State University by launching the **Global Freshman Academy** that allows students to complete the first year of a bachelor's degree through the MOOC provider. Since both entities joined forces, the Global Freshman Academy has enrolled over 230,000 students from more than 180 countries.[31] In 2016, Deakin University in Australia partnered with **FutureLearn**, a UK-based MOOC provider, to offer post-graduate master's degrees in cybersecurity, information technology, financial planning, property, and humanitarian and development action. **FutureLearn** offers a diverse selection of courses to over 110 leading universities and internationally renowned organizations and professional bodies from around the world.[32]

In 2013, Tsinghua University in Beijing, China, launched MOOCs that today offers over 60 courses in Chinese.[33] **XuetangX**, which means a place of learning in China, is one of the world's top five MOOC providers, with over 14 million users and 32 million enrollments offering over 1,700 courses. The MOOC provider has more than 500 partners and collaborating with prestigious Chinese universities such as Tsinghua University, Pekin University, and Fudan University and American universities such as **MIT**, University of California, Berkeley, and Rice University. The organization is developing Chines courses with **Stanford Online** and **Association of Chartered Certified Accountants** (ACCA) and offering an exchange program with **France Université Numérique** (FUN) France, and **National Institute of Lifelong Education** (NILE) South Korea.[34]

In 2018, **Coursera** announced six new master's degrees: A Master of Computer Science from Arizona State University, a Global Master of Public Health from Imperial College London, a Master of Computer Science from the University of Illinois, a Bachelor of Science in Computer Science from the University of London, a Master of Applied Data Science and a Master of Public Health from the University of Michigan. With a total of 10-degree programs offered on its platform, Coursera could become a premier destination for world-class degrees in the future.[35]

Studies consistently show that the quality of online learning is as good or better than the quality of face-to-face instruction, and education institutions design MOOCs mostly for distinct groups of professionals that traditional education systems cannot accommodate. The MOOCs offered by North Carolina State University, New York Institute of Technology and the American Museum of Natural History specifically target K-12 teachers and administrators.[36]

At Coursera, only one-third of the students are from the U.S while 68% of users come from outside the United States such as Brazil, India, and Russia where the number of jobs that require a higher education dramatically exceeds the number of people with the required skills to perform the tasks.[37] Students who take MOOCs at Harvard, MIT, and Stanford adapt the courses to meet the needs of their local communities and in the process, inducing change and transforming lives. The students combine screen time with face time and sometimes meet in small-group in informal and blended-learning settings with the support they receive from peers and mentors they compete well with their counterparts anywhere in the world.[38]

For many years, MOOC providers offered classes only in the English language. Education providers are addressing the cultural problems constraining students from non-English speaking countries by partnering with foreign universities in creating new courses and facilitating the translation of the existing curriculum into local languages.[39] For instance, **Coursera** works with universities in non-English-speaking countries to teach classes in native languages such as French, Spanish, Chinese, German, and Italian. The education provider has a network of "translation partners" that include non-profit organizations, companies, and universities that translate popular courses into a selection of languages such as Russian, Portuguese, Turkish, Japanese, Ukrainian, Kazakh, and Arabic so it can reach more students. **Coursera** also uses **Transifex** cloud-based localization tool that enables organizations and individuals to translate course content across multiple disciplines from anywhere.[40] As of January 2017, **Coursera** had partnered with over 148 top universities and organizations in 29 countries, offering more than 2000 online courses.[41]

Given the current state of higher education and the demand of students and employers, MOOCs could be the catalyst for competency-based education needed for the 21st-century economy and the solution to the escalating costs of higher education. MOOCs could open the floodgate of educational opportunities for disadvantaged students in countries where admission demand outpaces available space. As educational institutions embrace MOOCs, they must address the problem of converting MOOCs into credits without resulting in students taking multiple courses.[42]

Social Learning

Social learning is acquiring and sharing information through **social media**. The use of social media technologies in education has not only made learning exciting but teaches students communication, collaboration,

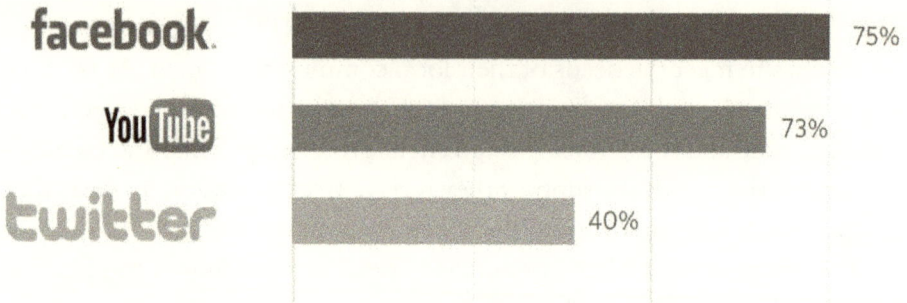

facebook. ████████████████████████████████ 75%

You Tube ██████████████████████████████ 73%

twitter ████████████████ 40%

Figure: 6.4   Social Media Use in the Classroom

College-Bound High School Students Use of Social Media

Source: BestColleges.com (2016)

and creativity skills needed in the workplace after graduation.[43] While preference for social media platforms change over time, social networks have become indispensable in acquiring knowledge and building professional skills. Today, social and professional networking sites such as YouTube, Facebook, Twitter, LinkedIn, Edmodo, Instagram, Vimeo, Pinterest, and messaging applications such as WhatsApp, Viber, Snapchat, WeChat, Facebook Messenger, Telegraph, and others are no longer used exclusively for informal conversations with friends and family, but educational purposes.

Among college-bound high school students, 75% use Facebook, 73% use YouTube, and 40% use Twitter (see figure 6.4). About half (51%) of the students visited a college's Facebook page, and about 30% of their parents browsed the page.[44] **The Pew Research Center** on social networking use shows that 74% of adults who use the Internet also use social media and higher among 18 to 29-year old, followed by the 30 to 34 age group.[45] The selling point for social networking sites is having the largest concentrations of people from different backgrounds under one roof. In July 2017, **Twitter** had approximately 328 million monthly active users, with 1 billion unique visits monthly, with 79% of them outside the United States. The social networking platform supports more than 40 languages, with 82% active users on mobile devices.[46]

In February of 2019, **Twitter** reported a 2% decrease in the number of monthly users down to 321 million from 2018 due to purging fake accounts from its platform. Nevertheless, the number of daily active users continues to grow, with a 9% increase in daily active users of 126 million while **Snapchat** had daily users of 60 million.[47]

As of September 2018, **Facebook** had an average of 1.5 billion daily active users and 2.27 billion monthly active users, with approximately 85.8% regular active users outside the U.S. and Canada.[48]

As education institutions integrate social learning into their instructional method, controversies have ensued whether social media is anathema to learning. While there are valid reasons to question the legitimacy of social media sources for knowledge acquisition, social media has become indispensable in areas where teachers and schools are in short supply. As the world's largest professional networking site, **LinkedIn** has more than 500 million registered members in over 200 countries and territories. The company has more than 40 million students, and recent college graduates are the fastest-growing demographic on the network.[49] In 2015, **LinkedIn** acquired **Linda.com** for $1.5 billion with a strategy of playing an active role in the education marketplace. Founded in 1995, **Linda.com** offers over 6,074 online courses in Business, Technology, Creative Skills, and other disciplines taught by industry experts that are available to individuals, higher education, and government.[50]

YouTube has millions of educational videos that students can watch online, and from the videos, they can obtain information to help them understand concepts better. In 2011, scholarly views on YouTube doubled, and in January 2012, such views accounted for 84% of the 181 million unique online video views. In December of 2011, YouTube introduced YouTube for Schools through which school administrators access videos on the **YouTube EDU** section of the site. In 2019, there were more than 10 million education videos on more than 14,000 channels for primary and secondary education and over 16,000 channels for university and 13,000 for vocational training from various **YouTube** educational partners.[51] The **School Tube** and **Teacher Tube** on the social networking site allow teachers and students to upload instructional videos and share information.[52]

A professor can integrate a topic trending on **Twitter** or **Facebook** to a lecture and ask students to share their views on the subject with the opportunity for students to enrich their knowledge of current issues, not only through their instructors but from millions of people around the world. At Iowa State University, students use **Twitter** and **Facebook** for discussions. Studies show that these platforms improve retention as students who use **Twitter** for studies are more likely to stay for their second year than students who do not.[53]

A study of social media in teaching by **Pearson Learning Solutions** showed that many of the social elements such as blogs, wikis, and podcasts are now standard in educational systems, and major e-learning manufacturers make social networking links a standard feature on their products. For instance, students can create a profile with their image and a brief biography on **Blackboard**. **Canvas** has external tools that help instructors live stream information and integrate content from **YouTube** and **Twitter** into lectures.[54]

Social learning enhances academic performance because it minimizes the loss of social interaction and allows students to personalize their learning experiences and presence, and often better than in a face-to-face classroom. Universities, academic departments, and support service offices (e.g., career centers, libraries) also use social media platforms to communicate with different stakeholders, including prospective and current students, as well as alumni and employers.[55] The University of Liverpool is adapting social learning pedagogies to the changing needs of students by focusing on customization, convenience, and real-time delivery of education. Students learn in an **asynchronous environment** with no fixed lecture times, and they can interact with instructors and fellow students at any time. Also, students can customize their degree programs to suit their educational needs and future professional careers.[56]

Gamification

Gamification is a "series of design principles, processes, and systems used to influence, engage, and motivate individuals, groups, and communities to drive behaviors and produce desired outcomes."[57] Games are created without any reference to reality and are governed by rules and structured with a goal or an intention to win, to be victorious, or to overcome an obstacle.[58]

The video game industry has grown tremendously, and the prevalence of smartphones with advanced capabilities has continued unrelentingly. **Entertainment Software Association** (ESA), finds that 58% of Americans played video games and spent a total of $20.77 billion in 2012 on games and accessories.[59] Apart from recreational games that individuals played for personal enjoyment, there are sophisticated **edugames** (educational games) for learning, and the game industry is expanding and growing each year.[60]

At higher education and K-12 levels, schools take advantage of the built-in reward system in games, which increases students' engagement and motivate them to learn and retain new information seamlessly.[61] For decades, instructional designers have integrated game elements such as stories, case studies into the curriculum, or used game-based mechanics, aesthetics, and game thinking to engage students, motivate action, promote education and solve problems in the classroom.[62] Studies show that games enhance learning in the cognitive, affective, and psychomotor domains.[63] Games-based learning takes into consideration the interactivity and engagement of learners first and the learning objectives second.[64]

In real life, individuals might not feel that they are as good as they are about their accomplishments or objectively rate their performance. Also, when confronted with obstacles, people might feel depressed, overwhelmed, frustrated, or cynical. In games, these feelings disappear because of the instant gratification that keeps people motivated to accomplish a task. Gamers have four common features that make them hopeful individuals: urgent optimism, social fabric, blissful productivity, and epic meaning.[65] The successful application of a simple game technique can transform a mundane task into an addictive regimen making a complex task attractive to accomplish. Gamification minimizes the negative emotions that one experiences in the traditional learning environment because of the **learn-by-failure** and the absence of embarrassment that sometimes accompany face-to-face learning. Games allow instructors to monitor and effectively track progress and use currency-based tracking mechanisms in meeting course objectives.[66]

Studies show that students tend to procrastinate and start assignments only two or three days before the deadline. Likewise, they find it difficult to identify critical concepts taught in lectures or recalling them if they don't apply the ideas immediately. In one study, the application of game mechanics in a traditional scheme-based introductory programming course, induced consistent behavior from students and exposed gaps in each student's learning progress.[67]

An educational game produces immersive experiences when incorporated with **augmented reality** (AR). In a game, Minecraft, jointly sponsored by the U.S. Department of the Interior and the National Park Service, the city of La Junta, Colorado., and a nearby community college, a local school district reconstructed the historic Bent's Old Fort in Colorado that students worldwide and the general public can explore virtually.[68]

Game-based learning is not exclusive to the education industry as organizations use games for onboarding and training employees. A study found that employees trained on video games learned more information, attained a higher skill level, and retained information longer than workers who learned in less interactive environments. Games provide a higher level of result because of the interactivity and the elements that make games engaging.[69]

For many years, game-based learning has been a staple in the U.S. military but increasingly becoming popular in organizations and consumer education.[70] **Volkswagen** used game-based learning to change consumer behavior so they could exercise more. In the campaign that went viral, **Volkswagen** installed a Piano Staircase at the Odenplan subway in Stockholm, Sweden. The Piano played a musical note every time a person moved up and down the stairs. The sound of the Piano with each step encouraged people to use the stairs instead of the escalator, and at the end of the campaign, 66% more people used the intriguing musical stairs over the elevator.[71]

In a Gallup's Employee Engagement Survey conducted by **Deloitte** in 2011, the company found that 71% of workers were "not engaged" or "actively disengaged" in their work. Also, the employees had a low interest in face-to-face training due to the loss of time and money coupled with printed materials that mostly go unused despite the huge money the company spent procuring them. **Deloitte** modified its training method by adding games to the online executive training that reward accomplishments with points and badges.[72] Within a short period, **Deloitte** recorded a 37% increase in the number of workers that completed their training programs and recorded a 40% increase in weekly visitors and those returning to its digital learning portal.[73]

In 2007, **United Parcel Service Inc.** (UPS) noticed that 30% of the driver candidates were not performing well in face-to-face learning. **UPS** introduced video games into its **340 Methods** training program that place candidates in the driver's seat, so they can identify obstacles and react to them while meandering through street corners. Since the introduction of video games, less than 10% of the driver candidates have failed the training.[74] As online education grows, learning will transition from instructions that seem like teaching toward learning that functions like games.

Simulation

Simulation is a simplified, dynamic, and precise representation of reality defined as a system. A simulation is judged by its realism, by its correspondence to the system which it represents and for optimization of the discovery of the relationships between variables and the confrontation of divergent approaches.[75]

Simulation and **games** share some commonalities, but in practice, they have different usages and serve different purposes. A game is created for entertainment and educational purposes and provides an artistic representation of some event while simulations are a deliberate effort to precisely represent a real phenomenon and used for evaluative or computational purposes.[76]

Research in education (including continuing education) demonstrates that simulations promote competency development, both in primary and complex subjects because it allows for efficient testing of the models used to predict events. **Simulation** possesses animations and graphics, and game-like exercises that immerse students in learning and help them complete tasks and understand the ramifications of their decisions and actions within a defined parameter.[77] A medical student will demonstrate competency better in an environment that uses various examples in a realistic context or an environment that provides educational activities of scenarios that imitate real-world situations that the student will face in the clinical setting.[78]

The reality-personified of simulations underpin its acceptance across disciplines because it mirrors the conditions students will confront in the workplace. **Harvard Business Publishing** developed simulations that cover a range of topics from entrepreneurship and finance to operations management and organizational behavior that provide students with the real-world experiences of the concepts learned in the classroom. The simulation in entrepreneurship used at Wharton School, University of Pennsylvania, immerses students in the fundamentals of forming a new company, and they can role-play as founders, investors, and potential employees. The students interact with their classmates to negotiate deals, calculate valuation, find the right staffing mix and debate financial gains versus organizational control.[79]

At the University of Colorado, Boulder, the **PhET** simulations allow students to visually explore concepts (such as balancing a chemical equation and Faraday's Law) in physics, biology, chemistry, and more.[80] In 2010, **Wiley Higher Education** partnered with **Stock Trak**, the world's leading provider of financial education simulations, and **Facebook** through **WallStreetSurvivor.com** to develop simulations on different investment options that provide students and instructors a better perspective on how they can impact the global economy.[81]

In the military, medicine, aviation, macroeconomics, and other fields, simulations provide the digital visibility of events before application because the least error in these sensitive fields could be costly and catastrophic. Simulations offer high-level interactivity and strengthen concepts and theory acquisition because it places objects or systems within the center of learning and promotes the development of mental models in learners.[82]

Personalized Learning

Personalized learning or **Personalization** is the tailoring of pedagogy, curriculum, and learning environments to meet the needs and aspirations of individual learners. Personalized learning is also called **student-centered learning** because the learning objective is to make students the primary focus in educational and instructional decisions, rather than what might

be preferred, more convenient, or logis-
tically easier for teachers and schools.[83]

In the 1970s, in the United States,
the idea of creating distinct courses and
formulating instructional strategies for
every student was famous for a brief
period. Educators abandoned the idea
when they realized that it was imprac-
ticable to develop unique academic
programs for dozens of students in the
same class.[84] In the traditional classroom
environment, the teacher provides all
students with the same instruction, the
same assignments, and the same assessments with no variation or modification
from student to student.[85] The traditional education model thrives under a
one-size-fits-all approach because teachers expect students to absorb content
communally irrespective of each student's learning capabilities and learning
preferences. Technology offers a different learning approach and provides
alternate learning experience because teachers can structure a course or
construct individualized learning pathways for a student thereby increasing his or her learning effectiveness through engagement and evaluation
measurements.[86]

A **Research and Development** (RAND) Corporation report showed
that K-12 schools that used personalized learning improved in mathematics
and reading and performed higher than schools without such emphases.
Personalized learning lets students work with the course material that meets
their needs and suit their abilities. Also, they can go at their own pace and
learn from anywhere, whether at home, in a classroom, at the library or
from other locations.[87]

The Multiple Intelligences (MI) Chart

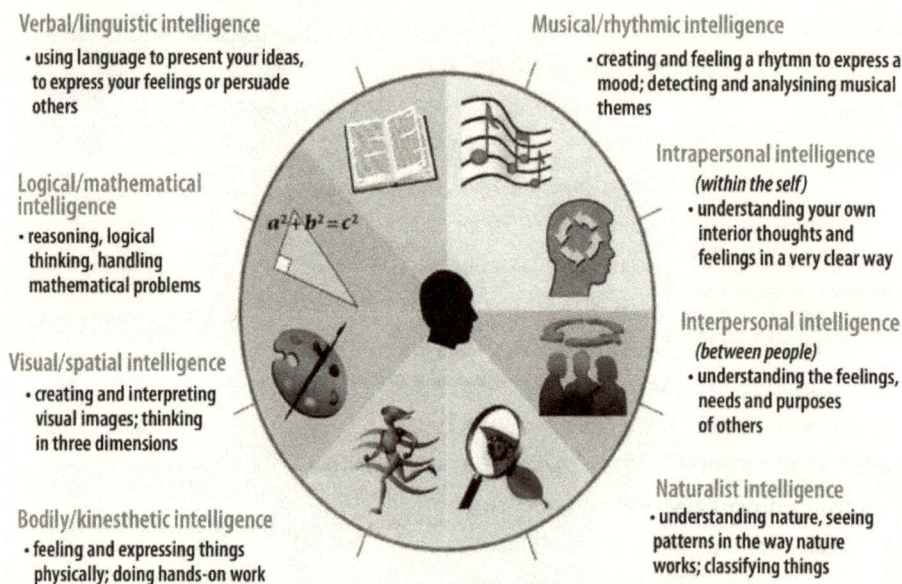

Verbal/linguistic intelligence
- using language to present your ideas, to express your feelings or persuade others

Logical/mathematical intelligence
- reasoning, logical thinking, handling mathematical problems

$a^2 + b^2 = c^2$

Visual/spatial intelligence
- creating and interpreting visual images; thinking in three dimensions

Bodily/kinesthetic intelligence
- feeling and expressing things physically; doing hands-on work

Musical/rhythmic intelligence
- creating and feeling a rhytmn to express a mood; detecting and analysining musical themes

Intrapersonal intelligence
(within the self)
- understanding your own interior thoughts and feelings in a very clear way

Interpersonal intelligence
(between people)
- understanding the feelings, needs and purposes of others

Naturalist intelligence
- understanding nature, seeing patterns in the way nature works; classifying things

Figure: 6.5   Dublin West Education Centre

Learning theories show that individuals learn differently and possess different **Intelligence Quotients** (IQs). A person's **IQ** determines and reflects on how the person absorbs, process, and retain materials and the way students A and B will absorb and process information will depend on their **IQs**. Students also face myriads of social, physical, and mental issues within and outside the class that impacts their academic performance, but teachers are generally ill-equipped in handling such problems. Under the conventional learning system, if student A has mastered a topic, and student B needs additional support, student A must wait for student B, who needs extra assistance. Technology has changed student possibilities because there are online tools that teachers use to track students' progress and present learning content based on each student's abilities and learning preferences. Through periodic assessments, teachers can evaluate the acquired knowledge with additional practice exercises given to struggling students so they can excel in specific areas of study.[88]

Personalized Learning and Concept Mastery

Personalized learning assesses students' present knowledge and assigns a specific learning path for them to develop a competency in a discipline that matches their future career choice. Personalized learning allows students to determine what they learn when they learn and how they learn and the opportunity to study in ways that suit their learning styles and multiple intelligences (Intellectual Intelligence, Emotional Intelligence, Social Intelligence, Change Intelligence).[89]

Personalized learning is often confused with **Self-study**, but broader than individualization of instruction. In personalized learning, students can listen to recorded lectures as many times as they deem fit and go back as many times as possible to clarify confusing areas. Likewise, they can repeat an exercise until they master it before moving on to the next section. Personalization enables students to control the learning process by setting their own goals, move at their own pace, and communicate with teachers when they need help and have a direct say in the methods and content provided.

The University of Hawaii's **STAR** graduation initiative has won accolades from **Complete College America** for dramatically increasing student graduation rates. The **STAR Guided Pathways Systems** use technology to give students a clear and streamlined route to graduation. Students track their progress, review requirements, and explore the impact of scheduling (and changes in major) or the time it will take them to graduate. In the early 2000s, Florida State University introduced a guided-pathway model that maps academic programs with mandatory advising at crucial points in a student's career. Since the school launched the program, the percentage of students graduating with excess credits dropped from 30% to just 5% between 2000 and 2009, while the four-year graduation rate rose from 44% to 61%.[90]

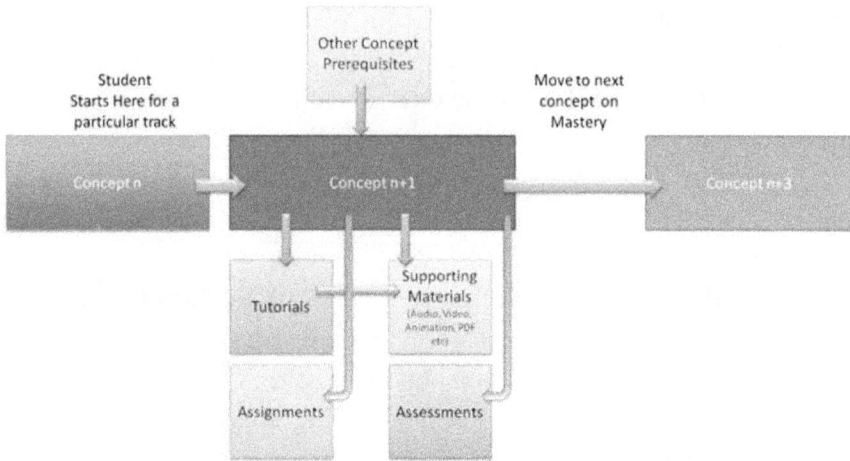

Figure: 6.6   Movement within One Track

Nedungadi, P. & Raman, R (2012)

Diagram 6.6 illustrates the pathway it takes to master a concept. In the figure, a student needs to get from mastery level Concept n to Concept $n + 3$. Concept n is what the student currently knows or the current mastery level. The student needs to move from Concept n to Concept $n + 1$ the next mastery level. If the student cannot master Concept $n + 1$, he or she stays at this level and may need the knowledge of other topics (Other Concept/Prerequisites), tutoring, or additional academic support to comprehend Concept $n + 1$. The student will repeat this process until he or she has achieved the required mastery before moving to Concept $n + 3$. Put differently, if there are 20 students in a class, based on the mastery learning approach, not all of them who begin from Concept n would get to Concept $n + 3$ at the same time unless all the students achieved the mandatory mastery at every stage of the learning track.[91]

Personalized learning encourages prospective and current students to make the most of their existing skillsets and pursue education formats that match their abilities and help them reach their learning goals.[92] Some countries see personalized learning as a real possibility to improve student's performance and learning outcomes in the classroom. Under the **Obama administration**, the United States Department of Education allocated

$500 million to personalized learning programs in 68 school districts in the United States, serving almost 500,000 students in 13 states and Washington, D.C. The state of Rhode Island plans to spend $2 million to become the first U.S state to make teaching in all schools individualized. **Bill & Melinda Gates Foundation** is one of the organizations that support personalized learning and other student-centered learning methods in the United States and other countries.[93]

As the work environment changes, personalized learning will expand because it assigns a specific learning path that students could take to attain mastery in an academic area and offers the opportunity for schools to monitor their performance at each level of the learning process.[94]

Adaptive Learning

Adaptive learning empowers students in taking ownership of learning and correct their mistakes as they occur without waiting for the instructor. Adaptive learning uses technology to personalize learning experiences based on the command of course material, enabling students to focus on the concepts they need to understand. In a multiple-choice test, for example, if a student chooses answer B over the correct answer C, the student will receive the appropriate feedback as soon as he or she submits the assignment indicating a fault in the student's thought process or hints as to why another choice would be more suitable. The instant feedback helps students to know the correct or incorrect answers and saves instructor time and energy they can devote to other learning areas in class.[95]

Adaptive Learning and Academic Achievement

Studies show a strong correlation between adaptive learning and academic performance. Three-quarters of students noted that adaptive learning helped them retain new concepts, and most parents welcome the use of adaptive digital learning in the classroom. Eighty-four percent of students that used adaptive learning noticed a moderate to a significant improvement in their grades, and 91% of them stated that it had a positive impact on their learning experience.[96]

Starting with the class of 2020, Bucknell University in the U.S. will use predictive modeling to identify students who need extra help getting through their first year of college. The model uses pre-enrollment data such as demographic characteristics and family income, and post-enrollment data such as academic and social experiences during the first semester, to arrive at a "success score." In the predictive model, students who achieved a first-year **grade point average** (GPA) of 3.0 or higher are likely to return for their sophomore year than their peers who scored less.[97]

In the fall of 2011, Arizona State University (ASU) introduced an adaptive learning system in mathematics class when the institution noticed that many newly admitted students were not college-ready for the course. The adaptive system assesses what a student knows and identifies proficiency gaps, and reassess student mastery of course concepts, giving each student a personalized learning path. Instructors know students that are doing well and those that are not doing well. Likewise, instructors see which concepts students are struggling with across the board and focus attention more on those concepts in class. Since **ASU** introduced the adaptive learning system in developmental math, students have performed better with fewer of them withdrawing, and more students completing the course on time.[98]

From elementary to higher education, schools use **Adaptive Learning and Assessment System** (ALAS) in identifying the skills mastered, diagnose instructional needs, and monitor academic growth over time. At the classroom, school, and district levels, educational officials use the data generated in making decisions that place students in appropriate instructional programs. **ALAS** automatically detects device types and adapt the content based on the device, allowing students to continue with their assessment and learning in almost any environment. **ALAS**, tracks input, including answers, hints requested, and time spent on an item, tutorials viewed, and so on. Teachers can compile learning activities and put appropriate mechanisms in place for students to achieve their learning goals based on needs and priorities.[99]

As adaptive learning becomes popular, more organizations support the educational approach in the United States. The **Association of Public and Land-Grant Universities** (APLU) established a **Personalized Learning Consortium** to help schools interpret student learning data and develop initiatives that support adaptive learning methods. Adaptive learning will continue to be crucial for knowledge development because of the need for continued education throughout one's career whether it happens in a formal college environment or varieties of professional development settings.[100]

Mobile Learning

Mobile learning or ***M-learning*** occurs when students access course information from arrays of mobile devices, including laptops, tablets, smartphones, and other gadgets. The use of mobile devices for educational purposes has gained currency from researchers for some time, and the interest has continued to rise unabated.[101] In 2016, more than 2.1 billion mobile devices had **HTML5** web browsers, up from 109 million in 2011.[102] Students and educators use tablets, smartphones, notebooks, e-readers, and other portable devices not only because they make learning engaging but to connect and collaborate with subject-matter experts on research projects. Instructors can use smartphones for instant polls, quizzes, and other assessments, and quickly determine which students need additional information or help. Equally, students can use video chats for conversations or work on projects or use them for writing, posting links or pictures and developing social relationships.[103]

Mobile telecommunication services are becoming ever more predominant in many sectors, including education. While fixed telephone subscriptions continue to decline with a penetration rate of only 12.4% in 2018, the number of mobile-cellular telephone subscriptions continue to increase and now higher than the global population of 7.5 billion.[104]

A decade ago, research in mobile learning, focused mainly on **personal digital assistants** (PDAs), and cell phones, with an emphasis on the hardware used for creating course content. Recent research addresses mobile learning from hardware and software contexts and how their functionalities align with pedagogy.[105] Internet-based services and programs have evolved into a high degree of interactivity, and advances

in computing power and bandwidth allow **e-learning** designers to create and deliver visual and interactive experiences **synchronously**. Performance support software, such as **Adobe Captivate,** and **Camtasia**, enable experts to package knowledge for **asynchronous** distribution, and educators of all types use **synchronous** and **asynchronous technologies** to create large repositories of knowledge. The prevalence of tablets and smartphones make learning and academic support available right when they're needed. Whether you're on a train, plane, or by the pool, mobile devices provide an easy way to answer a question, demonstrate a function, or collaborate with peers on an idea or concept.[106]

At the University of Washington in Seattle, device ownership among students increased more than was projected by **EDUCAUSE Center for Applied Research** (ECAR). In 2014, only 38.5% of students reported owning a tablet. By 2015 the percentage had risen to 45.2% while smartphone ownership among the students increased from 87.9% in 2014 to 93.0% in 2015.[107]

The use of mobile devices by students for non-class activities during lectures have been a source of concern lately. Paradoxically, smartphones can minimize distractions because when learning is engaging, students will be less desirous of using their devices for non-educational activities. At New Franklin R-1 School District in Missouri, high school students in anatomy and physiology classes used video chat to connect with a university and observe a cadaver dissection. The students virtually visited the Holocaust Museum, video-conferenced with other students in Argentina, and a former student studying in Costa Rica.[108] The immediacy of mobile devices for work and personal use makes them invaluable for research and for solving problems.[109] Studies show that when students use mobile devices in different learning contexts, either in the informal or formal learning settings, it increases their understanding of subjects like science, mathematics, language and art, social science, and engineering.[110]

Mobile Devices in the Classroom

Mobile devices will be a primary driver for multimedia learning content in the coming decades. Improvements in the fields of integrated circuits, cellular transmission, and human-computer interface systems will provide a broad range of services and interact with the thousands of content objects that are available on the Internet. Educators and students will build virtual communities around media sharing applications, social networks, and **Web 2.0 applications** (used in social networking and social media sites). Researchers and practitioners and instructional designers are providing greater insight into the best ways of using **m-Learning** and **Web 2.0** technologies collaboratively.[111] Mobile technologies will increase globally, especially in South Asia. In India, smartphone ownership was up 184%, with more than 200 million devices in 2014. **FutureLearn** has 250,000 registered learners on its platform, of which 30% of them access courses via a mobile device.[112]

Despite the aptness of mobile devices in learning, overreliance could be detrimental to student achievement if there is a mismatch between pedagogical details and learning environment. Studies show that m-learning is beneficial, but the use of mobile technology by itself does not guarantee success. **M-learning** only improves learner outcomes when it is appropriately matched by pedagogical practices that consider the characteristics and opportunities presented by m-learning and recognize the demands of the differentiated educational and cultural contexts of the users.[113]

The use of mobile technologies in academics will continue to increase globally. Although there is a need for more studies on the impact of m-learning on education outcomes, preliminary research shows that m-learning boosts lifelong learning habits and skills. Schools and teachers must cooperate in promoting mobile learning especially how students can use the technology to achieve success in the classroom.[114]

Consumer Technologies
> 3D Video
> Electronic Publishing
> Mobile Apps
> Quantified Self
> Tablet Computing
> Telepresence
> Wearable Technology

Digital Strategies
> BYOD
> Flipped Classroom
> Games and Gamification
> Location Intelligence
> Makerspaces
> Preservation/Conservation Technologies

Internet Technologies
> Cloud Computing
> The Internet of Things
> Real-Time Translation
> Semantic Applications
> Single Sign-On
> Syndication Tool

Learning Technologies
> Badges/Microcredit
> Learning Analytics
> Massive Open Online Courses
> Mobile Learning
> Online Learning
> Open Content
> Open Licensing
> Personal Learning Environments
> Virtual and Remote Laboratories

Key Emerging
Technologies

Social Media Technologies
> Collaborative Environments
> Collective Intelligence
> Crowdfunding
> Crowdsourcing
> Digital Identity
> Social Networks
> Tacit Intelligence

Visualization Technologies
> 3D Printing/Rapid Prototyping
> Augmented Reality
> Information Visualization
> Visual Data Analysis
> Volumetric and Holographic Displays

Enabling Technologies
> Affective Computing
> Cellular Networks
> Electrovibration
> Flexible Displays
> Geolocation
> Location-Based Services
> Machine Learning
> Mobile Broadband
> Natural User Interfaces
> Near Field Communication
> Next-Generation Batteries
> Open Hardware
> Speech-to-Speech Translation
> Statistical Machine Translation
> Virtual Assistants
> Wireless Power

Figure: 6.7   Key Emerging Technologies

(Larson et al., 2014, p. 35)

Summary of Main Points

- Blended or hybrid learning combines face-to-face instructions with technology and allows students to complete course activities online and spend some time in a face-to-face environment.
- A residency enables students to have face-to-face interaction with their classmates and other members of the academic community.
- Massive Open Online Courses or MOOCs is the learning delivered to hundreds and sometimes thousands of students either for free or for a fee with little or no interactions with a professor.
- Social learning entails acquiring and sharing information through social and professional networking sites such as YouTube, Facebook, Twitter, LinkedIn, Edmodo, Instagram, Vimeo, Pinterest, and other websites.

- Games enhance learning in the cognitive, affective, and psychomotor domains. The instant gratification keeps students motivated to accomplish a task.
- Simulation enables students to be more engaged in the classroom because the animations and graphics, and game-like exercises immerse them in learning.
- Personalized learning assesses present knowledge level and assigns a specific learning path that enables students to develop a competency and learn in the way convenient to them.
- Adaptive learning personalizes learning experiences based on the command of course material, enabling students to focus attention on the concepts they need help understanding.
- Mobile learning enables students to access course information from an array of mobile devices, including laptops, tablets, smartphones, and other gadgets from any location as long as they have Internet access.

Discussion Questions

1. Education institution combines face-to-face instruction with technology to enhance learning outcomes. Argue for or against the learning approach and provide the rationale for your position.
2. Opinions vary on the efficacy of MOOCs in higher education. Identify and discuss the potential risks or benefits of MOOCs and place in the future of higher education.
3. Identify the social and professional networking sites that you know, and in what ways can education institutions use those platforms for learning? Discuss the dangers that social media posed to education and offer suggestions that could mitigate the problem?
4. Games and simulations not only make learning interacting but reinforce the theories taught in class. Address how educational institutions should leverage games and simulations for learning.

5. Adaptive learning uses technology to personalize learning experiences. Based on your understanding of the learning approach, would you recommend it for education institutions? Provide the rationale for your answer.

6. Describe the mobile learning approach. Identify various mobile technologies and discuss their advantages and disadvantages. Argue for or against using mobile devices for learning.

7

ONLINE EDUCATION TECHNOLOGIES

Learning Objectives: After studying this chapter, you should be able to:

1. Describe the learning management systems
2. Understand the management systems features and functionalities
3. Explain the rationale for choosing course management systems
4. Describe the process of creating an online course
5. Understand the online education technology requirements
6. Explain the role of technology in online education

INTRODUCTION

Technology continues to impact online education as manufacturers develop new learning applications every day. In this chapter, we discuss various learning management systems (LMSs) and course management systems (CMSs). We look at how schools deploy them and the process they go through before launching an online program.

Learning Management Systems

Learning Management Systems (LMSs) are software or web applications written in the **hypertext markup language** (HTML) or other computer languages that allow course administrators or instructors to create online courses, store, manage, track, and facilitate discussions in a virtual classroom. Learning Management Systems are sometimes called **course management systems** (CMSs) or **learning content management systems** (LCMSs). Although these systems share some commonalities, their functionalities, and usages are generally different.

A learning management system operates on **PHP**, **.Net**, or **Java** platforms connected to **PostgreSQL**, **MySQL**, **databases**, or **SQL Servers**. We will not discuss the technicalities of these applications and databases in this chapter because they are outside the scope of our discussion in this book.

Open-source versus Closed-source Applications

At the beginning of an online program, an education institution selects the learning management system that best meets the needs of its academic community. Schools can choose **open-source** or **closed-source** systems that vary in cost, quality, and functionalities. Educational institutions can download Open-source programs for free online or purchase closed-source systems from e-learning manufacturers or vendors.

Choosing an open-source program over a closed-source application and vice-versa may not provide a cost or quality advantage either way. Schools need computer experts to install open-source applications and to run the program. Education institutions will pay more to use closed-source programs, but save money in the long run because of the free technical assistance they will receive from e-learning vendors.

Self-Hosting or Outsourcing

One of the challenging tasks that an institution faces at the beginning of an online program is choosing among numerous **LMSs** available on the market. Finding the right balance between quality and price is a tricky proposition because an institution can spend a considerable amount on LMS, only to realize that the system never fulfills the needs of the students.

When choosing an LMS, an education institution can pursue several options. The institution can self-host, meaning that the institution will shoulder the technical duties in-house through its **information technology (IT)** department. Alternatively, the school can outsource the maintenance functions to a third party or collaborate with a vendor in managing the LMS. Either way, the institution must consider the financial implications and available human resources and how they will add value to its academic programs.

Before proceeding with the implementation plan, a school must ask and answer some pertinent questions. How well does the LMS align with the business and learning objectives of the institution? Is the price affordable? Is there availability and opportunity for updates of the LMS? Is the vendor or the company that provides the LMS stable and solvent? What is the reputation of the company that hosts the courseware, the vendor, or the corporation behind its firewall if outsourcing the service?[1] An institution should know the storage capacity of the **webserver** and whether it can accommodate the potential increase in student enrollments and if the system is **Shareable Content Object Reference Model** (SCORM) compliant.

Education institution is a community, and everything is interconnected. Schools must anticipate how new technology will affect students and other stakeholders. Breaking down jurisdictional walls between competing interests within the academic community is critical to the success of an online education initiative.[2]

Shareable Content Object Reference Model (SCORM)

SCORM is a set of technical standards and specifications that allow e-learning content to work and communicate with other learning management systems.[3] In 1997, the **United States Department of Defense** (DoD) formed the **Advanced Distributed Learning** (ADL) for the portability of learning content across various systems and related information (such as student records) from one platform to another and to make course content into modular objects that institutions can reuse in other courses.[4] **SCORM** became the de facto industry standard for e-learning interoperability and compatibility enabling educational institutions to reuse instructional materials across multiple learning management systems and environments.[5]

A learning management system, whether a **closed-source** system or an **open-source** application, should provide the best learning experience for students, instructors, and other users. Some of the popular closed-source LMSs on the market are **Blackboard** and **Desire2Learn** (**D2L**), while the open-source **LMSs** include **Canvas, Joomla, Sakai, ANGEL**, and **Modular Object-Oriented Dynamic Learning Environment** (Moodle). **Sakai** has similar features as **Moodle**, but more suitable for research and group projects. For the most part, these learning systems have the same capabilities and perform the same functions.

Blackboard has been the leader in the e-learning market for many years. In 2006, Blackboard acquired **WebCT**, and in 2009 it purchased **ANGEL**. The other two popular LMSs in higher education are **Sakai**, and **Desire2Learn** (D2L) founded by John Baker in 1999 in his third year of Systems Design Engineering study at the University of Waterloo.[6]

THE CHARACTERISTICS OF A LEARNING MANAGEMENT SYSTEM

The characteristics discussed in this section are by no means exclusive or exhaustive because e-learning manufacturers frequently update their products and sometimes allow users to modify them to fit their needs.

Easy Graphical User Interface

Graphic user interface (GUI) makes the virtual classroom environment artistic but serves other useful purposes. A graphical user interface makes the virtual classroom easier to navigate and allows you to work quickly with a computer by using a mouse to point to small pictures and icons, or other visual indicators, rather than using the command line or text. All versions of **Microsoft Windows** have graphical user interface features.

Figure 7.1 shows a **Windows 7** operating system with a **GUI** capability with taskbar icons that you can click on to open a program or a file without using commands or memorizing complex programming languages.

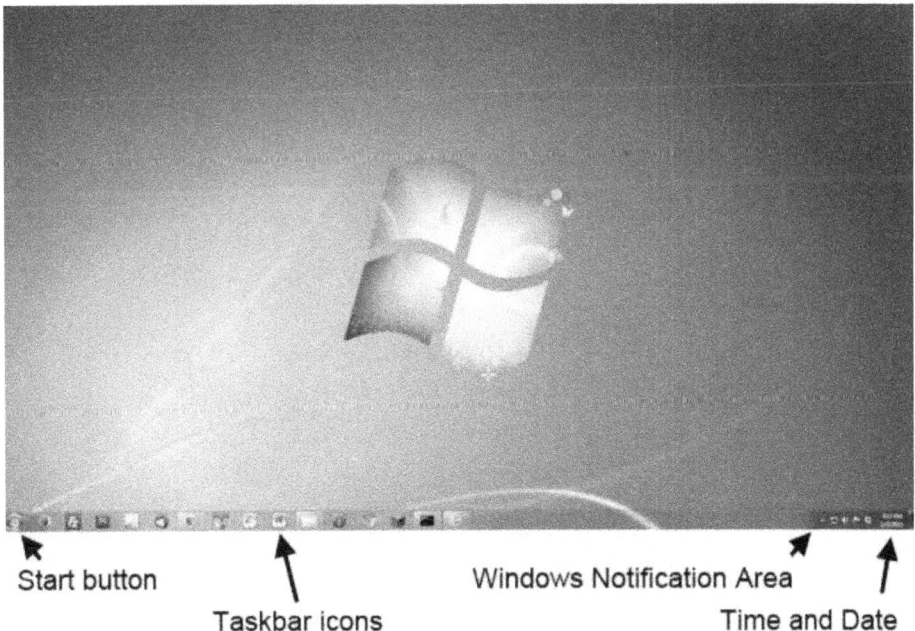

Start button   Taskbar icons   Windows Notification Area   Time and Date

Figure: 7.1   Window 7 Desktop with GUI Interface

Source: ComputerHope.com

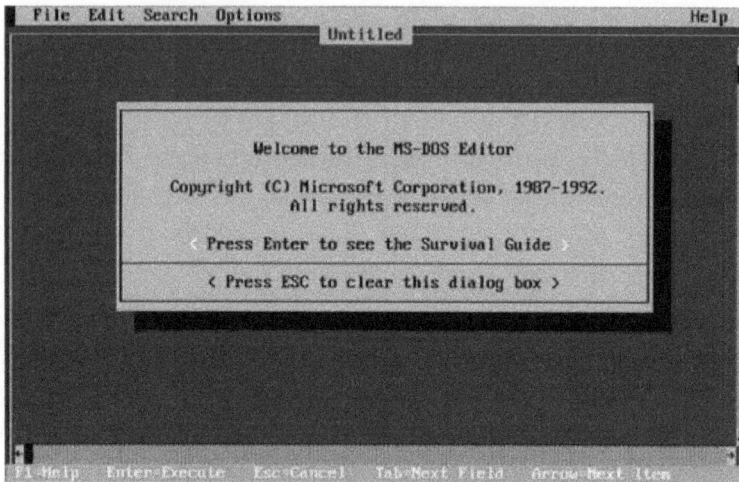

Figure 7.2   Microsoft DOS and Windows

Source: ComputerHope.com

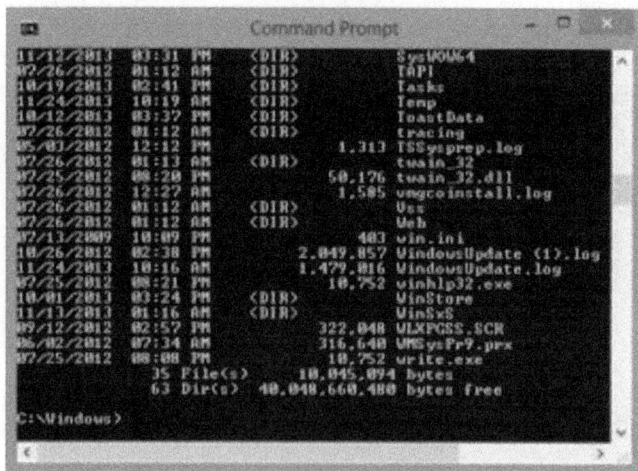

Figure 7.3   Command-Line and Prompt

Source: ComputerHope.com

GUI has become standard and dominant in **Microsoft Windows, Apple System 7** and **Mac OS**, and **Chrome OS** operating systems since Microsoft first released Windows in 1985.

Figures 7.2 and 7.3 show the **Microsoft Disk Operating System (MS-DOS)** and **Unix** with a **command-line user interface** (CUI) or **character user interface** (CUI). In contrast with **GUI, CUI** operates on **MS-DOS,** requiring inserting a disc into a computer and following the prompts before performing a task.[7] **Blackboard** recently introduced **Ultra** with a host of improvements in editing, rubrics, multimedia, and other features that enable instructors and institutions to collect data they can analyze to improve student online learning experience.[8]

Customization

Learning management systems are mostly designed for the mass market, but institutions can customize them to suit their educational needs. For instance, a school can change the language preference from English to Spanish or customize the discussion forum in ways that students must first post or contribute to the discussion forum before seeing what their classmates posted.

The flexibility to customize a learning management system depends on whether the program is an **open-source** or a **closed-source** application. **Moodle, Joomla,** and **Sakai** are **open-source** systems that education institutions can customize as necessary while schools might need permission before customizing **Blackboard** and other **closed-source** applications. **Moodle,** for example, provides a long list of customization options and has more than 1,000 plugins in 20 categories in activities, course formats, text editors, and reports. California State University Fullerton uses **Moodle** because of "easier to use interface" and "better integration with social networking sites" and the ability for administrators and instructors to modify the look, feel, and function of the learning environment.[9]

Another option is for a school to cannibalize **open-source** applications and combine different systems to create an entirely new LMS system. A school can develop propriety learning software from scratch; although much expensive than other options, such systems provide the freedom for a school to build applications that exactly meets the needs of students.

Courses or My Course

Courses or My Course is where the teaching and learning take place in the virtual classroom. Under the section, you will see the classes registered for and the instructors teaching them. The area also houses reading materials, lectures (videos and audios), supplemental materials, and links to external resources. **Courses** could have segments for invites and reminders for future course sessions if integrated with an online calendar system.

Social Networking

Social networking enables you to connect and share information on professional and social networking sites such as **LinkedIn**, **Facebook**, **Twitter**, and **YouTube**. Most **LMSs** now link the virtual classroom directly to these networking sites. Educational institutions use these platforms for discussions or share information with students, the academic community, and alumni or use them to promote their academic programs.

Enrollment

LMSs have a feature that enables you to self-enroll for classes and keep track of your academic performance. Also, you can pay for courses using a credit card, debit card, PayPal, and other online payment methods.

Communication

LMSs have internal email gateway systems for communicating in the virtual classroom. There are chat options and discussion forums for exchanging messages in class. An **LMS** can automatically notify you of upcoming events such as assignments due dates and future class sessions.

Reports

LMSs generate reports that you can export into Excel and other applications for analysis. Schools collect data on specific course areas to know the time students spent on reading course materials, discussion forums, and listening to lectures and then use the information to articulate a solution.

Testing

LMSs have areas for creating randomized questions to short essays. Schools can set a timer for the maximum number of times students can take an assignment. Testing has an auto-grading capability with the results of quizzes delivered and displayed on the screen immediately after submission. For essay assignments, instructors will manually input the grades, but students can receive notifications once instructors enter the points into the **grade book**.

COURSE MANAGEMENT SYSTEM (FEATURES AND FUNCTIONALITIES)

A **course management system** (CMS) contains essential features for taking online courses and making virtual classrooms easily navigable. The Teacher Education Center at Illinois State University, notes that learning management systems should have the announcements, calendar, grade book, asynchronous discussion boards, synchronous chat room, e-mailing (internal and external accounts), online journal, whiteboard, Dropbox, quiz, test, survey options, user-activity reports, team areas, document sharing, including digital pictures, audio, and streaming videos for collaboration, managed by the instructor.[10]

Announcements

The **announcement** is where instructors post course information and usually located on the course home page. As soon as you log into the virtual classroom, you will see the new information instructors posted since your last visit. The information may include assignment due dates, grading updates, general feedback, changes to the course guide, holiday schedules, and other relevant information.

Sun	Mon	Tue	Wed	Thu	Fri	Sa
			1	2	3	4
3		7	8	9	10	11
10		14	15	16	17	18
17	18		22	23	24	25
24	25			30		
31						

Calendar

The **calendar** will show the schedule of activities to accomplish in a course. The calendar will show the start and the end of a term, assignment, and exam due dates, discussion or chat sessions. Also, you can set the calendar to remind you of assignment due dates and other course activities.

Grade book

The **grade book** shows the breakdown of points earned in assignments, quizzes, projects, and class discussions. Depending on the grade book configuration, instructors can manually enter grades, or the systems can automatically grade multiple-choice assignments. Increasingly, some programs can grade short essay questions. However, technology is not error-proof, as glitches in the system could cause reporting errors. Also, instructors are not infallible to making mistakes when entering grades into the system. Frequent checking of the **grade book** will provide the opportunity to validate the authenticity of the information entered into the system.

Asynchronous Discussion Board

The **asynchronous discussion board** is where instructors post the weekly discussion questions and students can respond to classmates' postings. Depending on the course objectives, the discussion question may contain a single item or multiple subjects. The instructor will specify the number of students to respond to and when to respond to them. The syllabus should have instructions on class discussions, but instructors can post the information to the discussion forum.

Chat

Chat is a web application that allows you to communicate in real-time in the virtual classroom. In the synchronous environment, you can chat by text or by video. Although you will most likely use the chat option in a synchronous environment, you can use the chat feature in asynchronous environment for group discussions or one-on-one conversation.

Mail

The **mail** option enables you to communicate with professors, classmates, course administrators, academic staff, and others in the virtual classroom. The **mail** system works differently from the regular emails like **Yahoo! Mail, Gmail**, or **Hotmail**, because you can only send and receive messages from specific people on your contact list.

The internal email system provides some level of privacy and confidentiality because the messages go through a private server owned or maintained by a school. On the flip side, private servers are susceptible to hacking unless a school has strong firewalls that can prevent cyber-attacks and unauthorized access of information.

Online Journal

An **online journal** enables you to write down things that catch your attention as you work through various course activities. For instance, if you see a citation that you need for an upcoming assignment, you can write down the source and retrieve the information later. To make a journal relevant, you must set reminders for all entries so that it won't be efforts in futility.

Whiteboard

A **whiteboard** is akin to the **chalkboard** or **smartboard** used in the face-to-face classroom. In the synchronous learning environment, instructors can write or make graphical representations on a whiteboard using a digital pen or a mouse. For instance, an economics instructor can plot a graph of supply and demand on a **whiteboard**, showing where both variables intersect and their relationships with a price.

Dropbox

A **dropbox** is where you submit essay assignments or **PowerPoint** presentations for grading. Instructors can digitally or manually grade assignments submitted to the dropbox. Since every homework is different, instructors will provide instructions on the types of files to upload into the dropbox. Once the instructor returns a work, you will receive a notification on the grades earned in the assignment.

Document Sharing

The **document-sharing** is the feature that enables students and instructors to share and exchange learning resources in the virtual classroom. Students or instructors might have educational materials to share in class but would be distracting if they posted them to the discussion forum. They can share such resources in the **Document sharing** area.

Team/Group Areas

The **team** or **group** area is where you can engage in group discussions and collaborate with classmates in the virtual classroom. The learning objectives and the class size will determine the mode of group activities and the number of students in each group. Instructors can arrange groups alphabetically, such as A, B, C, and D, or numerically, such as 1, 2, 3, and 4. If an instructor assigns students to a group, members will see their names in their designated groups in the group area. To make discussions more intense, assuming there are 20 students in a class, the course instructor can divide the class into four groups with five students in each group. Instructors can further divide the four groups into sub-groups with two students in each sub-group.

Quiz, Test, Assignments

The **quiz, test**, and **assignments** area houses both objective questions and written assignments. Each assessment will have numeric points assigned and weighted percentages. The syllabus will contain information on quizzes and homework due dates. It is essential to crosscheck the due dates in the course guide with the information posted by the instructor and resolve any discrepancies that could cause late submissions or answering the wrong questions.

Survey Options

A **survey** is a tool that schools use for collecting and analyzing information in the virtual classroom. Schools collect various data that they analyze and interpret to improve learning outcomes or address a specific academic problem. At the beginning of an online course, a school can use a survey to assess students' familiarity with the online environment or gauge their expectations in the class.

At the end of an online course, a school will conduct **student opinion polls** (SOP) on the instructor, curriculum, and technology to know how each performed against expectations and to address deficiencies before the next class.

User-Activity Reports

User-activity reports summarize the areas of the virtual classroom that students visited, and the clock time spent in those areas. The user-activity reports would show the time spent listening to lectures, reading course materials, participating in class discussions, and engaged in other course activities. The instructor, academic staff, IT department, or anyone with access to a course can pull the user-activity reports and analyze the data for decision making.

Implementing Online Education Program

The planning and implementation of online education have essential interdependent processes that can either contribute to the success of the initiative or its failure. Before launching an online education program, a school must evaluate its financial position and know the available human and technical resources at its behest.

The collapse of **Fathom.com** exemplifies how a well-funded online education initiative could fail if a school fails to implement the right strategies in a rapidly changing environment. In 1999, Columbia University launched **Fathom.com** in conjunction with 13 other universities, including the University of Michigan, the London School of Economics and Political Science, and the American Film Institute.[11]

Fathom.com had a promising chance of making inroads in the bourgeoning online education market but failed to achieve the goal. Between 1999 and 2003, the Consortium offered over 2000 online courses and registered over 65,000 students. On March 31, 2003, **Fathom.com** abruptly folded-up, but not before $30 million had been spent.[12]

A report by Columbia faculty senate that probed the issue revealed that through 2001, the University spent $14.9 million but only generated about $700,000 in revenue.[13] Although the unenviable result of **Fathom. com** is not emblematic of most online education initiatives, its disappointing end is a reminder that a well-funded online education program could quickly unravel if there is a misalignment between planning and execution.

In the state of North Carolina, in the United States, the Guilford County School District learned its lesson the hard way when approximately 15,000 tablets deployed to middle schools in 2013 had hardware issues, requiring a recall which took another year before replacing them. In the multimillion-dollar technology initiative, the district gave only brief training to school staff without a pilot program before large-scale rollout. In a new agreement with the tablet vendor, the administration moved from massive deployment to slower, and incremental implementation with an initial pilot and device testing and expanded training for staff.[14]

ONLINE CLASSROOM MANAGEMENT

Building an Online Course

Building an online course begins with an objective of what students will achieve when they take the course. The quality of instructional materials such as text documents (.doc, .rtf, and .txt), PDF files, audio and video files, Microsoft PowerPoint presentations, simulations, games, graphics and images, and successful integration plays a significant role in the course quality.

A course designer can use textual materials in designing a course or use a **video content management system** to centralize, manage, and deliver video lectures. But not all video content management systems have the same capability or work the same way. For instance, **SharePoint**, **Cornerstone**, and **Saba** have video features, but these applications do not support large video files. If a school uses these applications as its primary learning platforms, the school must integrate video streams into its **courseware** for better quality.[15]

A course administrator must first create a **course shell**. A course shell is an empty template for building a new course. After a course administrator has developed a course, the course will be in the **place saver** or the **place holder** for later use. Depending on course objectives, the course builder can divide a class into weeks, sections, modules, topics, content, or use other descriptions. The administrator will upload the course content to the course area or enter the information into a **What You See Is What You Get** (WYSIWYG) editor (programs that allow a course builder to see courses as they build them instead of relying strictly on codes they type into the system). The course design, the materials uploaded must match the course objectives.[16]

Online Course Quality Management

Education institutions follow several processes before the start of an online class. The course administrator will upload the reading materials, PowerPoint, articles, journals, videos, simulations, pictures, games, and other instructional materials at the beginning of the session or the start of each week.

In the virtual classroom, quality management is a cyclical process. The effort begins before the start of a class, during the course, and at the end of a session. Some schools have quality teams that monitor the virtual classrooms to ensure the fidelity of their online programs. Schools often use the information collected from students through **SOP** to address areas of concern.

The Instructor's Role in the Virtual Classroom

Instructors play a critical role in online classroom management. They provide the required educational materials that students need before the first day of class and relay relevant information to them throughout the semester. Similarly, they answer questions that may be confusing to students and guide them to the appropriate departments before their problems metastasize. The problem some institutions confront is that instructors may find it challenging to learn new technologies, deploy new pedagogies, or follow new processes after years of doing things the same way.[17]

Faculty and educators must buy-in to technology not only by demonstrating how it can improve instruction, but they must be actively involved in the decision-making process. Professional development programs should be ongoing, not a one-and-done exercise to maximize the benefits of technology in the classroom. A mentor can show a new instructor how a learning tool works, then let the instructor take over when he or she feels comfortable using it. Additionally, education institutions can recruit "tech evangelists" among technically savvy instructors to lead informal workshops on how to use new technologies. Faculty can leverage professional networks found on **Twitter** and other social and professional networking sites to expand their knowledge on new applications for teaching and learning.[18]

Online Education Technology Requirements

Students need essential hardware and software programs before taking an online course. For **asynchronous classes,** the pre-installed applications on computers might suffice in taking online courses. For **synchronous** sessions, students may need other applications to use videos, audio, games, and animations. Usually, schools will advise if additional hardware and software programs are required for an online class.

Table: 7:1   Shows the minimum technology required in a typical online course.

Minimum Technology Requirements for Online Courses

Minimum Technology Requirements	Windows PC	Apple MAC OS X
Operating Systems	Windows Vista or better	OS X 10.7 (Lion) or better
Memory/RAM	2GB or more	2GB or more
Browser	Firefox 24.0 or higher Internet Explorer 10 or higher	Firefox 24.0 or higher Safari 6.11 or higher
Audio	Speakers or Headphones and Microphone (Built-in or External)	Speakers or Headphones and Microphone (Built-in or External)
Internet Access	DSL, cable, educational, or corporate connection. **Wired internet strongly recommended.**	DSL, cable, educational, or corporate connection. **Wired internet strongly recommended.**

Technology in Higher Education

The relationship between technology and higher education and specifically online learning can be partly seen from the instrumental perspective and partly from a substantive standpoint. The instrumental viewpoint translates into the academic and catalytic rationale (realizing educational change to better learning processes) and in the cost-effectiveness rationale (cost reduction). The substantive aspect translates into the social and vocational justification in using **ICT** as a learning tool in curricula (needed for societal and professional functioning).[19]

The use of technology in education continues to attract attention at professional conferences. In some countries, technology has become central to learning and teaching in higher education and the opportunity for increasing access to education and training. As societies transition into knowledge-based economies, information technology will become the driver of both economic competitiveness and social development. Because different learning technologies support different learning models, technology must align with the educational objectives of an institution. Education institutions with an **asynchronous learning model** use e-mail, threaded discussion boards, and newsgroups to communicate with students in the virtual classroom. A school with the **synchronous learning model** uses webcasting, chat rooms, and audio/video for communication, which allows students to collaborate and work in a group setting. While earlier online programs focused primarily on one of these communication technologies, more recent applications combine synchronous and asynchronous interactions and occasional face-to-face interactions.[20]

As higher education evolves, education institutions must teach students how to use **ICT** and the **Internet** in their future work either as an entrepreneur, researcher, or professional and as educated citizens. Higher education students must learn from the **Internet of people, and things** with ever-expanding technological possibilities, policy-makers, and education practitioners must rethink the role of **ICT** in the future of higher education and not just to improve learning.[21]

These elements are essential when a school is developing its technology architectures:

1. A university's constituents must have access to technological resources, including both full-time and part-time students, resident students, commuter students, distance learners, faculty, administration, staff, and alumni.
2. A full variety of technological resources must be available regarding admission, advising, career planning, registration, administration, the library, computer labs, technical support, and other resources.
3. Full access to university technology resources must be available in two ways: on-campus and via remote locations (i.e., the web).
4. Schools must provide access for extended hours (ideally, twenty-four hours a day, seven days a week).
5. Remote access and extended service hours must be available to campus-based students as well as distance learners because students will desire more convenience than is presently available.[22]

Summary of Main Points

- Technology plays a vital role in online education. A learning management system is the entire technology architecture used for managing online learning. A CMS is a part of the LMS which focuses on the course area or Courses in a virtual classroom.
- Education institutions have choices in choosing a learning platform, but they must choose the best platform that meets the needs of the stakeholders.
- A university can build its own CMS in-house or purchase the program from a third-party, but the application must meet the needs of various stakeholders.
- The planning and implementation of an online education program have several interdependent processes that must align for successful execution.

- A **CMS** has different features that students must be familiar with before taking an online course.
- Instructors have a critical role to play in the success of an online course by ensuring that the virtual classroom is ready for learning and required materials available on the first day of class.
- Students must ensure that their computers have essential software and hardware programs and meet the minimum requirements recommended by their institutions.

Discussion Questions

1. From your understanding of course management systems, which system (open-source or closed-source) would you recommend for an online program, and why? Discuss the benefits and potential downside.
2. Assume you are the leader of the project team for the implementation of an online education program in your school. Provide the steps you and your team members will take to implement the initiative. Discuss the financial, technology, and human resources that you might need to achieve the project objective.
3. Technology is an essential aspect of any online program. How much do you agree with this statement?
4. Assume that you are an engineer at a learning management company. Identify areas of online learning technologies that you can improve on, and how?
5. Identify the characteristics of a learning management system. Discuss how the features can contribute to learning outcomes in the virtual classroom.

8

BENEFITS OF ONLINE EDUCATION

Learning Objectives: After studying this chapter, you should be able to:

1. Understand the convenience and flexibility of online education
2. Describe the cost-effectiveness of online learning
3. Explain how distance education improves productivity in the workplace
4. Discuss how online learning enhances technology competency
5. Explain how the virtual classroom boost learning confidence
6. Understand how to tailor online learning in meeting a specific learning need
7. Describe how online education increases interactions among students
8. Understand how online learning enhances job performance in the workplace
9. Discuss how e-learning aids continuous training and professional development of employees
10. Explain how online learning induces collaboration in the classroom
11. Understand how online education support personalized learning
12. Discuss how online learning promotes intercultural understandings in the classroom

13. Describe how online learning supports quality control of the instructional process
14. Explain how online learning technologies provide instant grading and feedback

INTRODUCTION

Over the years, educators and policymakers had made several attempts to make traditional learning more effective and measurable. The effort fell short of expectation due to the haphazard nature of the paper-based process of conventional education. Technology has not only made learning more measurable, but it has standardized the learning process. Today, students can learn anytime and anywhere and receive immediate feedback on their performance. In this chapter, we discuss the benefits of online education and how schools and organizations use the learning technique in different settings.

BENEFITS OF ONLINE EDUCATION

Convenience and Flexibility

Online education provides the comfort to learn without the rigor of commuting to campus every day. The learning technique offers scheduling flexibilities with opportunities for schools to add unlimited course sections. In the Fall of 2014, 72.7% of undergraduate and 38.7% of graduate-level students in the United States enrolled in distance education courses.[1] According to the 2014-15 **Noel-Levitz report**, 90% of students who took an online course cited convenience and flexibility for their decisions, and 62% stated that work schedules and other obligations were the primary external factors for choosing an online class.[2]

Convenience and flexibility have become topmost for students in higher education, including those living close to the campus. In 2017, out of the 2.2 million undergraduate students in the United States who exclusively took distance education courses, 1.4 million took their classes in institutions located in their home states, while only 717,000 enrolled in institutions outside their states.[3]

The profile of incoming college students has changed over the years. In the United States, 44% of college and university

students are 24 years or older, with 30% attend class part-time, 26% work full-time while enrolled, and 28% take care of children and other dependents while pursuing post-secondary studies.[4] The **New American Foundation** reported that only 14% of all undergraduates in 2012 attended full time and lived on campus. The archetype of a typical college student to be a well prepared 18-year-old high school graduate who moves into a college dormitory and all expenses paid by the parents is not the reality.[5] A study showed that the average age of students at the University of Phoenix is 31 years, and many of them are working adults who cannot take time off work to attend traditional institutions.[6]

In the United States, the enrollment for both full-time and part-time students has generally increased since 2000. Between 2000 and 2010, full-time enrollment increased by 45% (from 7.9 million to 11.5 million students), and part-time enrollment increased by 27% (from 5.2 million to 6.6 million students). In 2016, the total undergraduate enrollment in degree-granting post-secondary institutions was 16.9 million students, an increase of 28% from 2000.[7] Between 2012 and 2015, the total number of students studying on campus (those not taking any distance course or taking a combination of distance and non-distance courses) dropped by almost one million (931,317).[8]

Higher educational institutions, from private for-profit and nonprofit institutions to public institutions, offer online learning to meet the needs of students who increasingly seek flexibility in learning. The University of North Carolina offers online programs in sixteen of its campuses across the state for students whose work and family obligations prevent them from coming to school.[9] The University of London provides distance learning to students across the globe so they can study without leaving their countries.[10]

For organizations, convenience has become a corporate priority in the 21st Century as workers increasingly becoming dispersed. Organizations offer **e-learning** to reduce the stress that employees undergo when they travel outside their primary job locations for training. More than eleven-thousands of **Johnson & Johnson**'s forty thousand employees worldwide use the company **e-university** educational resources each quarter.[11] The United States Army offers distance learning, so the servicemen stationed abroad can receive training without traveling to their headquarters in the United States.[12] In New Zealand, the **Institute of Chartered Accountants** (ICA) offers online training for its members all over the country. Eighty-one percent of members who participated in previous **e-learning** programs were satisfied with their virtual classroom experience because it reduced the inconveniences they faced each week when they traveled to the Institute's headquarters for training. E-learning motivated more members to participate in training activities and more committed to other programs organized by the Institute.[13]

Cost-Advantage

Online education provides the most cost-effective way to learn, given the high tuition cost of higher education. **E-learning** offers an alternative that is not only faster but cheaper and potentially better than face-to-face learning. A survey by the **Pew Research Center** showed that 84% of college graduates disclosed that college education was a good investment, but 75% of the respondents acknowledged that college education was too expensive.[14] Online learning can reduce tuition costs, relocation cost, commuting cost, loss of income, the loss of quality family time, and other out-of-pocket expenses.[15]

As figure 8.1 depicts, in the United States, the tuition fees in the public four-year college in the 2017-18 academic year were 3.13 times higher than it was in the 1987-88 academic year. While this figure speaks directly to the cost trajectories in the United States, similar patterns have emerged in other countries. The unsustainable trend makes online education an inescapable option for education institutions looking for ways to lower their tuition

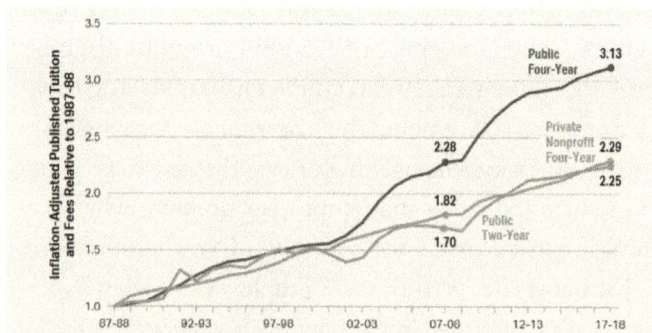

Figure: 8.1 **Inflation-Adjusted Published Tuition and Fees Tuition and Fees (Relative to 1987-88 to 2017-18**

Source: The College Board (2017)

fees. In 2014, Georgia Tech's Computer Science Department developed the online version of its Master of Science in Computer Science in partnership with **Udacity** and **AT&T**. The online section costs about $7,000 compared to $45,000 that students pay for the campus version of the program.[16]

Education institutions need physical infrastructures and constant maintenance to deliver face-to-face lectures successfully. Education institutions can reduce capital expenditure on the construction of physical classrooms because a well-designed online program can address the academic needs of a large number of students, providing schools the opportunity for economies of scale.[17] The **Southern Regional Education Board** notes that a state can realize significant cost efficiencies over time by creating and managing a virtual state school because, with each online course developed or acquired, the state can copy and reuse the course and exercise quality control over course content, evaluation of teachers, and monitoring student success.[18] Equally, e-learning providers can reduce operational costs because employees can work from home, and book publishers can reduce the economic loss of transporting and storing textbooks and other educational materials by digitizing them.[19]

Increased Productivity in the Workplace

The acceptance of computer hardware and software products, including digital telecommunication equipment in the workplace, have changed the way employees work and increase their productivity. Companies now use web-based tools such as multimedia, databases, and telecommunications infrastructures such as networks and the Internet for training. In 1997, Alan Greenspan, former chairman of the **Federal Reserve** of the United States, averred that "we should expect the widespread and practical application of information and technologies to increase productivity and reduce business costs

significantly…with the result that business services and financial transactions are transmitted almost instantaneously across global networks."[20]

His prediction over twenty years ago couldn't be more valid today, given technology pervasiveness and how it has transformed business. Interestingly, technology has not only changed business operations but transformed education. In the 21st-century, technology will promote skills collaboration, civic literacy, global awareness, and a constructivist pedagogy that requires higher-order thinking. Likewise, it will induce creative problem-solving mechanisms and aptitude needed in the knowledge economy.[21] E-learning enables organizations to communicate new ideas quickly and provides the platform in achieving uniformity in training programs. Today, organizations headquartered in New York City, United States, can deliver the same training program, with the same consistency and rigor to employees in Melbourne, Australia, in spite both cities are thousands of miles apart with a fifteen-hour time difference.

Proficient in Using Modern Technology

The virtual classroom offers opportunities to develop technical competence that are not available in the face-to-face class. In the virtual environment, you can use different web communication tools such as e-mail, chat, video-conferencing, discussion board, and simulations to communicate in class.[22] The knowledge of computer programs and the opportunity to navigate a website enhances computer skills, while an Internet-based course increases the chance to participate in virtual workgroups and being part of a learning community.[23] Social media resources also provide networking opportunities to pursue professional careers in various disciplines.[24]

Assertiveness and Confidence in Learning

In the face-to-face class, if you're shy and not comfortable speaking in front of a large group, you might hesitate to participate in class discussions. The virtual classroom is less intimidating because you can express yourself without facing the unease of someone mocking you. The text-oriented communication approach in the virtual classroom allows you to take as much time as you need to form your opinions and contemplate fellow students' responses. The online classroom environment provides a social-leveling platform that blurs gender, racial, and other barriers because no one cares how you look, talk, or dress compared to the face-to-face classes, where you don't have much anonymity.[25]

Easy Course Adaptability

In today's fast-paced environment, knowledge has become so transient that what you know a few seconds ago can become outdated the next minute. Online education provides for just-in-time learning because the virtual classroom is open twenty-four hours a day, seven days a week. Instructors can update syllabi, lectures, learning materials, discussion forums, and other course areas anytime and track learning activities without disrupting the classroom flow.[26] Available technologies enable instructors to update and share content within a matter of seconds, thereby saving the time and efforts, it would require to print and distribute hard copies.[27]

Online education also supports scalability because schools can modify and break down a course into smaller modules, with each module packaged to fit the needs of a specific audience. A few years ago, the University of Phoenix Online piloted a master's in International Management program specifically designed for students from abroad to meet the need of organizations in international contexts. The institution offered courses in finance and strategy and had students from many countries to ensure diverse perspectives and exposed the students to the global business best practices.[28]

Likewise, organizations use e-learning to meet the needs of specific employees. The **Foodservice Equipment Distributors Association** (FEDA) in Chicago, specially designed a virtual university for employees in the food-service equipment and supplies distribution business, focusing on profit management for dealers, customer service, and negotiations.

Employees who work in the industry can receive training in specific areas relevant to their jobs.[29]

Promotes Active Learning and Collaborations in the Classroom

In the virtual classroom, where little or no face-to-face interactions exist, creating a climate conducive to open expression, trust, and interdependence, and designing instructional materials that encourage active learning is essential.[30] Online education promotes an open exchange of information because, in the virtual classroom, students confront different points of view, accommodating, challenging, rejecting, and integrating new information. The online environment also provides a channel through which information flows from instructor to student, student to student, and student to instructor.[31]

Fifty percent of online students surveyed noted that online courses gave them more opportunities to interact with their classmates, and 60% believed that online courses gave them better learning opportunities compared to face-to-face classes.[32] In an online course, students use live chats, discussion boards, videos, and text messaging to communicate with classmates from any location and at any time. By collaborating and engaging in shared tasks in class (whether it's a project or a lesson), students learn and gain a variety of skills from classmates.[33]

Continuous Learning and Professional Development

In today's global and competitive environment, job responsibilities change, new careers emerge, old jobs disappear, and often, the only way to prepare for these changes is through continuing education.[34] In the 1980s, corporate universities emerged and created continuous training opportunities for a workforce that was increasingly dependent upon technology and knowledge acquisition.[35] In 2001, ninety-two million U.S. adults, or 46% of the population, received informal education to keep their skills current, accommodate new job requirements, earn an advanced degree, or broaden their knowledge.[36]

In the United States, nurses complete more than 1.7 million hours of online education every year to maintain their certifications and enhance their employability. The health agencies measure the quality of the instruction through countless lives saved and patients who regain their health every day. More than 3 million U.S. skilled professionals annually complete technical industry certification courses in programming, database management, network administration, information technology, heating, ventilation, and air conditioning (HVAC), telecommunications, automotive repair, building trades, and other areas through distance learning.[37]

Employees must continue to learn to remain employable in today's volatile economic environment. As organizations face budget constraints, distance learning becomes the most efficient, scalable, and sustainable way to prolong the value of current and future workforce.[38] In 2011, **BEST** and **Global 500** (G500) organizations reported high usage of e-learning. **BEST** organizations delivered 50% of their training online, while **G500** organizations offered 42% of their learning hours online. The consolidated group reports showed both entities provided 39% of formal learning hours online.[39]

Developing the knowledge and skills of the workforce continue to be topmost for organizations as they make sizeable investments in employee training. In 2016, a survey of more than 300 organizations of various sizes, industries, and locations showed that organizations spent about $1,273 per employee on direct learning expenditure, compared to $1,252 spent in 2015, and they delivered nearly half of the training online.[40] Online learning allows companies and employees goals to move in concert with employees using their current jobs as learning laboratories and directly applying course lessons to solving organizational problems. The benefits are immediate, with employees developing both theoretical and practical knowledge in the context of their current employers' business interests.[41]

Fosters Diversity and Intercultural Understanding

As education institutions extend their recruitments beyond their immediate territories, the proclivity of students from different cultural backgrounds learning together couldn't be higher. As in the face-to-face environment, cultural misunderstandings can create tension in the virtual classroom. However, the benefits of students with different cultural experiences learning together outweigh any potential drawbacks. A study showed that students who had regular contact with diverse ideas and different people achieved higher growth in their active thinking processes and recorded superior levels of intellectual engagement and motivation in the classroom than their counterparts who did not have the same experience.[42]

Students have different life experiences, and when they bring diverse perspectives to class discussions, it broadens their knowledge and exposes them to new frontiers of learning and professional development.

DIVERSITY IN THE VIRTUAL CLASSROOM

The story here exemplifies the advantage of cultural diversity in the virtual classroom:

Mona is a military officer who combined education with her profession. A few months after she enrolled in a graduate program, her Agency deployed her to Italy on an overseas assignment. Because the school she attended in the United States offered online programs, she continued her education when she arrived in Italy.

In one of Mona's classes, most of her classmates were from the United States, but some came from other countries. Mona shared her experience living abroad with her classmates and the cultural dichotomies between Italy and the United States, where she grew up. The information that Mona shared deepened her classmates' knowledge of Italy and the United States, especially her classmates, who had never been to either country. Likewise, her classmates shared information about their countries that benefited Mona and her professor.

The instructor who taught the course was a Hungarian living in Wales. The professor shared her experience growing up in Eastern Europe and life in the United Kingdom with Mona and her classmates. In the middle of the course, the professor traveled to Northern Ireland but taught her class while she was there. At the end of her one-week visit, she shared information about some of the exciting things she saw at various historical sites that she visited.

Greater Quality Control of Instructional Materials

Innovation in online learning has taken traditional education to a whole new level because there are many tools for creating interactive courses, standardized tests, and a better understanding of the educational process. Learning analytics ensures the quality and efficiency of learning and teaching by injecting simple elements into otherwise rigid and cumbersome traditional learning processes.[43]

Technology promotes quality and adherence to best practices in education as curricula are guaranteed, instruction closely monitored, and assessment of rubrics common and consistent.[44] For example, the Western Governors University uses assessment-based coaching reports to develop and customize study plans for students. Marist College, in New York, uses a predictive model to provide students with feedback and address any issues before it is too late. The school saw a 6% improvement in the final grade of at-risk students who received early learning intervention. Purdue University can identify at-risk students as early as the second week of term, prompting actions to help the students improve their performance. At New York Institute of Technology, 74% of students who dropped out had been predicted as at-risk by the data model.[45]

Online assessment tools can prompt students about what they know, and how to improve on what they don't know. Instructors can track and collect data on what students know, so they can tailor learning activities to ensure their continuous improvement at every level. Online education tools allow authentic, project-based assessments that focused on higher-order thinking and the use of common rubrics in class.

From a financial standpoint, schools can determine the economic impact of at-risk students. A study of about 20,000 students at an Australian University showed that, on average, each time a student dropped out, the university loses about $4,500. But when the institution received a notification on the at-risk students and worked to retain them, during the first year of study, it realized about $4000 in revenue, during the second year $2,675 and the third year $3,479 per student.[46]

Instant Grading and Just-in-Time Feedback

Students receive feedback from instructors either quantitatively or qualitatively, showing their areas of strengths and weaknesses. Quantitative feedback involves assigning a numeric point to work, while qualitative feedback entails giving a written comment on an assignment.

In the face-to-face environment, when students submit an assignment, instructors would grade and return the work the following week. The lag time between when a student completes a task and receive feedback could determine whether the student will repeat the same mistakes all over. The auto-grading feature used in the virtual classroom provides instant feedback immediately students submit work.

Learning tools and data-driven processes enable institutions to implement educational strategies for all the stakeholders, from school administrators to the students. The **Universidad Internacional de La Rioja** in Spain uses the **A4 Learning** system that synchronizes data techniques with information visualization and provides students with ongoing information that enables them to think critically about their learning progress and goals. The **Local Interpretable Model-Agnostic Explanations** (LIME) allows teachers to make personalized recommendations to students.[47] The **Educause Horizon Report** 2016 showed that students have a desire for immediate feedback as they learn and almost two-thirds of the students surveyed believe that immediate feedback had a positive result in their academic performance.[48]

Summary of Main Points

- E-learning provides convenience for students to learn and reduces the stress that employees undergo when they travel outside their primary locations to attend off-site training.
- Online education provides the most cost-effective way to learn, given the current high tuition costs.
- Companies achieve higher productivity when they use web-based and telecommunications infrastructures in their training programs.
- The virtual classroom provides a less intimidating learning environment because you can freely express yourself without anyone jeering at you.
- Online learning technologies allow course content to be updated and disseminated promptly. Also, instructors can quickly distribute instructional materials with the possibility of real-time tracking and reporting.
- Online learning supports collaborative learning synchronously or asynchronously and increases the opportunity to gain knowledge in a specific subject area.
- Organizations use e-learning to support the continuous training of employees and enhance their professional development at work.
- Online education promotes intercultural understanding because students from different cultural backgrounds can share ideas.
- E-learning ensures adherence to best practices in teaching because schools can closely monitor instruction and develop assessment rubrics consistent for all students.

- Online learning supports instant grading and just-in-time feedback because students can receive immediate feedback as soon as they submit an assignment.

Discussion Questions

1. Compare and contrast traditional education with online education. Discuss the benefits of online education vis-à-vis traditional education.
2. Identify the type of technology that education institutions can use to enhance learning and their specific advantage.
3. In what ways can online education help schools and organizations reduce operational costs?
4. Discuss the benefits of online education to students and organizations. How true is it that the benefits of online learning outweigh its disadvantages? Discuss.
5. Online learning is a good substitute for face-to-face learning. How much do you agree with this statement? Defend your position with appropriate examples.
6. What is the advantage of diversity in the virtual classroom? Identify the steps you would take to minimize the frictions that cultural differences may induce in the virtual classroom?

9

CHALLENGES OF ONLINE EDUCATION

Learning Objectives: After studying this chapter, you should be able to:

1. Explain how learning styles affect performance in the virtual classroom
2. Understand apathy towards online education
3. Explain computer illiteracy in the virtual classroom
4. Discuss hardware and software issues in the virtual classroom
5. Understand how poor Internet connection hampers online learning
6. Explain the cost associated with online education
7. Examine the incongruence of online learning with hands-on learning
8. Explain the cultural issues in the virtual classroom
9. Describe the legal and regulatory issues facing online education
10. Discuss the health risks associated with technology
11. Understand plagiarism and impact on learning
12. Explain retention issues in the virtual classroom
13. Understand how humans and the environment impacts online learning
14. Discuss the personal matters that affect academic performance

INTRODUCTION

The flexibility and convenience that online education offers do not mean that the virtual classroom is problem-free. Most of the issues that are hardly noticeable in a face-to-face environment become magnified in the virtual environment. In this chapter, we discuss the challenges of online education and how to overcome them.

A Mismatch between Learning Styles and Instructional Methods

A learning style is a person's preferred method of gathering, organizing, and thinking about information.[1] Learning styles could be information processing-based, personality-based, or multi-dimensional/instructional-based. **Information processing-based learning styles** evaluate someone's cognitive approaches to comprehending and incorporating information and the way the person sense, perceive, solve problems, organize, and remember information. A **personality-based learning style** analyzes a person's personality in incorporating content and measures his or her reaction in various learning conditions. **Multi-dimensional/instructional-based learning styles** evaluate a person's preferred learning environment.[2]

Table: 9.1   How People Learn

LEARNING STYLE	Learning style is an individual's natural or habitual pattern of acquiring and processing information in learning situations. A core concept is that individuals differ in how they learn
VISUAL	Visual Learning is a teaching and learning style in which ideas, concepts, data and other information are associated with images and techniques
AUDITORY	Auditory Learning is a learning style in which a person learns through listening.
TACTILE	Tactile learners learn physically by touching manipulating objects
KINESTHETIC	Kinesthetic learning is a learning style in which learning takes place by the student carrying out a physical activity, rather than listening to a lecture or watching a demonstration
ANALYTIC	Analytic learners focus on the details of language, such as grammar rules, and enjoy taking apart words and sentences
GLOBAL	Global learners focus on the whole picture and do not care so much about specific details. They do not want to get bored with slow moving lessons and enjoy interesting and attractive materials.

Docebo (2016)

As table 9.1 shows, individuals learn and absorb information differently. A student's preferred learning style is the environment that fits his or her learning personality. Learning theories show that some students learn best from experiential exercises, others from the reflective method, while some learn better in a face-to-face setting.[3] Students who learn from experiential activities may prefer learning in a face-to-face setting than in the virtual classroom, while students who learn by reflection could do well both in a face-to-face setting and online environment.

As different environments and learning styles produce different learning outcomes, so do the curriculums. The design of online courses can impact academic performance because education institutions often create online programs in standard formats for a large and diverse population of students. For instance, education programs developed in the more developed countries are often available to learners in developing countries, which are home to a large and growing percentage of end-users of distance education. But curricula, methodological approaches, and content developed abroad often do not adequately address or reflect regional interests and values, contradicting what professors teach from what students learn.[4]

Apathy Towards Online Education

The opposition to online education programs often occurs among students, parents, educators, and administrators due to competing priorities. The **information technology** (IT) department might introduce new technology without adequate consultation with instructors, curriculum developers, and students, causing them to dissent.[5]

The level of skepticism about online education among faculty has remained high because the traditional educational approaches often don't reflect new technological realities. Only 29.1% of academic leaders report that their faculty accepts the "value and legitimacy of online education."[6] In the traditional education system, faculty design, develop and implement courses while online education empowers students and provides variability in structure and autonomy and mass-customization of knowledge. Faculty entrenched in the pre-modern education system often have difficulty accepting online learning as a post-modern practice in the age of technology.[7] Although, the degree of acceptability of online education vary between schools that do not have online learning programs at 11.6% and schools with distance education enrollment at 60.1%, ironically, the group that benefits most from educational innovations is the audience that must be convinced on how it enhances the learning experience in the classroom.[8]

Students can resist online education due to a lack of academic support, bad experiences in previous online classes, and other reasons discussed in this chapter. However, schools provide advising, tutoring, counseling, and other interventions to help students overcome those problems.

For decades, organizations have been the most significant users of online educational resources. Employees may not be receptive to **e-learning** if they cannot align online training with business objectives. Organizations can reduce employee apathy by educating them about the benefits of online training and how it aligns with business goals and how it could enhance their efficiency in the workplace.[9]

Lack of Computer Skills

Over the past few years, computers have significantly advanced as manufacturers add new features every day to enhance the quality of their products. Most computers come with hundreds of pre-installed applications with the opportunity for users to install dozens of additional programs. However, those enhancements have made computers more complicated for an average user to operate unless they have basic computer training. Also, e-learning manufacturers frequently update and upgrade their products by adding new features and replacing old ones. Students must not only understand how to navigate the **learning management systems** but know how to use various search engines to conduct academic research.

Computer Hardware and Software Issues

A computer is perhaps the most uniquely valuable technology you need when taking an online course. But a laptop can develop hardware problems such as hard-drive failures, keyboard issues, defective batteries, broken screens, or software issues such as application errors, virus issues, and outdated programs anytime. In either circumstance, accessing the virtual classroom, participating in online class activities, or submitting assignments will be impossible. Although you might be able to diagnose and fix some hardware and software glitches quickly, others will require the service of computer experts. Depending on a glitch, it could be cheaper to buy a new computer because, in some instances, the costs of labor and parts would be too high that buying new equipment would be a better option.

Before buying a new computer or taking it to a repair shop, check and see if your school has a system problem. If your school has a server problem, it will be difficult to access the school website or log-in to the virtual

classroom while the problem persists. In this instance, you should contact the **IT** department in your school for advice or resolve the issue.

Poor Internet Connections and Lack of Access

The speed of the Internet connection will determine how fast to complete a task, upload information, and navigate the virtual classroom. If the Internet is slow, the web pages will load slowly, and using animations, graphics, or audio and video clips will be difficult.[10] Although the Internet is prevalent, its availability does not automatically translate into education opportunities due to numerous regulatory, administrative, technical, and logistical challenges that hinder the use and the deployment of Internet technologies.[11]

In some countries, including advanced countries, many students don't have access to high-speed Internet connections, especially those living in rural communities. The 2010 census showed that roughly 27% of students in America lacked broadband access at home and, 20% of American households don't have an Internet connection due to a personal decision, geographic location, or socioeconomic status.[12] In December 2018, the developing countries achieved Internet penetration of 45.3% from 7.7% in 2005. The **International Telecommunication Union** (ITU) noted that attaining the 50/50 milestone was both historical and monumental because Internet availability will enable people to obtain essential services online, including education and healthcare. While Internet penetration continues to increase, affordability remains an issue, especially in Africa. The region has the most expensive mobile data packages with prices for one gigabyte, costing as much as $35 or 5.5% of the monthly income over the 2% of monthly gross income recommended by the **UN Broadband Commission**.[13] In Sierra Leone, the cost of Internet connection for subscribers is 118% of the annual per capita income, compared with subscribers in Australia, where it is only 1% of their yearly income.[14]

Internet connection remains slow in some countries ranking well below the average speeds of above ten megabits per second, which is the minimum needed for consumers to take part fully in a digital economy. In some cases, governments do not promote connectivity in rural, remote, and deprived urban areas even when they have the financial means to do so.[15] In most markets, broadband-based on **Digital Subscriber Line** (DSL) technology remains limited, and where available underdeveloped because telecommunication companies offer the service on **fixed-line networks**. In Africa, although the future of connectivity in the rural and semi-urban areas lies in mobile broadband, the cost is traditionally far more expensive than the price of fixed-line networks.[16]

The discrepancy in **Information and Communications Technology** (ICT) quality and access manifest not only across regions and national boundaries but also in rural and urban settings within the same country, and the service charges are considerably higher to those with fewer resources than for those with the necessary financial means. The telephone and Internet access, power supply (and reliability), and essential infrastructures are generally available in the main urban areas and major cities where the largest student populations in distance education still reside, creating a notable imbalance in the distance (and higher) education access within the same country.[17]

Lack of Timely Feedback from Instructors

Instructors provide two types of feedback in the classroom to encourage students for higher performance—corrective and motivational feedbacks. Corrective feedback lets students know how well they perform on assignments, quizzes, projects, or class discussions. Motivational feedback helps students to complete tasks and work harder to achieve higher performance.[18]

In the face-to-face learning environment, students could walk into the professors' office to clarify confusing areas if they have questions on their assignments. In the virtual classroom, students don't have such luxury. Students can only communicate by technology, and if a professor doesn't respond within a reasonable timeline, students will likely to repeat the same mistake on the next assignment.

Education institutions usually have policies on the timeline that instructors should respond to students in the virtual classroom. For general questions, they expect instructors to respond within 24 hours during the week and 72 hours on weekends. Feedback on graded assignments could take up to a week, depending on the assignment criteria. Students must follow up if they didn't hear from their instructors within a reasonable timeline.

Cost of Online Education

Online education is convenient but necessarily not cheaper than face-to-face learning. As the trend shows, most traditional education institutions offer online programs and charge the same fees, whether students take courses online or in a face-to-face classroom. If a student enrolls in a blended course, the student will incur traveling, accommodation, parking fees, and other out-of-pocket expenses, and need computers, Internet service, for the online session. These expenses could run to thousands of dollars each quarter.

Affordability is the greatest challenge for international students seeking higher-education opportunities outside their countries. The students usually pay higher tuition rates and out-of-state-fees to study abroad. In the United States and other advanced countries, students have access to financial aids, loans, grants, scholarships, and employer educational reimbursement programs that are mostly not available to international students.[19]

From an operational perspective, education institutions need capital and human resources to implement online education. The initial investment often creates entry barriers for smaller institutions and inhibits them from growing existing programs.[20] Only schools that have the capital to implement online education will gain from their investments through higher student-to-teacher ratios and reduction in the construction of physical facilities.[21]

Unsuitability for Hands-On-Learning

Hands-on learning is education that individuals demonstrate through work, play, and the sharing of life experiences. The virtual environment may not accommodate courses that require practical demonstrations of skills or need laboratory experiments. A culinary student can watch a video on how

to prepare a specific dish, but the student cannot determine the quality of the food without tasting it.

In recent years, the use of **artificial reality** and **simulations** in producing real-world experiences is on the rise. There are specialized areas in natural and social sciences that technologies cannot replace without consequences. A pharmaceutical company can use technology to research a new drug before bringing it to the market. The company cannot determine the health risks of the medication without knowing the effects on human beings or testing the medicine in a controlled laboratory environment.

Cultural Issues

Culture is the dominant pattern of living, thinking, feeling, and believing developed by people over many years and transmitted consciously or unconsciously, to successive generations.[22] The culture that people embrace is often the lens through which they view others. The virtual classroom allows students from different cultures to learn together. Students who feel they have a superior culture will see things through their cultural lenses and expect their classmates to conform to their **values, assumptions, beliefs,** and **expectations** (VABEs). Instructors can play an active role in dousing cultural tensions in the virtual classroom by reinforcing online classroom etiquettes and educating students on how they can benefit from diversity and the experiences of their classmates who are culturally different from them.[23]

Information and communications technology (ICT) is rapidly breaking down old patterns of education that were long driven by colonial language ties. Language barriers are the most significant cultural challenges that online students face. English has emerged as the dominant language of scholarship, research, business, and diplomacy, and English-speaking countries such as the United States, United Kingdom, Canada, and Australia have positioned themselves to operate in the distance-education sector far beyond their national borders. English-language materials and instruction have successfully infiltrated many parts of the world that have traditionally delivered higher education in other languages. Distance education thrives under an economy of scale, but curricula and methodological approaches designed in standard format in advanced countries for the use of students in developing countries that are home to a large number of online students often don't address the local needs, interests, or values of students in those countries.[24]

Regulations and Standardization Issues

Globalization is eliminating business and economic barriers, making it easier for educational providers to operate across borders. However, most providers are often not answerable to the jurisdictions of the national regulatory systems of users, nor are they entirely controlled in the countries where they operate.[25]

Accreditation organizations verify that schools offer quality education and develop a set of standards that, if followed, should provide excellence in instructional delivery.[26] In the United States, the six regional accrediting bodies that accredit postsecondary institutions operate independently and develop their standards and procedures for measuring program quality. Professional associations accredit programs in some fields, while the **Council for Higher Education Accreditation** (CHEA) serves as a clearinghouse and umbrella organization for legitimate accrediting bodies. However, most educational institutions that recruit students from abroad have no established methods of verifying the identity of students they admit and often lack the mechanisms to enforce entry requirements for such students.[27]

Some countries lack regulations in coping with the emerging issues related to distance education and where quality-assurance and accreditations agencies function, they often lack clear mandates on matters of program delivery beyond regional or national borders. Some countries also have limited resources in tracking fraudulent entities and diploma mills, or capacity to take appropriate measures in curbing illegal practices of bogus educational providers.[28] In the United States, and other advanced countries, the copyright and plagiarism laws that protect authors and writers, and unauthorized use of academic property do not exist in many countries and violators may not face prosecution at home or abroad.[29]

In recent years, the accreditation process has come under intense scrutiny both locally and internationally. In the United States, the government shut down accredited schools like Corinthian Colleges due to questionable educational practices.[30] Globalization, regional integration, and the ever-increasing mobility of students and scholars have made internationally recognized standards among nations more complicated, and the exponential growth of new education providers with different educational models have raised further questions about quality. Although the consumers of education (students, parents, employers) are demanding quality from institutions and the degrees they award, mechanisms for establishing international comparability are vague and mostly untested.[31]

In a country like the United States, which boasts a robust tradition of quality assurance and accreditation compliance, the widely reported fraud case and diploma-mill activity by the defunct Saint Regis University is a prime example of how a phony operation can leverage the relatively weak oversight of distance education. The expansion and growth of private distance education providers have also brought new kinds of accrediting institutions, often driven by financial gain making the task of identifying legitimate institutions, programs, and providers difficult.[32]

To ensure confidence in online education, educational institutions must communicate not only about how their instructions and academic programs compete with other institutions, but also how their curricula differ from degree mills hawking certificates on the Internet.[33] The relative ease of entry into the online education market and the ability of educational institutions to recruit students from abroad will force regulators to demand new requirements from educational institutions. The online education industry is developing procedures for the design and delivery of online courses to conform to specific standards, such as **Shared Content Object Reference Model** (SCORM), which tracks students' progress, achievement, competency, attendance, and other areas of learning in the classroom.[34]

The Health Risks of Technology

Technology has simplified life in a lot of ways, but studies show that the uncontrollable use of technology is hazardous to human health. Studies show that exposure of humans and animals to **electromagnetic fields** (EMFs) affects the **central nervous system** (CNS), causing headaches, sleep apnea, anxiety, cognitive dysfunction, and neurogenesis impairment. Starring on a computer for an extended period can cause severe eye strain, and there are causal relationships between times spent in front of a screen and psychological health problems such as depression and anxiety among the youth.[35]

The prospect of using mobile devices to connect to **WIFI** anywhere continues to expand. On the other hand, it has elevated the risk of exposure to some severe unknown physical health hazards, including procreation.[36] In 2003, a study found damaged rat nerve cells after exposure to microwaves from **Global System for Mobile** (GSM) communication. Other studies revealed the biological effects of microwaves on mice and other animals and a possible effect on fertility and carcinogenetic (an agent directly involved in causing cancer) of **Universal Mobile Telecommunications Service** (UMTS) wavelengths of **Radiofrequency** (RF).[37] Research showed that exposure to **EMFs** with a **specific absorption rate** (SAR) of 2 W/kg (watts per kilogram) was permissible and not risky to humans, but the study did not exclude **UMTS** at high energy absorption rates of 10 W/kg (watts per kilogram).[38]

In 2016, the study published in the Journal of Public Health and Environment that analyzed 79,241 malignant brain tumors over 21 years period found the rise of an aggressive and often fatal type of brain tumors known as **Glioblastoma Multiforme** (GBM) due to radiation exposure. In England, cases of **GBM** increased from approximately 1,250 a year in 1995 to almost 3,000 in 2016. Although the overall fall in other types of brain tumors masked the increase in **GBM**, equally, it has increased the suspicion that mobile and cordless phone use causes gliomas. The study conducted by the European Commission Scientific Committee on Emerging and Newly Identified Health Risks in 2015 did not find increased risks of brain tumors or other cancers of the head and neck region when exposed to cell phone radiofrequency electromagnetic radiation.[39] The research, however, did not address the long-term effect of **GBM** on humans or rule out the specific health risks of **UMTS**.[40]

Technology will continue to be part of everyday life, and its use for business and learning will continue to expand. Personal responsibility will be paramount in reducing the associated health risks. Experts recommend the 20-20-20 rule for those who frequently use computers and other mobile devices to reduce eye strain. They should look at something every 20 minutes from 20 feet away and at least for 20 seconds. Also, taking intermittent breaks when using computers will relax the brain and minimize the dangers technology poses to humans.

Privacy and Security Issues

Privacy and security concerns have heightened in recent years due to increases in cybercrimes, virus attacks, and hacking not only against organizations but academic institutions. In Australia, cyber-attacks have become so worrisome that the Law Council in the country called on the government to launch an awareness program to combat the epidemic.[41]

In 2008, the **Identity Theft Resource Center** that tracks data breaches in the United States reported 446 incidents of exposed private information that contained more than 127 million records.[42] In 2018, the number of data intrusions reported was 1,244. The 2018 figure was a decrease of 23% from the number published in 2017, but the consumer records containing sensitive **personally identifiable information** (PII) such as names, social security number, date of birth, place of birth, mother's name, biometric records, and private information such as medical, educational, financial, and employment records increased by 126% from 198 million records in 2017 to 447 million in 2018.[43]

In higher education, data privacy continues to be a primary concern as educational institutions collect more data from students and stored them in the cloud. Faculty, students, and other stakeholders use various devices to connect to campus networks, making them targets and more susceptible to cyber-attacks. Smartphones and other mobile devices are an easy target for hackers because they are not nearly as secure as the computers that schools provide in their computer centers or personal computers owned by individuals. Large institutions often have different departments and off-campus divisions such as medical centers and research institutes and manage multiple computer networks, which increases their vulnerability and risk of exposures to cyber attacks.[44]

In 2005, hackers breached a computer at Boston College, exposing the addresses and Social Security Numbers of 120,000 alumni.[45] In March 2018, the **United States Department of Justice** (DOJ) reported that more than 300 universities in the United States and abroad were victims of cyber-attacks and system intrusion. The hackers infiltrated 144 U.S. universities, 176 universities in 21 other countries by spear-phishing emails to trick professors and other university affiliates into clicking on malicious links and entering their network login credentials. The hackers stole 31 terabytes of data, estimated to be worth $3 billion in intellectual property. Of 100,000 accounts the hackers targeted, they gained access to about 8,000, with 3,768 of them at U.S. institutions.[46]

The increased cyber-attacks against schools means they need more than just smart passwords and the latest antivirus software programs against today's more powerful hackers.[47] Education institutions must build robust technology infrastructures to inoculate them against increasingly sophisticated hackers of today. Schools must create a **data governance plan** they can use in the event of system intrusions. In the United States, education institutions must stay abreast of **FERPA** (Family Educational Rights and Privacy Act), **COPPA** (Children's Online Privacy Protection Act), **CIPA** (Children's Internet Protection Act) and **HIPAA** (Health Insurance Portability and Accountability Act), including other state and federal laws governing student privacy to limit their legal exposure.[48]

Several companies such as **ForeScout Technologies** have security programs that help schools detect vulnerabilities of any device connected to their systems. **TrendMicro**, for example, developed a hacking software that allows students and faculty to access a virtual server from an **iPad** and work without able to make changes to the central system.[49]

Retention Problem

Retention of online students is a growing concern among chief academic leaders. As figure 9.1 shows, in 2004 and 2009, only 27% and 28% of educational leaders respectively thought that retaining online students were more problematic than keeping traditional students. In 2013, the number of academic leaders that agreed increased to 41%.[50] Although comparing the retention of campus-based students with online students could be misleading because both groups intersperse from time to time, and the experience of a school in running distance learning program differs, a 68% increase within ten years deserves scrutiny.

Schools can use various academic and administrative programs to solve retention problems. The **Arizona State University Foundation** and the **Boston Consulting Group** (BCG) identified seven best practices that colleges and universities could initiate to increase students outcome in the virtual classroom:

1. Develop a digital learning strategy that addresses the needs of different student populations.
2. Invest in instructional design, learning science, and digital tools to ensure quality.

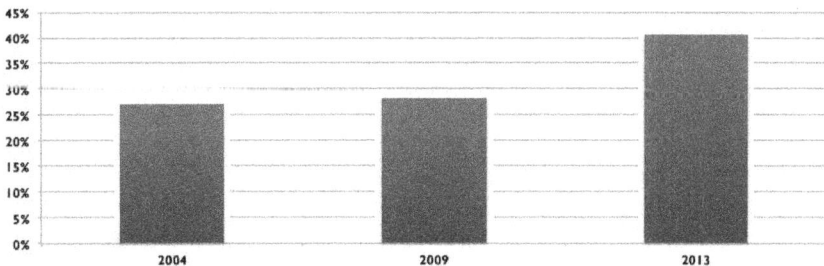

Figure: 9.1   Comparison in Retaining Students in Online Courses and Face-to-Face Courses: 2004, 2009, and 2013

I. Elaine Allen; Jeff Seaman, 2014.

3. Provide students with remotely accessible support.
4. Treat faculty members as partners– let them participate in critical decisions, offer professional development opportunities, foster an innovation culture.
5. Build a central team infrastructure to sustain long-term momentum.
6. Take advantage of outside vendors– when they can be helpful and additive.
7. Develop research and analytical prowess and find ways to translate plans into action.[51]

Plagiarism

Plagiarism is unethical academic practices of presenting someone else's work as one's own. The manifestation includes cheating in exams or assignments, theft of other students' work, paying others to complete a task, downloading whole or part of work from the Internet, falsification of information, misrepresentation of records, or other actions that undermine academic integrity.

Plagiarism is not exclusive to the academic environment but a cankerworm that infests organizations at every level. A survey showed that 33% of 3,600 mid-career and 4,160 early-career scientists in the United States had engaged in questionable research practices relating to data, methods, policy, use of funds, outside influence, peer review, giving credit, and "cutting corners."[52] In academics, plagiarism has become so pervasive that it diverts teachers from performing their primary role of developing students' writing, reading, and critical thinking skills to playing an adversarial role of "plagiarism police in the classroom."[53]

There are two types of plagiarism–intentional and

unintentional. Intentional plagiarism involves students deliberately copying another person's work or ideas and presenting them as their own. Unintentional plagiarism is the most common and occurs when students improperly cited authors or incorrectly referenced them in their work. Improper citations and erroneous authorial attribution do not remove the guilt of plagiarism even when students act in good faith but fail to acknowledge others' work accurately. The consequences for academic dishonesty could be severe, ranging from work resubmission, a permanent failing grade to suspension or expulsion. The University of Iowa provides examples of plagiarism and cheating, but the act may include other academic infractions not listed:

1. Presentation of the ideas of others without credit to the owner;
2. Use of direct quotations without quotation marks and attribution to the source;
3. Paraphrasing without credit to the author;
4. Participation in a group project with plagiarized materials;
5. Failure to provide adequate citations for content obtained through electronic research;
6. Downloading and submitting work from electronic databases without citation;
7. Submitting content created/written by someone else as one's own, including purchased term/research papers;
8. Copying from someone else's exam, homework, or laboratory work;
9. Allowing someone to copy or submit one's work as his/her own;
10. Accepting credit for a group project without doing one's share;
11. Submitting the same paper in more than one course without the knowledge and approval of the instructors involved;
12. Using notes or other materials during a test or exam without authorization;
13. Not following the guidelines specified by the instructor for a "take-home" test or exam.[54]

Combating plagiarism is a collaborative effort that involves students, instructors, and schools. There are things that students can do before writing a paper while writing the essay, and after the work has been completed. Students can avoid unintentional plagiarism by using the approved writing style when completing written assignments. Instructors also must not jump to a conclusion without detailed reviewing student work for plagiarism (e.g., uncited or incorrectly cited source material) and cheating (e.g., unauthorized collaboration). In the event of a possible infraction, instructors should follow the established plagiarism guidelines for fairness and due process. Educational institutions must specify the writing format such as APA, MLA, or Chicago Manual of Style that students should use when writing assignments to reduce intentional and unintentional plagiarism.[55]

Depending on the gravity of plagiarism, instructors should work with affected students in resolving the problem before escalating the issue to a higher academic officer because unintentional plagiarism can look intentional, and often schools don't have a clear policy on plagiarism, and when available, the adjudication process not transparent.

Environmental and Natural Catastrophes

Nature and technology have adversarial relationships and, by extension, learning. Natural calamities such as thunderstorms, tornadoes, hurricanes, floods, wildfire, or snowstorms are generally unavoidable. When these natural disasters occur, they can take down technology grids, power lines and interfere with Internet connections making it difficult to access the online classroom and complete the required assignment. In these circumstances, students should contact their instructor for accommodation. For the most part, instructors will accommodate late submissions if students can provide genuine evidence of a severe problem.

Personal Problems and Miscellaneous

Family emergency, death, health problem, relocation, job loss, career change are part of daily life. These life-altering situations can significantly impact academic performance. For example, if an employer assigns a student to a rural area in the middle of a course where there is no Internet connection or the quality is poor, it will be problematic for the student to keep up with classwork or complete the required assignments. In this instance, the student is in an untenable position because of the conflicting priorities. Students who combine work with education could anticipate such problems but must have a plan in place in dealing with them when they arise.

Summary of Main Points

- Learning styles could be information processing-based, personality-based, and multi-dimensional/instructional-based style.
- Matching learning styles with the learning environment is essential to success in an online course.
- There is apathy among instructors, and students can resist online education as well.
- The lack of computer knowledge is a barrier to success in the virtual classroom.
- Hardware and software glitches can impede the learning experience in the classroom.
- Poor Internet connections can slow down the ability to complete course activities on time.
- Lack of active participation in class discussion could impact online learning experience.
- Failure of instructors to provide motivational and corrective feedback promptly would cause mistakes to reoccur.
- The cost of taking an online course could be astronomical when students take a blended course.
- Online education is not suitable for natural science or social science courses that require face-to-face interactions.
- Cultural problems can induce misunderstanding in the virtual classroom unless instructors enforce strong classroom etiquette.
- Cybercrimes such as hacking, virus attacks, and phishing against academic institutions continue to be a concern.
- Retention of online students could be problematic unless schools develop initiatives to address the problem.

- Educational institutions face legal and regulatory challenges as they extend their academic programs outside their primary catchment areas and abroad.
- Plagiarism has intensified due to the ubiquity of the Internet and the availability of written materials online.
- Natural disasters such as thunderstorms, tornadoes, hurricanes, floods, wildfire, snowstorms could take down the technology grid, causing outages and disrupting learning.
- Personal problems such as family emergency, death, health problem, relocation, job loss, and career change could take a toll physically and mentally, making it difficult to focus on learning.

Discussion Questions

1. Identify and discuss the most critical challenges students face in the virtual classroom. Recommend strategies to overcome the problems.
2. Identify and discuss the technical and technology issues you are most likely to encounter in the virtual classroom. How can you overcome them?
3. Discuss why students and instructors might resist online education. What can educational institutions do to make them more comfortable in the online environment?
4. Identify and discuss the cultural problems that students might face in the virtual classroom. Suggest ways to improve cultural understanding in the virtual classroom.
5. Identify and discuss the legal and regulatory issues that online education providers face at home and abroad. What can education institutions do to overcome those issues?
6. What does plagiarism mean to you? What tools can schools use to detect plagiarism, and what can students do to avoid intentional and unintentional plagiarism?
7. Technology is essential to learning, but with potential risks to human health. Suggest ways to minimize the dangers technology pose to human beings.

10

STRATEGIES FOR SUCCESS IN THE ONLINE ENVIRONMENT

Learning Objectives: After studying this chapter, you should be able to:

1. Understand the importance of goal setting in the virtual environment
2. Discuss why time management is essential in the online environment
3. Explain the role of technology in the virtual classroom
4. Understand self-discipline and educational achievement
5. Explain the role of educational institutions in academic attainment
6. Understand the importance of social support in the virtual classroom
7. Describe effective communication in the virtual classroom
8. Explain the need for computer competency in an online class
9. Understand the value of social connection in the virtual classroom
10. Discuss the attributes of independent learners in the virtual classroom
11. Describe the effect of the learning environment on academic performance
12. Discuss the technical skills required to be successful in an online class
13. Understand accreditation issues in higher education
14. Discuss the questions to answer before taking an online course

INTRODUCTION

Strategies are a set of actions that, if implemented, will produce the desired outcome. In this chapter, we discuss evidence-based strategies that students need to be successful in the virtual environment. But there are salient questions that students should ask and answer before taking an online course.

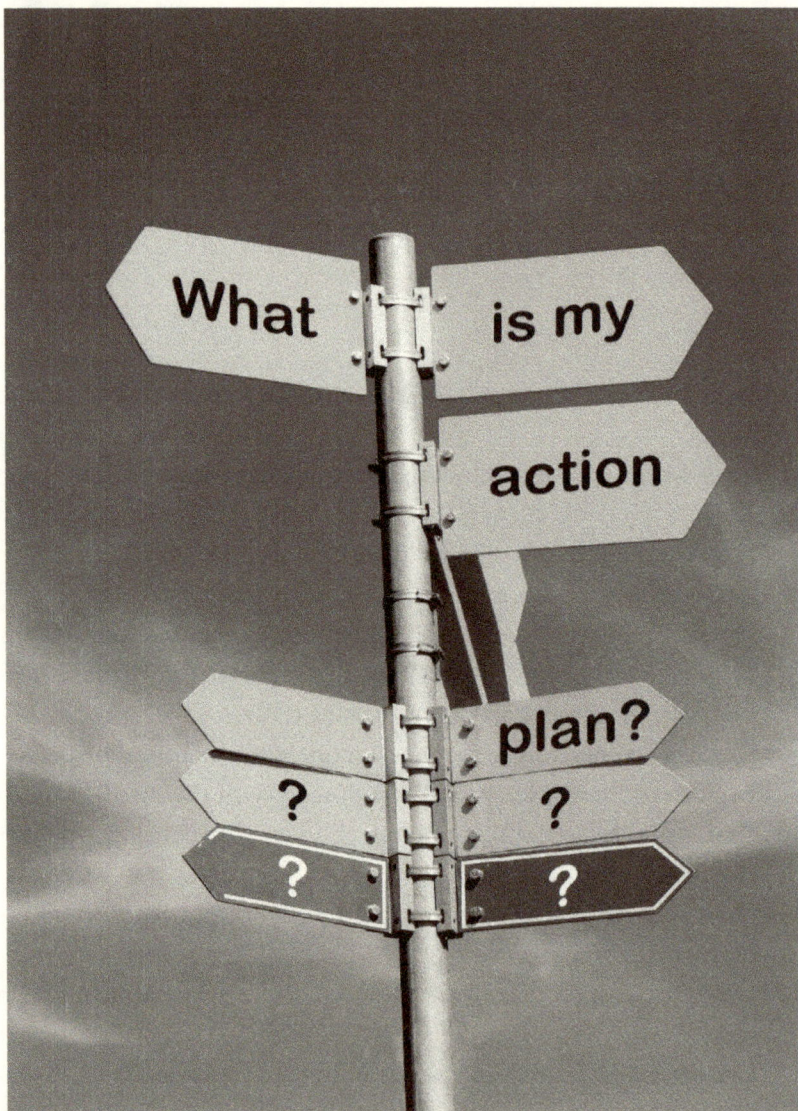

THE FORMULA FOR SUCCESS IN THE VIRTUAL CLASSROOM

Set Achievable Goals

Goal setting is the first task to prepare for an online course. The goal should not be too easy or too ambitious to achieve. If you wish to make an A in a course, you must begin preparing for the grade before the first day of class, meaning that you must have a computer ready and a spare. As soon as practicable, you must register for your courses, pay the required course fees, and familiarize yourself with the course management system used in class. Also, you must get high-speed Internet service from a reliable provider and get the learning materials ready.

There is a **SMART** (Specific, Measurable, Attainable, Realistic, and Timeliness) way to achieve a goal. A goal should be **Specific**, meaning that if you plan to make an A, you must be specific and focus on the grade from the beginning of the course to the end.

There are two ways to measure performance—during and after completing a task. As a course progresses, you should **Measure** your progress against your goal. The progress report will show gap areas between your goal and achieved results and what you can do to get back on track if you're trending in the wrong direction.

Attainment is the peak of a goal and the actualization of an effort.

Being **Realistic** is how well you think you will perform based on your academic strengths and weaknesses. Making an A depends on your efforts, and partly controllable and uncontrollable situations, which you will face within and outside the class.

Timeliness is the time it takes to accomplish a task. A course has a start and an end. Timeliness requires that you complete and submit all the assignments as due to achieve your goal.

Effective Time Management

Time management is the act of prioritizing tasks around the available time. The limitless access to the Internet and the availability of mobile devices has made life more comfortable and the ability to get things done expeditiously. Equally, the pervasiveness of smartphones and other mobile devices has complicated life because of the accompanying distractions, making time management a challenging endeavor. A survey showed that 92% of college students used their devices for checking email, texting, or Web browsing during class and accessed information on their mobile devices more than 30 times per day.[1]

Time is perishable, and once you lose it, you cannot regain it, causing you to reschedule tasks to accommodate for the lost time and postpone things that you previously planned to accomplish.

In the virtual classroom, you control when to attend class and complete your assignments. The onus to manage time and understand which tasks come first and those that can wait falls on students. For instance, socializing with friends is necessary but optional if it will distract from completing the required homework. Apart from educational implications, poor time management often induces anxiety, stress, high blood pressure, and other health problems. The College Student Journal recommends the following strategies for proper time management:

1. Use the syllabus and planner to sketch out the semester.
2. Organize and prioritize tasks.
3. Plan homework time around a work schedule if necessary.
4. Study at an office or library to avoid distractions at home.
5. Study after children goes to bed (if you have children).
6. Work on assignments several days before they are due. If there are any problems or you need clarifications, you will have enough time to contact your professor for assistance.
7. Be disciplined, read the online discussions, and do some work each day.[2]

Reliable Technology

Reliable technology ensures that you can listen to lectures, submit assignments, conduct research, share files, participate in class discussions, check grades, and perform other learning activities. If your computer lacks the required hardware and software programs or the Internet connection is weak, it will prevent you from performing these course activities.

Education institutions need a reliable Internet connection for Wi-Fi-enabled devices for students because most students arrive on campus with all manner of Wi-Fi-demanding gadgets from laptops, tablets, smartphones, wireless printers, e-readers, and gaming machines to fitness bands and other wearable devices. A survey shows that most students have approximately three to five mobile devices, and the number will increase in the future. Multimedia content, such as video streaming and videoconferencing that students use in classrooms, require strong connection capabilities, and as thousands of students take online courses and other standards-based assessments at once, institutions need network infrastructures to handle the increased traffic without affecting the student experience. Schools should continually upgrade their networks, add more wireless access points to extend signal reach, and using solutions such as software-defined networking, cloud-based management, and desktop virtualization programs to accommodate and meet the increased demand of students. Service providers can work with education institutions in providing wireless service and offering technical support to support new education networks.[3]

Periodically, students will have problems with their computers, mobile devices, and other technologies. The good news is that most higher education institutions allow external visitors to use their library resources, including computers, for free after proper identification or registration. In some areas, there are public libraries and Internet cafés and workspaces that students can utilize while they resolve their technical problems. Frequent program updates will not only make computers work smoothly but prevent most virus incidents.

Self-Discipline

Self-discipline is the willpower that individuals have in controlling their behaviors. While it takes a long time to reach the comfort zone on the

self-discipline level, it takes a short period to drop off the scale. Self-discipline determines if a student will spend hours watching movies during the week or work on assignments due at the end of the week. Although watching movies could release stress, recreation time should not conflict with study time.

In the virtual classroom, and outside the class, students face myriads of unrelated issues. For most academic matters, schools will provide the necessary support, but schools cannot control what happens outside the class or how students spend their free time. The **locus of control** determines how individuals handle personal issues. People with an **internal locus of control** take responsibility for their conduct. People with an **external locus of control** look for excuses and blame others for their problems. Taking control of personal issues by looking inward for motivation is a prerequisite to success in the virtual classroom.

Institutional Support

Educational institutions provide technical support, academic assistance, career counseling, library services, students' rights, and responsibilities, and offer necessary administrative support to ensure that students succeed in an online class.[4] Educational specialists support students in developing learning strategies to meet their needs and ensure that proctors are available during examinations and handle other critical administrative issues so in-class student to student and instructor to student interactions can flow smoothly.[5]

The educational and administrative services that schools provide can only go as far as students take advantage of them. Knowing who to contact for a specific issue can go a long way in an online class. For example, an academic advisor may share their opinions on a course syllabus, instructors are in a better position to address curriculum-related matters. Although technology plays an essential role in today's educational process, a school cannot exclusively rely on technology without some face-to-face interactions. Some local representatives must be available to answer questions, organize exams, provide feedback, offer a back-up service, and generally follow up with students' issues and deal with their everyday academic problems. Learning is a group activity and collaborative effort that involves students, professors, communities, governments, and organizations. Affiliated universities, local research centers, colleges, and branches of organizations are indispensable in assisting students pursuing distance education programs in different contexts.[6]

As online education becomes a global phenomenon, colleges and universities form strategic alliances to enhance academic quality and student experience. Education institutions must communicate with the internal stakeholders (students, faculty, and administrators) on the standard of excellence that nurtures and promotes academic quality as follows:

1. Encouraging contact between students and faculty.
2. Fostering reciprocity and cooperation among students.
3. Using active learning techniques.
4. Giving prompt feedback.
5. Emphasizing time on task.
6. Communicating high expectations.
7. Respecting diverse talents and ways of learning.[7]

A Supportive Social Community

Personal problems such as sickness, family issues, job loss, relocation, or death of a loved one are part of everyday life and inevitable. Although schools can counsel to cushion the effects of personal problems, only family, friends, managers, colleagues, social, and religious organizations can provide the required emotional support. Students should engage their social networks when in distress, but it is necessary to bring them along early in a degree program so they can be available when the going gets tough.

Effective Communication

In the virtual classroom, you can use discussion forums, telephones, email, videos, chat, and text messages to communicate with instructors, classmates, academic advisors, and other stakeholders. Using the right communication tool will determine how quickly you will get a response and have your issues addressed. The telephone may be the quickest way to reach a professor but may not be the most efficient because you may need to schedule a meeting before a telephone conversation. Email may not be the fastest but could be the most effective because instructors check their emails several times a day. Online forums are also efficient because professors will visit a class at least once a day though some instructors have a preferred method they want students to communicate with them.

Computer Literacy and Skills

The knowledge of computer programs such as Windows Office, Internet Explorer, Google Docs, Adobe, and other applications is essential when taking an online course. Although e-learning manufacturers improve their products every day in ways that make them user-friendly, educational institutions ensure that students can log-in to class and navigate the learning systems easily. As Edmonds Community College in Washington notes, the comfort of students with computers and uninterrupted Internet access enables them to manage files and install required software programs.[8]

As online education becomes standard practice in learning, instructors must have the computer skills and web-design knowledge to teach online courses. Most educational institutions provide online teaching training, instructional materials, teaching assistants to help instructors successfully manage student issues and enhance the virtual classroom experience.[7]

Stay Connected

Social interaction is essential when you take an online course due to the

lack of face-to-face opportunities in the virtual classroom. A survey showed that 74% of students believed they "missed out" educationally because they took an online course.[9] You can use chat, discussion board, videos, whiteboard, e-mails, telephone, chat, videos, blogs, or text messaging to connect with classmates, instructors, advisors, and other school stakeholders. E-learning systems now link directly to social and professional networking sites such as **Facebook**, **Twitter**, **Google+**, **Instagram**, and **LinkedIn** while education institutions have social media pages through which they connect with current students and alumni. As education institutions combine residencies with their online programs, students meet in a face-to-face environment and build relationships that often continue after graduation.

The following are additional strategies that can boost success in the virtual classroom.

1. Be open-minded about sharing life, work, and educational experiences as part of the learning process.
2. Ability to communicate through writing.
3. Self-motivation and self-discipline.
4. Speak up when there is a problem.
5. Be willing and able to commit four to fifteen hours per week to study.
6. Able to meet the minimum program requirements.
7. Accept critical thinking and decision making as part of the learning process.
8. Have access to a computer and the Internet.
9. Able to think ideas through before responding in the discussion forum.
10. Feel that high-quality learning can take place without going to a classroom.[10]

QUESTIONS TO ANSWER BEFORE TAKING ONLINE COURSES

Are You an Independent Learner?

An independent learner is a student who can study on his or her own with little or no handholding by a professor. Students must be able to navigate the academic and administrative issues they face in the virtual classroom personally. Some matters may only require going over the syllabus or reading the announcements posted by the instructor, or a simple google search would clear some confusing areas. Nonetheless, being an independent learner doesn't mean that students should not reach out to their schools or keep quiet when they have problems.

Are You Self-Disciplined and Self-Motivated?

Online education provides the convenience to learn anytime, but self-discipline is crucial to success. In one study, 64% of students noted they needed more discipline to succeed in the virtual classroom than in the face-to-face course.[11] In another study, self-discipline was ranked the highest among the barriers to the widespread adoption of online learning.[12] Online education is more suitable to highly motivated, self-directed adult learners who have a substantial stake in their educational outcomes.[13] In 1980, Knowles developed five assumptions of adult learning which are relevant to online education:

1. Adults arrive at a self-concept and capable of self-direction;
2. Adults accumulate various life experiences that add to the classroom experience;
3. Adults need (not) to be assured and reinforced about why a subject matter is essential to learn;
4. Adults are solution-oriented and desire practical application; and
5. Adults influenced by intrinsic motivation rather than extrinsic motivation.[14]

Based on Knowles's assumptions, students must exude some qualities before taking an online course. For example, the University of Phoenix requires students seeking admission into its online program to be at least twenty-one years old and working full-time. The average age of students who attend the institution is 31 years, and many of them have acquired substantial professional experience before starting their degrees. The students are motivated and committed to pursuing their academic careers and realizing their educational goals because of their desire to advance and grow professionally.[15]

Does Your Academic Program Require Hands-On Learning?

Technology has transformed learning, and sophisticated computers are now available that can analyze big data in ways that the human brain cannot comprehend. Simulations can predict events before they occur, and games can enhance learning in the cognitive domain. However, these educational tools cannot replicate the real-world experience in certain situations. In natural sciences, such as botany and zoology and physical sciences such as chemistry, physics, and astronomy, students need both theoretical and practical demonstrations in these disciplines. In sociology, psychology, anthropology, and other social science disciplines, computers can collate and analyze data on a given phenomenon, but conclusions will be theoretical at best without physical interactions with human beings or the environment that produced the event.

Are You Looking to Develop Your Educational Career Along with Your Professional Career?

Online education enables working adults who want to achieve their academic dreams to do so without quitting their day job. As the job market changes, organizations partner with educational institutions to deliver professional development programs. Many schools now focus on career-oriented programs that help employees develop in several areas of their professional careers. **Starbucks**, a U.S based retail coffee company with more than 24,000 stores in 70 countries, recently partnered with **Arizona State University** (ASU). Part-time and full-time employees at Starbucks and eligible U.S. partners can earn a bachelor's degree delivered online by **ASU** with full tuition coverage for every year of college attended through the **Starbucks College Achievement Plan**. The military veterans and active service members with their family members take advantage of the program to achieve their dreams of a college education as well.[16]

How Comfortable Are You with Technology?

Comfort with technology is a precursor to success in an online course. It is crucial to know how to navigate the course management system, participate in class discussions, submit assignments, download, and upload information. Also, you must know how to use various online communication tools in communicating with instructors and classmates and know how to install some hardware and software programs.

Are the School and Your Program of Study Accredited?

Accreditation is a seal of approval given to a school after the institution has passed through a peer-review process and met the requirements established by a regulatory authority. In some countries, the government or the department of education handles accreditation issues. In the United States, the U.S. Department of Education approves the non-governmental accrediting agencies that accredit higher education institutions.[17] Many unaccredited colleges masquerade on the Internet as authentic degree-granting institutions, and their presence poisons the waters for the accredited institutions as people tend to lump them together.[18] Although accreditation is not synonymous with quality, degrees earned at an accredited institution provides the confidence that employers will recognize the degree, or students can transfer to another school or pursue a higher program in the future.[19]

Summary of Main Points

- Set an achievable goal before the start of an online class by knowing your strengths and weaknesses.
- Effective time management lets you prioritize your activities based on relevance and urgency.
- A reliable computer enables you to enjoy your online learning experience.
- Self-discipline ensures that you can make the right decision given the alternative options.
- Educational institutions provide academic and administrative resources to help students succeed in the virtual classroom.
- Family, friends, co-workers, managers, social and religious organizations offer social support to get them through personal problems.
- Using the right communication tool determines how quickly one receives feedback in the virtual classroom.

- Computer literacy enables you to navigate the virtual classroom successfully.
- Students can use discussion boards, videos, whiteboard, e-mails, telephone, videos, blogs, text messaging, and social media platforms to stay connected with the school stakeholders.
- Understand your professional goal and how online education can enhance your career goal after graduation.
- Institutional accreditation validates the quality of an academic program and provides the opportunity to transfer credits to another school and pursue higher degrees in the future.
- Connecting with classmates and alumni through **Facebook**, **Twitter**, **Google+**, **Instagram**, and **LinkedIn**, and other social media outlets.
- Comfort with technology is a precursor to success in an online course.
- Online education enables working adults to achieve their academic goals in conjunction with their professional careers.
- Accreditation provides the confidence that employers will recognize the degree, or students can transfer to another school or pursue a higher degree in the future.

Discussion Questions

1. Identify and discuss the strategies required to be successful in an online course. How would you apply the tactics in an online course?
2. Most people struggle with time management. Discuss how you can effectively manage your time in the virtual classroom.
3. What is self-discipline, and how can it help students when they take an online course?
4. What academic and administrative resources and support should schools provide to make online education exciting? Provide specific examples and justify your recommendation.
5. Discuss the technical knowledge required for success in the virtual classroom. Identify different school stakeholders, and what

role should each play in ensuring that students succeed in an online course?

6. Identify communication tools, including social media platforms that students can use in staying connected in the virtual classroom. Discuss the specific use of each instrument or platform and why the connection is essential?

7. What are the questions students should ask before taking an online course, and why should they ask those questions?

11

BEST PRACTICES IN ONLINE EDUCATION

Learning Objectives: After studying this chapter, you should be able to:

1. Understand how to prepare for an online class
2. Discuss the virtual classroom etiquettes
3. Explain active participation in the discussion forum
4. Discuss how to communicate with instructors
5. Understand the communication taboos in the virtual classroom

INTRODUCTION

Best practices are behaviors successfully demonstrated in one environment that individuals could transfer or replicate in similar situations. As students move from one course to another, they will encounter different situations and gain different experiences. Some experiences will be positive, while others will be negative. We identify and discuss the behaviors that students can transfer from one class to another and those they should jettison.

PREPARATION FOR AN ONLINE CLASS

Planning is the process of setting a goal and obtaining resources to achieve the goal. Although planning itself does not guarantee success, people that plan have a better chance to succeed than people that don't. In the virtual environment, there are things discussed in this section that you must do before the start of a course, while the class is going on, and at the end of the course.

Early Course Registration

In an online course, a day late to class could be a day too many because some of the performance issues that will crop up in the middle of a course could have their genesis in late registrations. Apart from the academic consequence, last-minute enrollment induces stress or hyperventilation, especially students that are sensitive to strenuous conditions.

Procrastination is the cause of most late registrations. At the start of an academic session, schools will publish course curriculums and the order to take them. In certain situations, academic departments handle course registrations, but in some cases, students can self-enroll. Whatever the process, the earlier student registers for a class, the sooner the academic department will process the information in the system.

Ordering Course Materials

After course registration, getting the learning materials is the next step. The task involves obtaining the authors' names, book titles, editions, and **International Standard Book Number** (ISBN) and the publishers' names, including the approved sellers. Some textbooks come with access codes for online activities, and some will only be available in digital format. In most cases, schools will provide relevant information about learning materials and how to obtain them.

For hard copy materials, timely purchases save money on delivery. As a best practice, students should order course materials four weeks before the start of a course. The longer the wait, the higher the risk of not getting the books before the start of class.

Meeting the Technology Requirements

Having necessary hardware and software programs, including computers and the Internet connection, enable students to listen to lectures, participate in class discussions, submit assignments, and perform other course activities. Some schools offer scholarships to help students alleviate the costs of purchasing mobile devices or provide students the ones they can use outside the class. Some schools include technology fees with tuition and give

Table 11.1

Minimum Technology Requirements for Online Courses

Minimum Technology Requirements	Windows PC	Apple MAC OS X
Operating Systems	Windows Vista or better	OS X 10.7 (Lion) or better
Memory/RAM	2GB or more	2GB or more
Browser	Firefox 24.0 or higher Internet Explorer 10 or higher	Firefox 24.0 or higher Safari 6.11 or higher
Audio	Speakers or Headphones and Microphone (Built-in or External)	Speakers or Headphones and Microphone (Built-in or External)
Internet Access	DSL, cable, educational, or corporate connection. **Wired internet strongly recommended.**	DSL, cable, educational, or corporate connection. **Wired internet strongly recommended.**

students the required tools for free. For instance, Indiana State University has a laptop scholarship program for incoming students. Other colleges, such as Wake Forest University in North Carolina, issue devices to students at the beginning of their course but require the students to return them at the end of the academic session.[1]

Table 11.1 shows the necessary software applications, internet browsers, and operating systems that students should have on their computers whether students buy them or their schools give them for free.

Knowledge of the Course Management System

Education institutions use various **course management systems** (CMSs) from the **closed-source** systems such as **Blackboard** and **Desire2Learn** (D2L) to the **open-source** systems such as **Canvas, Joomla, Sakai, ANGEL**, and **Moodle**. A school can build its learning system from scratch, as noted in the previous chapters. For the most part, most **learning management systems** work the same way and have the same features, but a school can provide tutorials on how to navigate its learning system.

Once you logged into the learning system, you should familiarize yourself with the announcements, syllabus, lectures, discussion boards, grade book, team groups, emails, and other course areas. Understanding the system will get you ready on the first day of class. If you cannot access the system, you must contact the technical department in your school immediately.

Understanding Course Expectations and Requirements

Once you gain access to a class, you must read the announcement posted by the instructor. If there is no information about course expectations and requirements, you should follow the syllabus guidelines. However, you can ask an instructor what he or she expects beyond what is in the course guide.

Typically, the course expectations and course requirements would have the course objectives, reading materials, assignment submission guidelines, and due dates, participation requirements, assessment and grading criteria, attendance rule, and institutional policy. At the beginning of the week, you should go over the course guide and understand the assignments for the week. However, you should have a view of the tasks for the upcoming weeks, so you can mentally prepare and strategize on how to accomplish them.

Class Introduction

At the beginning of an online course, you should introduce yourself in the **Introduction Forum** to the instructor and your classmates. You can share personal information but avoid sensitive information that can compromise your privacy and safety. At the minimum, you should state your names or alias, and upload your picture (if required). The photo must be professional and nothing inappropriate. You can share your family story and your hobbies and work experience (if any), academic goals and academic achievements, future career goals and aspirations, course expectations, and other exciting information about you. You should make the introduction on the first day of class but no later than the end of the first week.

In the **Introduction Forum**, classmates and professors will introduce themselves but pay attention to their biographies in case they make specific requests or have preferences, such as their preferred names and aliases. In an online class, you must respect the privacy and confidentiality of information that classmates and professors share. As a best practice, you cannot store or share personal information unless you obtain approval from the owners because unauthorized use of private information could be illegal or constitute grounds for disciplinary action.

POSTING ETIQUETTES IN THE DISCUSSION FORUM

In an online course, the discussion forum is where you will have the highest interactions with classmates. There are acceptable standards when answering the discussion questions or responding to classmates in the discussion forum.

Font Size

A font is a set of characters such as typeface, size, and spacing that appear when you type a message to the **digital box** (see figure 11.1). Using appropriate font sizes ensure that classmates and instructors can read your text without straining their eyes. If fonts are too small or too big, it makes reading difficult. Although fonts appearance can vary from one computer to another, Arial or Times New Roman sizes 2 and 3 or 12' should suffice when posting to the discussion board. Schools usually preset fonts to a specific standard, so students don't have to reset them before posting to the **digital box**. It is not a bad idea to experiment and see what works or use the previous experience as a guide in future postings. If your school recommends a specific font size, you should follow the recommendation.

Posting to the Digital Box

A digital box is a rectangular box mainly used for discussion postings, emails, and chats in the virtual classroom (see figure 11.1). You can either type directly to the digital box or attach a file, depending on the task at hand.

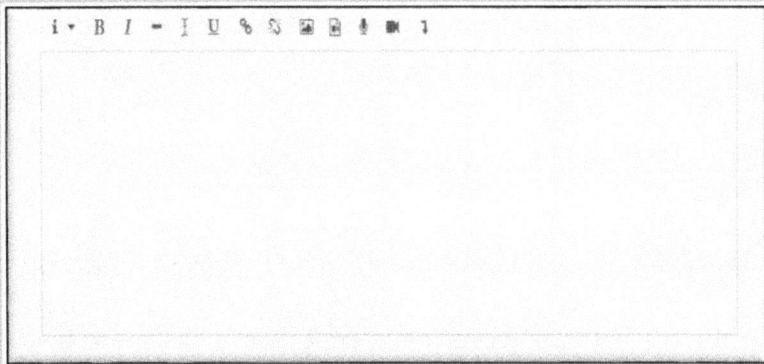

Figure: 11.1   A Digital Box

Diagrams, tables, and formulas may not look good on the **digital box**. If your postings contain these elements, you can attach them in a file or provide links to them. For best practice, you should first type in the Microsoft Word and edit before posting to correct any spelling errors and have the opportunity to recover your text if the **learning management system** malfunctions.

Grammar and Writing Mechanics

The quality of writing and organization will determine whether one will continue reading a post after the first sentence. In the discussion forum, it is essential to communicate clearly and concisely so everyone can understand the content. If a passage is too wordy or sentences not broken down to manageable paragraphs, it makes reading difficult and confusing.

Lately, short-hand words like "&" in place of "and" or "thru" instead of "through" used in texting have become common in academic writings. Short-hand words are not standard worldwide and could mean something different in other languages. Students must use academic language when communicating in the virtual classroom.

Substantive Post

A substantive post contributes to a discussion through a thorough and constructive analysis of an issue. Although a substantive post is about the quality than the volume, responses such as "good response" or "I disagree" must proceed with one or two sentences illuminating areas of agreement or disagreement. Generally, the original posting is about 250 to 750 words, and responses 250 words or less, but instructors will provide posting requirements as appropriate. Some discussions will require external sources for substantiation. In such situations, you must cite the authors, and if using information from previous class discussions, you must cite yourself.

Regular Class Attendance

Punctuality is a precursor to success in an online class. Students who attend classes regularly perform better than their peers who habitually miss classes. In the virtual classroom, schools track attendance when students logged into the system and complete required course activities.

Extenuating circumstances such as sickness, family emergencies, and other personal problems could cause a student to miss class. In these instances, the student must contact the instructor and provide the reason for absence so they can jointly formulate a solution. If a student is going to be out for an extended period, the student must contact the academic office or an academic advisor because of the educational and financial implications of nonattendance. A school can administratively withdraw students from a course if they repeatedly missed classes, but still be responsible for the full course fees and fail the course.

Active Participation in the Discussion Forum

Learning involves observations, interactions, and sharing of experiences to develop new ways of thinking and strategies for self-improvement.[1] At the beginning of each week, instructors will post questions for students to address in the discussion forum and their classmates will share their opinions by either supporting the views shared in a post or presenting alternative theses. Instructors can further enhance the discussion by offering their perspectives or asking students to expatiate their points.

In some schools, the course week starts on Monday morning and ends Sunday at 11.59 p.m. Some course week begins on Sunday at 12.am and ends on Saturday at 11.59 pm while some schools start their week on Tuesday and end Monday. In a self-study class, the week can start any day of the week and ends when a student has finished the required course activities and met the course objectives. Whatever the criteria, the expectation is for discussions to stop at the end of the course week.

Instructors will provide the timeframe to answer discussion questions and respond to postings. Sticking to the time will enable everyone to read and respond to postings or ask questions before the week runs out. If a student participates late in the week, classmates won't have enough time to read and respond to his or her postings. Also, instructors won't have the opportunity to provide feedback that could help the student understands the discussion topic better. There are also timeframes to complete group projects that students should abide by in the virtual classroom.

Respect Classmates and their Opinions

In the virtual classroom, you should treat others the way you want them to treat you, not only because it is the right thing to do, but because of the unintended consequences. In the face-to-face environment, you can clarify remark and apologize if a classmate finds it objectionable. In the virtual classroom, there is less opportunity to retract information once you post it.

Race, religion, ethnicity, sexual orientation, and politics are sensitive subjects that often provoke strong feelings will come up in the virtual classroom. But there could be collegial discussions on these hot-button issues without stymie opposing viewpoints. The virtual classroom is where students confront different perspectives, accommodating, challenging, rejecting, or integrating new information.[2]

Need to Communicate with Instructors

In the virtual classroom, communication seeks to achieve the following objectives:

1. Elicit knowledge from students so instructors can see what students already know and understand, and students *owned* education as well as teachers;

2. Respond to things that students say, not only so that students get feedback on their attempts, but also so that teachers can incorporate what students say into the flow of discourse and gather students' contributions together to construct more generalized meanings;

3. Describe the classroom experiences that students share with the instructor in such a way that the educational significance of those joint experiences is revealed and emphasized.[3]

In an online class, you can use e-mails, chats, discussion boards, telephones, videos, or text messaging to communicate with professors and classmates. Since each communication tool has strengths and weaknesses, how you leverage them will determine how quickly you will receive feedback and have your issues addressed. Telephone and videos have two-way communication capability, but you might need an appointment with a professor before a phone or a video chat.

Emails are one-way communication and slow, but instructors will likely respond immediately after reading them. With the convenience of emails, students see online education as an individualistic enterprise, and their attitude extends to their relationships and expectations in how they communicate with their professors by failing to read online postings before sending emails to them. Often, professors receive the same question from multiple students requiring multiple responses.[4]

COMMUNICATION TABOOS IN THE VIRTUAL CLASSROOM

Shouting/Yelling

A **shout** or **yell** is when one communicates in UPPER-CASE letters. Sometimes, you might use upper-case letters to emphasize a point, but if you compose an entire message in upper-case letters, it crosses the boundary of emphasizing to yelling. Also, sentences written in upper-case letters are difficult to read and often make spelling errors challenging to detect.

Let us consider the tenor of a statement written in UPPER-CASE and another written in lower-case letters.

The following quote is in UPPER-CASE letters:

IN THE ONLINE ENVIRONMENT, THERE ARE THREE TYPES OF INTERACTIONS—LEARNER-INSTRUCTOR, LEARNER-LEARNER, AND LEARNER-CONTENT. LEARNER-INSTRUCTOR INTERACTION OCCURS BETWEEN STUDENTS AND THEIR INSTRUCTORS. LEARNER-LEARNER INTERACTION TAKES PLACE BETWEEN STUDENTS AND THEIR CLASSMATES. LEARNER-CONTENT INTERACTION OCCURS BETWEEN STUDENTS AND THE COURSE CONTENTS.[5]

Let us consider the texture of the same quote in lower-case letters.

In the online environment, there are three types of interactions—learner-instructor, learner-learner, and learner-content. Learner-instructor interaction occurs between students and their instructors. Learner-learner interaction takes place between students and their classmates. Learner-content interaction occurs between students and the course contents.[6]

The statement in the second example produced different effects though the content is the same because you don't have to squint or strain your eyes to read the passage, unlike the one in upper-case letters.

Colors

We have preferences from the colors of clothes we wear to the colors we paint our houses. In different societies, colors mean different things to people. In most Western countries, white color symbolizes purity and peace, while in some Asian countries, white represents evil omens. Among the Yoruba people in Nigeria, widows wear black attires to mourn the death of their husbands.

In the virtual classroom, when students compose an entire message in red and send it to their classmates, it signifies anger, even if the intention is to the contrary. Students can use red ink occasionally for emphases, but if the entire message is a red color, it moves the conversation to the anger zone. The best practice is to use black color on a white background in composing messages or postings in the virtual classroom.

Smileys, Emojis, and Emoticons

In the face-to-face environment, people use nonverbal cues such as postures, facial expressions, or gesticulations to express feelings or react to situations. In the online environment, smileys and emoticons can produce the same effect. There are different signs, symbols, and objects to communicate from static pictures to animations. Although a little humor in the virtual classroom can compensate for the loss of face-to-face interactions, the use of smileys and emoticons are not standard practice in the discussion forum, but informal conversations outside the discussion forum. Sometimes, instructors will use smileys and emoticons to motivate, empathize, or sympathize with students in the virtual classroom.

Flames

Flames are a disruptive behavior perpetrated when a student or a group of students send offensive messages to their classmates. A war of words can ensue if students apply passion instead of reasoning to discussing divisive and sensitive issues. In the virtual classroom, an unsavory comment can

go viral and become problematic because multiple students can read and share it within seconds.

Instructors must address disruptive behavior as soon as they see it because it can easily split a class. Likewise, students should report disruptive behaviors because of the potential spillover effects on them. Some schools consider offensive remarks bullying with possibilities for disciplinary action, and victims could take legal action against a perpetrator. Schools must establish procedures in dealing with disruptive behavior in the virtual classroom and make them known to students.

Acronyms

Acronyms are formed from the initial letters of compound terms instead of spelling out the entire words. There are abbreviations generally used in informal conversations that are not permissible in the discussion forum. The acronym "lol" usually stands for "laughing out loud." A student who is not familiar with the abbreviation could misinterpret it to mean "lots of love." Students should write out their words and avoid acronyms that can cause a problem.

Acronyms such as **CEO** (Chief Executive Officer), **IT** (information technology), **UN** (United Nations), **OPEC** (Organization of the Petroleum Exporting Countries), **EU** (European Union), **AU** (African Union), and **USA** (United States of America) represent positions, organizations, and countries and universally recognized in academic writings that won't create controversy when used by students.

Shorthand Words

Shorthand words are abbreviated versions of commonly used words and phrases. There are shorthand words used in text messaging or when communicating with friends such as "D tech dept is resp 4 d problem" (the technical department is responsible for the problem), or "see u be4 I go to schl dis wk" (I'll see you before I go to school this week). These shorthand sentences are not allowed in the discussion forum because they are not scholarly writings. If a phrase says, "his prof is interesting." Does that mean his professor or his profession is interesting? Confusion will arise when words are condensed and not completely spelled out.

Summary of Main Points

- Early course registration, ordering course materials on time, meeting the technology requirements are essential at the beginning of an online course.
- Effectively communicating with the instructor is essential because it determines how quickly you will receive feedback.
- Respecting classmates and their opinions make discussions flow smoothly in the virtual classroom.
- Using the right font size and posting directly into the digital box makes postings readable.
- Using scholarly language is essential when posting to the discussion forum to avoid confusion.
- Avoid yelling, red colors, smileys and emoticons, and unfamiliar acronyms and abbreviations in the virtual classroom.

Discussion Questions

1. Discuss the best practices in the virtual classroom and how they could enhance success in the virtual classroom.
2. What type of planning and preparations do students need before taking an online course? In what ways could the planning and preparations help them succeed in class?
3. Identify and discuss the types of support that students need in a virtual classroom.

4. Why is active participation essential in the discussion forum, and what roles should students, instructors, and school play in ensuring active participation in the virtual classroom?

5. Discuss the communication taboos in the virtual environment, and why is it essential to avoid them?

12

THE FUTURE OF HIGHER EDUCATION

Learning Objectives: After studying this chapter, you should be able to:

1. Understand how technology will impact higher education in the future
2. Discuss the role of artificial intelligence and virtual reality in education
3. Explain globalization and internationalization of higher education
4. Understand partnerships and collaborations in higher education
5. Discuss the role of transnational education (TNE) in the future of higher education

INTRODUCTION

The traditional education is changing, and nowhere is the transformation palpable than in higher education. As the work environment changes, students are not only looking for flexibility and convenience but learning that will equip them for the 21st-century economy.

The development of new technologies, artificial intelligence, globalization, internationalization, collaborations, and transnationalism is forcing education institutions to recalibrate their academic programs and educational strategies. Some of the phenomena discussed in this chapter have been manifesting for some time, but others will take several years before coming into a full circle.

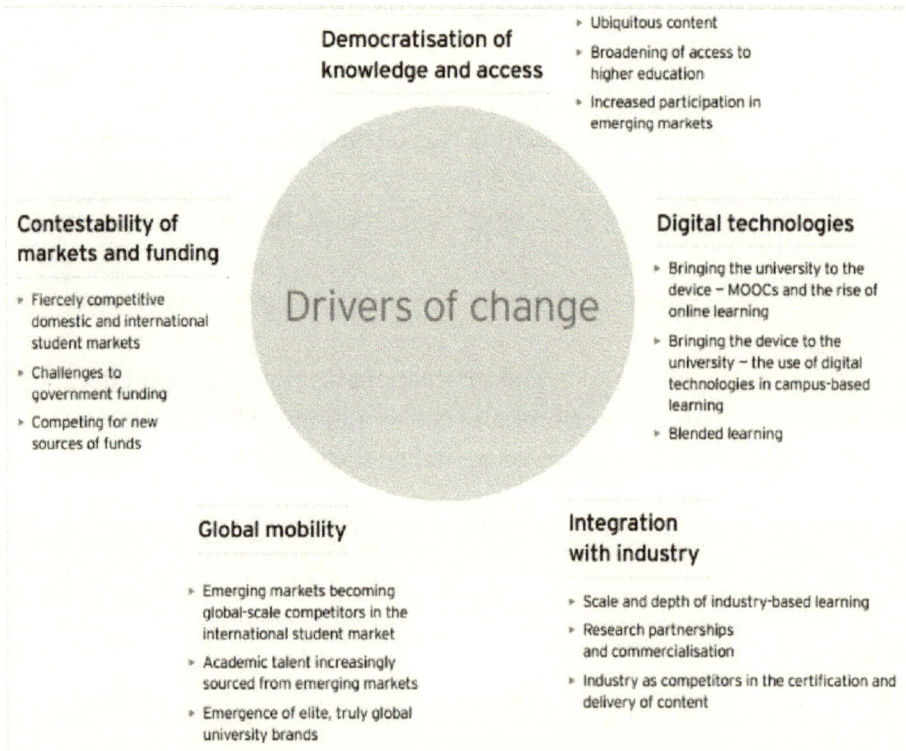

Democratisation of knowledge and access
- Ubiquitous content
- Broadening of access to higher education
- Increased participation in emerging markets

Contestability of markets and funding
- Fiercely competitive domestic and international student markets
- Challenges to government funding
- Competing for new sources of funds

Drivers of change

Digital technologies
- Bringing the university to the device – MOOCs and the rise of online learning
- Bringing the device to the university – the use of digital technologies in campus-based learning
- Blended learning

Global mobility
- Emerging markets becoming global-scale competitors in the international student market
- Academic talent increasingly sourced from emerging markets
- Emergence of elite, truly global university brands

Integration with industry
- Scale and depth of industry-based learning
- Research partnerships and commercialisation
- Industry as competitors in the certification and delivery of content

Figure: 12.1   The Future of Higher Education

Source: Ernst & Young, Australia, 2012, p. 6.

Information and Communication Technologies

The availability of broadband internet, digital videos, and increased owner-ship of personal computers and tablets have made online education more accessible than ever. In the future, technology will improve, and interactive media will offer better, new, and exciting features.[1] As telecommunications advance and transmission rates increase, emerging software programs will impact online education significantly.[2]

International Telecommunication Union (ITU), the United Nations specialized agency for information and communication technologies, fore-casted that by the end of 2018, 51.2% of the global population, or 3.9 billion people worldwide, would be using the Internet. Broadband access continues to grow while fixed-broadband subscriptions continue to increase. In 2017, there were more fixed-broadband connections than fixed-telephone con-nections, and in 2018 the number reached 1.1 billion compared with 942 million in 2017. The increase in active mobile-broadband subscriptions has risen faster, with penetration rates increasing from 4.0 subscriptions per 100 inhabitants in 2007 to 69.3 in 2018. Also, the number of active mobile-broadband subscriptions surged from 268 million in 2007 to 5.3 billion in 2018. The developing countries are seeing faster growth in mobile broad-band subscriptions, where penetration rates reached 61 per 100 inhabitants in 2018 with evidence of stronger growth in the future.[3]

As computers and wire-less networks become cheaper, and ownership grows across the globe, online education deliv-ery will be weaned from desktop computers and transmigrated to smartphones, tablets, and other handheld devices.[4] **International Data Corporation** (IDC) pre-dicted that the number of **per-sonal computers** (PCs) would fall from 28.7% in 2013 to 13% in 2017 while the tablets market would increase from 11.8% in

2013 to 16.5% by 2017, and the smartphone market increased from 59.5% to 70.5%.[5]

The five-year forecast (2019–2023) shows that smartphone shipments worldwide will reach 1.49 billion units in 2023, resulting in a **Compound Annual Growth Rate** (CAGR) of 1.2% from 1.38 billion units shipped in 2019. The shipments of 5G mobile devices will increase significantly from 2020 and beyond. China will lead other countries in 5G shipments, but the United States, Korea, Canada, and the United Kingdom will contribute to the volume increase, and the availability of more affordable 5G handsets with cheaper services will drive the market.[6]

Mobile devices, including tablets and cell phones, have transformed learning because of their capabilities in receiving educational materials on-demand. The newly developed wireless mobile devices have digital functionalities that house thousands of electronic books and journals at any given time. In January 2010, Apple unveiled the **iPad**, a wireless device that the company described as revolutionary in how people would experience the web, e-mail, photos, and video going forward.[7] Since the launch, the company has released newer versions, and other wireless tablets, such as the **Samsung Galaxy**, **Motorola Xoom**, **Blackberry Playbook**, **Google Nexus**, and **Microsoft Surface** have been introduced into the market by other companies.

In September 2011, Amazon added the **Kindle Fire** to the family of its Kindle digital e-readers, with additional capability for videos, movies, music, and other functionalities. In the future, mobile devices will become widely available that no longer will be fashionable for students to own them but required in the classroom for learning. **NPD Group**, a global provider of market research data to **Fortune 500** companies, reported that companies in 2011 shipped 72.7 million units of tablets. The company forecasted that by 2017, the number would grow to as many as 383.3 million units.[8] As the **IDC** report shows, by 2019, the number of smartphones shipped worldwide was 1.38 billion units.

In Auburn, Maine, in the United States, the school board recently distributed the **iPad** to kindergarten students in place of crayons for finger painting. Although critics questioned the **return on investment** (ROI) of the initiative, especially at the kindergarten level, supporters defended the program because the equipment hold hundreds of teaching applications and have the imagery and sound capabilities that can bring learning to life.[9]

In 2002, Maine was the first state in the United States to distribute Apple laptops to seventh and eighth-graders, and because of its success, the state expanded the program to cover high school students.[10] Dozens of other school districts in the United States, such as Omaha, Nebraska; Columbiana, Ohio; Huntington, West Virginia; Paducah, Kentucky; Charleston, South Carolina; and Scottsdale, Arizona, have initiated a similar program by providing wireless tablets to students, including kindergarten pupils.[11]

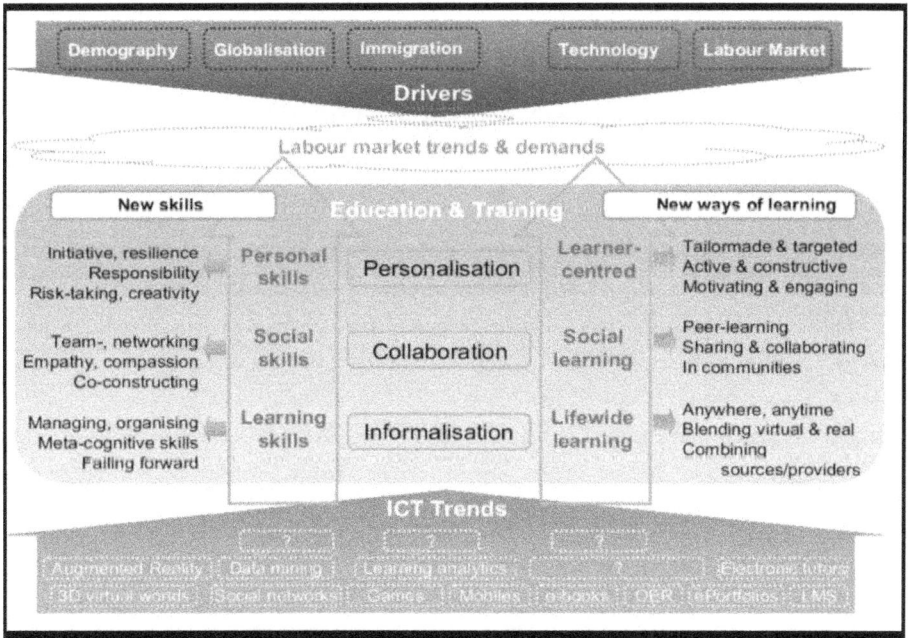

Figure: 12.2   Conceptual Map of the Future of Learning

Source: Redecker et al. (2011, p. 9).

Most school districts provide mobile devices for students not only because of their versatilities and multi-dimensional functionalities but save governments money in procuring textbooks. As a prelude to how computers and wireless devices will transform learning, most school districts in the United States have launched a **Bring Your Own Device** (BYOD) program that allows K-12 students to bring their laptops, tablets, and smartphones to school. A recent study from the **Pew Research Center** shows that 91% of students between ages 16 and 17 in the U.S have cell phones, of which 68% of the devices are smartphones.[12]

Artificial Intelligence

Artificial intelligence is the "science and engineering of making intelligent machines," especially computers that can think like humans.[13] Over the past few years, there has been an emergence of powerful computers that can analyze big data and forecast events with greater accuracy. The prediction by experts that **AI** would abet long-anticipated changes in formal and informal education systems is upon us and manifesting. In 2018, 979 experts including technology pioneers, innovators, developers, business and policy leaders, researchers and activists agreed that artificial intelligence increased human effectiveness on complex decision-making, reasoning and learning, sophisticated analytics and pattern recognition, visual acuity, speech recognition, and language translation in ways that match or exceed human intelligence.[14]

In education, artificial intelligence enhances the performance of teachers in the classroom and present information with greater efficiency and consistency. The **IBM Watson Tutor** (intelligent tutoring system) uses natural language conversation and guides students through a review session to perform at the top of their abilities.[15] Several universities now have powerful computers that can absorb seemingly infinite information that students use to search for information on various topics in the context that computers can understand. In the coming years, **AI** will enrich learning and deliver data in ways that humans cannot replicate.[16]

Virtual Reality and Augmented Reality

In higher education, **virtual reality** (VR) and **augmented reality** (AR) is creating new opportunities and solutions for teaching and learning. Immersive technologies and displays help students to learn concepts in multiple reference frames. For example, **VR** and **AR** can show the relationships between different locations on the planet, or the changes in a city over time.[17]

At Hamilton College, students use **virtual reality** and **simulations** to study the human body and organs.[18] Students and researchers at Villanova University in Pennsylvania can take virtual trips to the Grand Canyon in Arizona or St. Peter's Basilica in Vatican City, Rome, using Cave Automatic Virtual Environment (CAVE). The 18-ft wide by 10-ft deep by 7.5-ft high **CAVE** consists of a room with **three-dimensional** (3D) image projection walls that displays images on the floor or a retractable ceiling, and stereo audio played to create the full experience of being in a physical location.[19]

Higher-technology devices are coming to the market that will transform education, and vendors are already deploying robots that teach foreign languages or automata that can help special needs students in the classroom. Lifelike and life-sized robots can respond to students' facial expressions, and with built-in interactive tablets, they can communicate with students. Science and engineering students can practice coding and programming with robots, and students can attend classes or meet virtually by "seeing" what's happening through a tablet's forward-facing camera and participating in online discussions. Rock Valley College was the first education institution in Illinois, the U.S., to use the technology in the classroom. Technology develops students into independent, creative thinkers, instructors, administrators, curriculum designers and **information technology** (IT) personnel must be aware of technology's promise and take practical steps to embrace it. Communities and education leaders must collaborate in initiating educational projects and technology-based instructions that benefit everyone.[20]

Observers predicted that by the middle of this century, most post-secondary education would take place online, while others argue that with the rising profile of online learning, intellectual capital may have already abandoned the traditional schools. Those who would not go that far have acknowledged that the days of face-to-face learning is coming to an end because the teaching method is no longer adequate in meeting the needs of today's students, especially the generation who grew up with computers.[21]

Globalization and Internationalization of Education

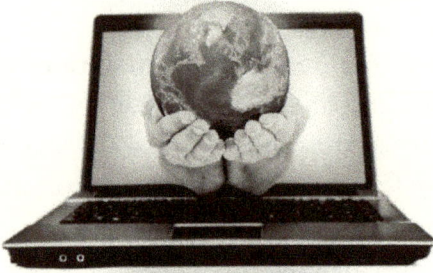

In higher education, although **globalization** and **internationalization** have symbiotic relationships, both concepts refer to different phenomena and seek to achieve different objectives. **Globalization** is "the broad economic, technological, and scientific trends that directly impact higher education and are largely inevitable in the contemporary world."[22] Globalization has changed how higher education institutions market their academic programs.[23] In 2006, over 2.5 million students studied abroad, and the number estimated to grow to 8 million by 2020. Globalization focuses on the movement of students across geographic boundaries. Students that will travel abroad for at least some portion of their education will increase by over 50% over the next decade.[24]

In the past few years, the increased youth populations in China, India, and other Asian nations have been driving international student mobility as students from the region travel abroad for education or to seek a better future. Although the number of institutions and countries competing for students in Asia has increased dramatically, the continent will remain a leading source of international students for many years. Africa is another region that will become a magnet for the next wave of student mobility. The number of students in sub-Saharan Africa that left their countries to study abroad increased from 296,395 in 2012 to 374,425 in 2017, a 26% increase. As the number of college-aged populations in Africa rises in the face of the decline in admission opportunity the number of students that will seek higher education outside the continent will grow bigger.[25]

Internationalization focuses on the "specific policies and programs undertaken by governments, academic systems and institutions, and individual departments to deal with globalization."[26] Internationalization reflects how universities tailor their core activities, especially teaching and research to meet the demands of the global society.[27]

The United States was the world's leading host country for international students in 2015. The number of international students enrolled in U.S higher institutions grew by 10% in the 2014/2015 academic year, which marked the ninth consecutive enrolment growth and the highest jump in 35 years. **National Association of Foreign Student Advisers** (NAFSA) reported that 974,926 international students enrolled in U.S universities in 2014/15 with the economic impact of the sector estimated at US$30.5 billion supporting 373,381 American jobs. In 2012/13, the United Kingdom experienced its first decline in international student enrolment in nearly three decades but recovered in 2013/14 with a 3% increase in non-European Union enrolment. The **Institute of International Education** (IIE) estimated that the total number of international students in the UK (including those from the European Union and elsewhere) in 2014 was 493,570. The **Higher Education Statistics Agency** (HESA) reported that the United Kingdom higher education had 310,195 in non-EU students with economic impact at more than £7 billion per year (US$10.4 billion).[28]

Educational institutions pursue internationalization for different reasons. **New York University** (NYU) has one of the most aggressive internationalization programs of any university in the world, with campus locations sprawling across six continents in major cities like Accra, Buenos Aires, London, and Prague, with approximately 60% of the institution's students in the United States spending a semester abroad.[29]

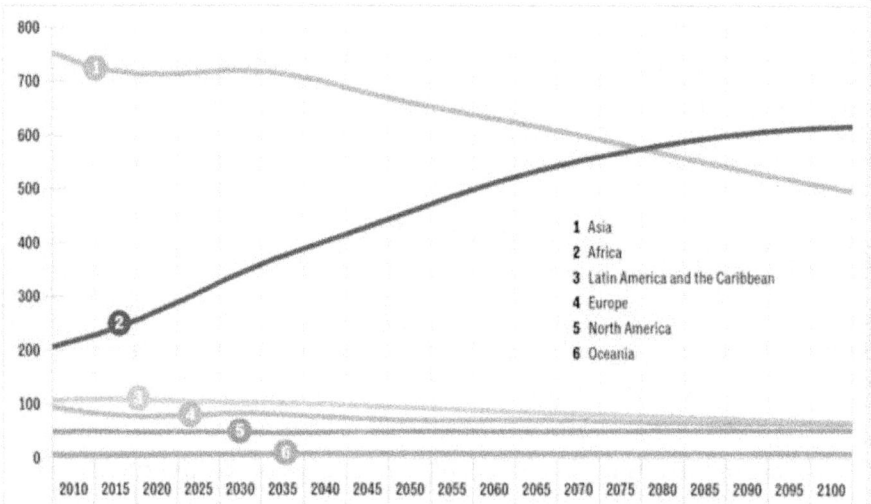

Figure 12:2   Global actual and projected populations (in millions) of 15–24-year-olds by region, 2010–2100

Source: United Nations 2019 World Population Prospects

By 2020, demographic and economic drivers, bilateral trade patterns, growing global competition, the rapid expansion of tertiary education capacity, and changes in inbound and outbound student flows will impact higher education. Demographically, four countries– India, China, U.S., and Indonesia will account for over half of the world's 18–22 population by 2020. A quarter of the number will come from Pakistan, Nigeria, Brazil, Bangladesh, Ethiopia, the Philippines, Mexico, Egypt, and Vietnam.[30] China's 18–22 population is forecast to remain large at over 90 million in 2020. The number will fall by over 20 million over the next decade, based on the number of 8–12-year-olds in the country. Russia's 18–22 population will drop, but in Nigeria, India, Ethiopia, Philippines, and Pakistan, the 18–22 demography will grow by 3.9 million, 2.9 million, 1.9 million, 1.2 million, and 0.9 million respectively over the next decade. Overall, the global 18–22 age group population outlook will expand rapidly marking a significant change from recent decades.[31]

In the past, education institutions primarily focused on recruiting students from the catchment areas they traditionally serve. Globalization and

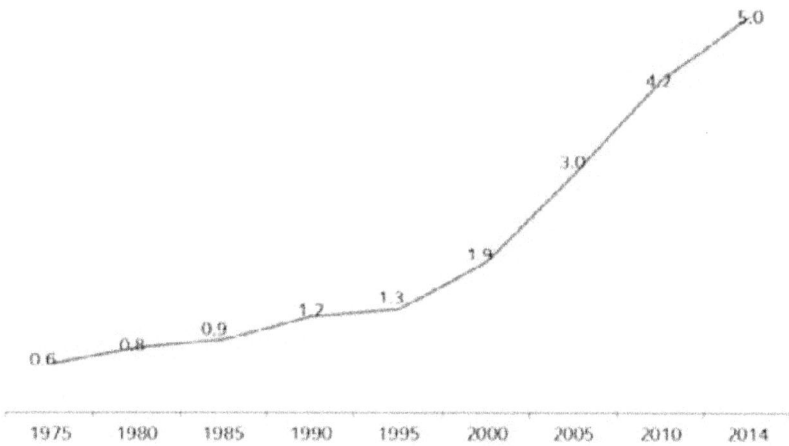

Figure: 12.3 Higher Education Students Enrolled Outside their Home Country (millions)

Source: University of Oxford (2017)

technology have changed the long-standing tradition and recruitment strategy because over one-half, or 58.2% of the academic leaders reported that students outside their normal service area were a primary target in their online course design, while 23.7% listed international students as a specific target for their online programs.[32]

In the United States, all 50 states report some out-of-state enrollment exclusively in distance education courses. Out of the 2,129 degree-granting institutions surveyed, 45% enrolled students outside the United States solely in distance education programs. The leading states are California with 125 institutions, New York with 57 and Texas with 54 institutions. Some of the institutions that admitted students from abroad enrolled and served almost as many students from other countries as students within the United States. In North Dakota, fourteen institutions served out of state students (students living in the United States from other states), while ten institutions served students from other countries. Higher education institutions in Arizona had about one-third of the total student population in the state from other countries.[33]

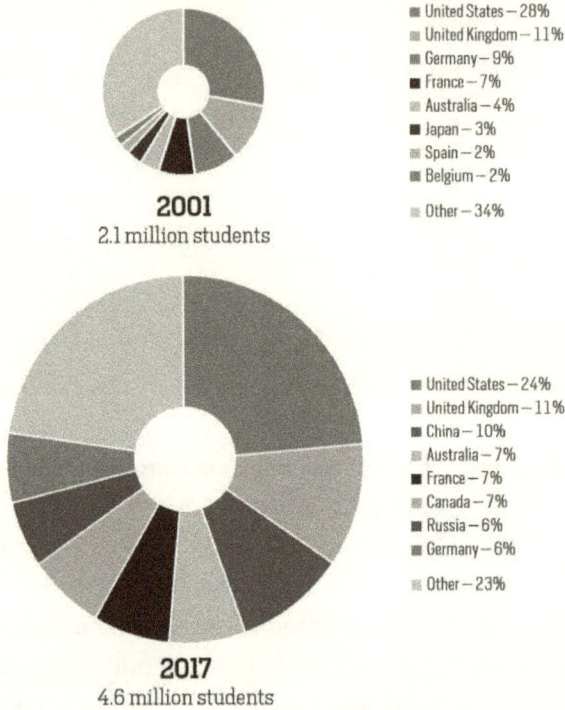

United States — 28%
United Kingdom — 11%
Germany — 9%
France — 7%
Australia — 4%
Japan — 3%
Spain — 2%
Belgium — 2%
Other — 34%

2001
2.1 million students

United States — 24%
United Kingdom — 11%
China — 10%
Australia — 7%
France — 7%
Canada — 7%
Russia — 6%
Germany — 6%
Other — 23%

2017
4.6 million students

Figure: 12.4   Top Host Destinations, 2001 & 2017
Source: Project Atlas, 2017; UNESCO, 2017

As globalization intensifies and web technologies improve, more students from Africa, South and Central America, and other countries will attend schools in the United States, the United Kingdom, Australia, and other advanced countries from the comfort of their homes. In the United Kingdom, education exports in 2008–09 were estimated to be £14.1 billion (and are forecast to rise to almost £27 billion by 2025). The 2008–09 figures equaled 1.0% of the GDP and 8.4% of total service exports.[34]

Africa is witnessing the sharpest increases in mobile data use in the world. Forecasts suggest that mobile internet traffic across Africa would double between 2014 and 2015 and increased by 20% by the end of the decade. Services based on 3G networks would expand within three years, replacing older and more limited 2G technology. By 2020, about three-quarters of all mobile connections will be on 3G or 4G, and operators will use the available spectrum to expand **Long-Term Evolution** (LTE) networks beyond the urban cities.[35]

Depending on the relative strength and standing of specific higher education institutions and systems, **globalization** and **internationalization** make it possible for wealthier nations and institutions to attract and retain human capital desperately needed elsewhere, causing "brain drain" and imbalance in the global population.[36] In 2004, 80% of the students from China and India who went abroad to study did not return home immediately after completing their education, while 30% of highly educated Ghanaians and Sierra Leoneans lived abroad. The side effect of internationalization is the "loss of cultural identity" and the rise of "elitism" in the developing and middle-income countries, especially in Latin America, the Caribbean, and the Middle East where people have more cultural affinities and sensitive to cultural issues.[37]

Educational Partnerships and International Alliances

Partnerships and collaborations have become standard practice as educational institutions collaborate in program developments and implement student exchange programs to promote cultural understandings and expose students to the global environment. Colleges and employers see career readiness programs as a shared responsibility, enabling corporate-academic partnerships to help students achieve their academic and career goals. Companies provide "free" tuition or a discount for specific programs or specialty and team up with schools in designing curriculum to meet their needs. A full-and part-time employee at **Starbucks** can obtain a bachelor's degree at Arizona State University (ASU) online through the **Starbucks College Achievement Plan. Walmart** offers partial tuition grants to eligible employees and their families to pursue associate, undergraduate, and graduate programs at American Public University System. **Southern New Hampshire University** (SNHU) offers associate and bachelor to **Anthem Inc**'s employees in its **SNHU**'s competency-based College for America program. Also, what began as a corporate training partnership between **Chrysler** and **Strayer University** has transitioned to academic degrees where dealership staff members pursue online and on-site programs at Strayer as an employer benefit, covering their tuitions and textbooks.[38]

Walden University partnered with six hospitals and health systems across the United States—Adventist Healthcare, Atlanta Medical Center, Greater Hudson Valley Health System, Lancaster General Health, Methodist Hospital of Southern California, and Valley Regional Medical Center. Employees from these organizations can pursue bachelor's, master's, or online doctoral degrees in nursing, focusing on emerging issues in healthcare.[39] Cardean University offers an online MBA program developed by professors from the University of Chicago, Columbia Business School, Carnegie Mellon University, Stanford University, and the London School of Economics.[40] Laureate International Universities Network have over sixty accredited campus-based and online universities with over 675, 000 students in twenty-nine countries throughout North America, Latin America, Europe, Northern Africa, Asia, and the Middle East.[41]

Online education is rapidly translating into new alliances between traditional education institutions, businesses, governments, and international organizations. Educational partnerships and collaborations are no longer **business-to-business** (B2B) but **business-to-government** (B2G) and **government-to-government** (G2G) both at national and international levels. The eighteen western states in the United States, which comprises the states of Alaska, Arizona, Colorado, Hawaii, Idaho, Indiana, Montana, Nebraska, Nevada, New Mexico, North Dakota, Oklahoma, Oregon, South Dakota, Texas, Utah, Washington, Wyoming, along with the territory of Guam formed the **Western Governors University** (WGU) and supported by over twenty leading U.S. corporations and foundations offers various degree programs to students within and outside the United States.[42]

Education institutions are also collaborating in sharing educational best practices. The **University Innovation Alliance** (UIA), with 11 member universities work together to identify innovative programs that can improve student success. The alliance plans to implement academic programs across member campuses that will impact the learning outcomes of over 68,000 students by 2025. Three-member schools—Georgia State University, Arizona State University, and the University of Texas at Austin developed predictive analytics for better decision-making and academic planning. Other **UIA** members will use the lessons learned in developing similar initiatives at their respective institutions.[43]

Partnerships between colleges and high schools are becoming common in easing the transition of high school students to higher institutions. A survey by **YouthTruth** showed that 87% of high school students wanted to go to college, but only 45% felt prepared to succeed there. Besides being academically unprepared, most high school students enter college with little knowledge of courses to take, the available financial aid options, or the professional careers they want to pursue after graduation. Also, most incoming students lack the emotional stamina that college life demands. On average, three out of four students who entered **City University of New York** (CUNY) in 2010 needed developmental or remedial education in at least one subject. **CUNY** initiated the **At Home in College** (AHC) program for New York City public high school students on track to graduate but had not met traditional benchmarks of college readiness, such as adequate **Scholastic Assessment Test** (SAT) scores. Students that participated in the **AHC** program scored 10 to 20% points higher on the **CUNY** placement exam than students who did not enroll in the program. Students enrolled full-time in associate degree programs with **AHC** advisement had a 16% higher retention rate than those in associate degree programs who did not participate in the **AHC** program. In Montana, the University of Montana works with high schools across the state to help students better prepare for college-level math coursework because 71% of students in the Montana State University system do not make it through college math classes within two years. The **EdReady Montana**, introduced by Montana State University system, provides a free online, personalized math curriculum for students from middle school through college. The initiative assesses a student's current math skills and provides a tailored learning path to help them achieve their educational goals. **EdReady** is now available in more than 290 schools across Montana, and the result from a 2014 survey showed that students who used **EdReady** before their college math classes, earned .25 to .75 higher average **Grade Point Average** (GPA) in their first semester of college than students who did not participate in the program.[44]

Another emerging trend is the **Early College High Schools** (ECHS) program that enables students to earn college credits while in high school. In Texas, high school students, starting from the 9th grade in small public schools can take college courses at the University of Texas at El Paso

(UTEP) and El Paso Community College (EPCC). The **Early College High Schools** program emphasizes that if you engage underrepresented students in a rigorous curriculum, with strong academic and social support, tied to the incentive of earning college credit, they are more likely to pursue higher education. In El Paso, students earn associate degrees while also completing high school; they then move on to **UTEP** as college juniors. The study conducted by **American Institutes for Research** (AIR) showed that students who attended early college high school were significantly more likely to enroll in college; 25% of them went on to graduate, compared to just 5% of students who did not participate in early college high schools' program.[45]

At the regional level, countries join efforts in promoting educational achievements among member nations. The **European Union** (EU) members are collaborating in achieving integrated distance learning policy and infrastructure, including working out the issues in cross-national credentialing through numerous cross-national commissions and summits on distance learning topics. The **Instituto Latinoamericano de la Comunicacion Educativa** (ILCE) comprises 13 countries that collaborate in offering distance learning programs throughout Latin America.[46] The **African Virtual University** (AVU) initially launched in Washington, DC, in 1997 as a **World Bank** project now headquartered in Kenya as an independent intergovernmental organization work to promote distance education across Africa. Over the past several years, the University has acquired the largest network of open, distance, and e-learning institutions in Africa, working across borders and language groups in Anglophone, Francophone, and Lusophone African countries. **AVU** has a presence in over 27 countries with over 50 institutions as partners.[47] In March 2017, **AVU** launched a Certificate Program in Teacher Education delivered simultaneously in English, French and Portuguese with 11 Partner Institutions across Africa.[48]

Organizations are also coordinating quality assurance activities based on shared interests and geographical proximity with support from the **World Bank**. The **Asia-Pacific Quality Network** (APQN) was established in 2003 to provide training and support quality assurance efforts in Asia. **Red Iberoamericana Acreditación Calidad Educación Superior** (RIACES) translated to mean the Iberoamerican Network for Quality Assessment and Assurance in Higher Education, was established in 2004 as a forum for cooperation in Latin America and the Caribbean countries. The **Arab Network for Quality Assurance in Higher Education** (ANQAHE) was established in 2007 to provide quality oversight for higher education programs. The **International Network for Quality Assurance Agencies in Higher Education** (INQAAHE), formed in 1991, has the broadest reach and promotes quality assurance activities on the global level. **INQAAHE** has members from regional, state, and professional quality assurance agencies that liaise between international organizations such as the **World Bank, UNESCO**, and **OECD** and their members. The organization supports new quality assurance agencies, offering forums where members can share experiences and information, and encouraging cooperation among members.[49]

The collaborations among educational institutions at national and international levels reflect the expanding and the changing dynamics in the relationships between the education community and the business world in areas of resource collaboration and the pursuit of common goals of providing quality education across the globe.[50]

Transnational Education (TNE)

Transnational education (TNE) is the practice where educational institutions establish campuses in other countries or where the learners are not from the homeland of the institution awarding the degree.[51] Globalization has intensified competition as higher education institutions pursue global strategies by opening branch campuses outside their countries.[52]

The UK universities have a broad and diverse range of **TNE** partners, including private companies, private for-profit education companies, public universities (autonomous and under state control), and

Physical presence
8%

Distance/online
learning
52%

Local delivery
partnership
40%

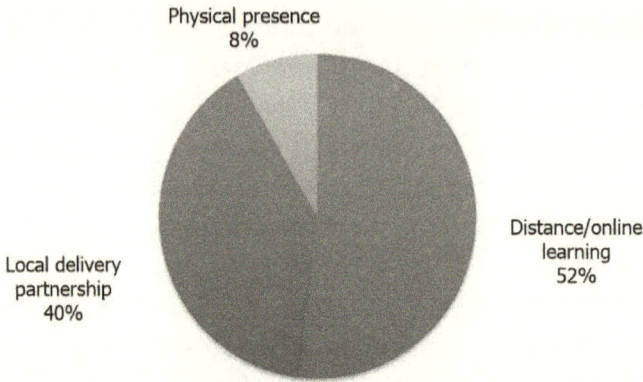

Figure: 12.5   TNE Delivery Method in the Top Five Countries of Delivery

Source: UK HE International Unit (2016)

government ministries. The London Metropolitan University joined with public Nanyang Polytechnic and public health care provider Singapore General Hospital. The University of Nottingham has campuses in Ningbo, China, and Semenyih, Malaysia. In 2009, Manchester Business School and Middlesex University, as well as Lancaster and Strathclyde universities, agreed to establish campuses in Pakistan. Aberystwyth University opened a campus in Mauritius in 2014. The University of Liverpool and Xi'an Jiaotong University in China formed Xi'an Jiaotong-Liverpool University (XJTLU), based in Suzhou, Jiangsu, China. Although the UK's existing and currently planned branch campuses are concentrated quite heavily in the **United Arab Emirates** (UAE), China, Malaysia, and Singapore, UK universities have schools in other countries. For example, Westminster University has a campus in Uzbekistan.[53]

As figure 12.5 shows, in recent years, **TNE** providers have depended on online learning to support their internationalization strategy rather than establishing schools or partnering with local universities. Additional entry methods such as franchise, validation, joint, multiple, dual or double, and concurrent degree programs are also popular. Nigeria and the United States are among the top five host countries with the most **TNE** students using distance education to earn a UK higher education degree.[54]

TNE is a win-win for students, tertiary institutions, and host countries if structured properly and policy frameworks developed to support outbound domestic students and inbound overseas students. In China, the government often mandates foreign institutions to partner with local providers, a policy geared towards protecting and improving the quality standards of the domestic education market. Australia has one of the most ambitious overseas presences of any country relative to the size of its local tertiary institutions. About a quarter of all Australian universities have campuses outside Australia, and their top partners for joint and double degrees are China, Singapore, and Indonesia, its closest neighbors.[55] **TNE** enhances cultural understanding and promotes economic activities in countries with a strong higher education sector, research, and science base. The educational model can rebalance the global higher education market, allowing more students to study in their own countries, saving them money and reducing the 'brain drain' epidemic in the developing countries on the one hand, and provide the labor skill needed by government, local and international organizations in the host countries on the other hand.[56]

Globally, over 200 branch campuses of universities operating in other countries now exist, serving over 120,000 students, with 37 more set to open by 2013. The **UAE** is the most popular host country (with 37 campuses), and the U.S the most popular source (accounting for 78 universities worldwide). In 2010 and 2011, over 500,000 students studied entirely overseas for a degree delivered in full or in part by UK institutions. **TNE** is expected to grow, especially in East Asia mainly through online learning.[57]

Table: 12.1   Major Categories and Examples of Impacts on Host Country

Category of impact	Examples of potential benefits	Examples of potential risks
Academic	• increased access for local students to higher education • updated teaching and learning, curriculum development, and evaluation practices • exposure to new quality assurance and qualification recognition policies and practices • increased capacity in program management and implementation • diversification of academic programs offered to students • Professional development opportunities for local faculty.	• lower quality provision if quality assurance and accreditation systems are not in place • the curriculum not relevant to local context and culture • competition, not collaboration, between domestic and foreign providers "canned courses." • sustainability of academic programs if low enrolments • local HEIs responsible for providing programs which require significant investments in equipment, labs, facilities • international qualifications not recognized.
Economic	• revenue generation from increased enrolments in collaborative programs • decrease outflow of currency • less expensive for students to study at home than go abroad • income from potential commercialization of joint research projects • contribution to the country's shift to knowledge/service-based economy • Increase trading education services for economic free zones.	• higher delivery costs for collaborative programs delivery • sending countries have more significant potential for revenue than host countries if memorandums of understanding do not address the issue • branch campus development is not attracting foreign direct investment.
Human resource development	• better trained workforce • mitigate brain drain if domestic students stay in the country • Potential brain gains if a nation retains international students.	• education/training is not meeting labor market needs and skills gap • Potential brain drain to neighboring countries.
Social-cultural	• exposure to teaching/learning in a different language to facilitate job mobility • Contact with faculty and students from other countries and cultures.	• overuse of foreign languages as medium of instruction • tensions between different cultural and value norms in and outside of classrooms • Potential change/loss of cultural identity.
Status	Increased status through a link with highly ranked foreign HEI.	• Reputational risks if the quality is not assured.

Source: British Council (2012)

Summary of Main Points

- Technology that offers better, new, and exciting features, especially in interactive multimedia, will impact online education in the future.
- Artificial Intelligence will change the traditional role performed by teachers and present information with greater efficiency and accuracy beyond human comprehension.
- Globalization and internationalization enable education institutions to enter new markets and provide opportunities for students to seek education opportunities abroad.
- Higher education institutions collaborate in program developments and exchange programs to expose students to the global environment and promote intercultural understandings.
- Globalization enables educational institutions to establish campuses outside their countries and provides opportunities for students in the host countries to receive foreign degrees without leaving their countries.

Discussion Questions

1. Identify and discuss the significant events that will impact education in the future.
2. Identify and discuss the new technologies that will impact learning in the future.
3. In the education context, what do you understand by globalization and internationalization? How would these phenomena impact higher education?
4. How do partnerships and collaborations impact higher education? Provide specific examples to illustrate your point.
5. Describe transnational education. Discuss the advantages and disadvantages of the learning strategy to the home and the host countries.

CREDITS

Credits and acknowledgments for pictures, tables, and other resources used in this book appear on the appropriate pages within the text.

- Pictures licensed by Fotolia
- Diagrams and tables with permission from Babson Survey Research Group

GLOSSARY

Academic e-learning: An educational program delivered by schools to students online.

Accreditation: A seal of approval given to a university, college, or any higher institution after undergoing a review process and met the minimum criteria of academic quality in its educational programs.

Adaptive learning: The process of adapting course materials so students' needs so they can focus on the concepts they need to understand.

Asynchronous: Asynchronous learning takes place over the Internet and allows students and instructors to participate in class activities at different times of the week.

Audio Conferencing: A type of communication facilitated and delivered through telephone lines or delivered on the web.

Attachment: A data file, such as a document, photos, and other materials, that individuals send through an e-mail message.

Augmented Reality (AR): Technology that superimposes information and virtual objects on the real-world environment. The technology uses the existing environment and adds sounds, videos, graphics to produce a new artificial environment.

Artificial Intelligence (AI): The programming of computers to think like humans and mimic their actions.

Bandwidth: The amount of data transmitted at a given time and measured in bits-per-second. The more the data, the slower the speed it travels. Text can transfer more quickly than audio or video because it carries fewer bits.

Best Practices: A set of behaviors demonstrated in one environment that students could adapt in another situation.

Big Data: A structured and unstructured large data sets that may be analyzed to reveal patterns, trends, and associations relating to human behavior and interactions.

Blended Learning: The integration of traditional face-to-face learning with online education. An example is attending lectures online and taking examinations in a face-to-face environment.

Blog: An updatable website where individuals post commentaries on issues of interest. Users can change information posted on a blog.

Brick-and-Mortar: An organization, school, or business that operates from a physical location.

Broadband: A high speed direct serial line (DSL) or a cable for fast transmission of big data. Broadband usually operates at a speed of 200 Kbps or more.

Browser: The software used for searching and viewing information on the Internet either from a computer or other electronic devices. An example of a browser is Internet Explorer or Mozilla Firefox.

Bulletin Board: The electronic board used for posting information and engage in conversation online.

Chat: A process engaging in a live conversation using online communication tools.

Chat Room: An area in a virtual classroom where live communication takes place.

Cohort: A small group of students enrolled in the same program and moved through the program together.

College: An institution that offers an associate, bachelor, master, or doctoral degree. A college could be a division within a university system, such as a college of medicine, college of arts, or college of business.

Corporate Training: Training organized by an organization for employees either in-house or through a third-party vendor. Corporate training could be virtual or face-to-face.

Communication: A process for transferring messages from a sender to a receiver. Communication could be oral, written, or body language. The channels of communication include face-to-face meetings, e-mail, telephone, videos, chats, text messaging, or fax.

Correspondence Course: A course facilitated by the mailing of academic materials such as textbooks, lectures, and assignments to students.

Course Management System (CMS): A web application that enables course administrators or instructors to create online course content, manage a course, and facilitate discussions in the classroom.

Course Materials: Learning materials includes but not limited to textbooks, articles, journals, pictures, software programs either available electronically or in hard copies.

Course Management System Features: The functionalities that enable you to perform different learning activities in the virtual classroom.

Coursework: A series of assignments, quizzes, projects, and other activities required to complete a degree program.

Courseware: See *Course Management System (CMS)*

Closed-source LMSs: Proprietary LMS applications that manufacturers licensed to education institutions or they purchased from a vendor.

Corporate e-learning: The training that organizations offer to employees to gain a specific skill and acquire the knowledge to perform their functions effectively.

Compound Annual Growth Rate (CAGR): The rate of return on investment over a period, usually from the beginning balance to its ending balance, assuming the profits reinvested at the end of the investment period.

Computer Hosts: A computer connected to a client, server, or any other equipment with a unique identifier that allows different computers to request and receive information from the network.

Database: A searchable online data stored on a computer so that it can be easily accessed, managed, and updated.

Degree Program: An academic program leading to an associate, bachelor, master, or doctoral degree.

Degree Mill: Any unregistered institution or organization that awards degrees or diplomas online for a fee with little or no academic rigors before obtaining such degrees.

Digital Box: A rectangular box students use for postings in the virtual classroom.

Discussion Board: An area in the virtual classroom where instructors post weekly discussion questions and students respond to comment posed by their classmates.

Discussion Forum: (see *Discussion Board*)

Distance Education: Learning or training delivered primarily via the Internet at remote locations, including homes. Online courses could be offered synchronously (real-time) or asynchronously (delayed time). There is the hybrid or blended (technology with face-to-face) format, which requires students and teachers to meet once or periodically in a physical setting.

Distance Learning: See *Distance Education*

Discussion Questions: Questions posted to the discussion board by a professor or a course administrator. Typically, discussion questions focus on areas of lectures covered in class during a particular week.

Download: A file or information pulled from one device to another.

E-book: A digital version of hard copy text that you can read on a computer, wireless tablet, or e-book readers.

E-Learning: See *Online Education*

Face-to-Face Classroom: A classroom environment where students and instructors can see each other and interact live.

File: A collection of information stored on a computer or external storage device for use at a later date.

Firewall: A program that provides a defense for a computer from unauthorized users or filters information to and from a computer. Data can pass through the firewall if authorized by a system administrator.

Flash Drive: An external device used for storing data and information for later use.

Gamification: A series of design principles, processes, and systems used to influence, engage, and motivate individuals, groups, and communities to drive behaviors and produce desired outcomes.

Graphic user interface (GUI): The feature that allows you to work quickly with a computer by using a mouse to point to small pictures and icons, or other visual indicators, rather than using only text through the command line.

Grant: A type of funding and educational assistance provided by the government or an organization to students who demonstrate financial needs. Students may not be required to pay back the money.

Gross Domestic Product (GDP): The total monetary value of all final goods and services produced (and sold on the market) within a country during a period (typically one year). GDP provides an economic snapshot of a nation for estimating the size of an economy and growth rate.

Hands-on Learning: A learning that involves practical demonstration of knowledge rather than listening to lectures.

Hypertext Markup Language (HTML): A type of code or language that allows the creation of a website. The programming language also allows the creation of layers of web pages on a website.

Hybrid Learning Format: See *Blended Learning Format.*

Hyperlink: A graphic or text that links to another web page so individuals can access specific information.

Internet: A global system of interconnected computers that communicates with each other.

Intranet: A private network used by organizations in communicating and sharing information with employees internally.

Internet Service Provider (ISP): A company that provides Internet service to individuals and businesses.

Informal e-learning: The instruction offered by individuals and organizations to the public for free or for a fee online.

Internet Protocol (IP) Address: A numerical label assigned to each device connected to a computer network that uniquely identifies the device and distinguishes it from other computers on the Internet.

Intelligence Quotient (IQ): A number used to measure the level of intelligence based on a standardized test. The score measures a person's cognitive abilities ("intelligence") vis-a-vis their age group.

Java: A programming language and computing platform that runs on operating systems (OS) such as Windows, Linux, and Mac OS using English-based commands instead of writing in numeric codes.

LCMS (Learning Content Management System): See *Course Management System* (CMS)

Learning Management System (LSM): See Course Management System (CMS)

Local Area Network (LAN): A network of computers in the same proximity, usually within a home, school, or an organization.

Mobile learning: Learning that occurs through mobile devices, including laptops, tablets, smartphones, and other gadgets.

Machine Learning: The application of artificial intelligence (AI) to improve the learning experience. The program adapts data to learning without human interference.

MOOCs: Massive Open Online Courses or MOOCs is the learning delivered to hundreds and sometimes thousands of students either for free or for a fee with little or no interactions with a professor.

Multimedia: The integration of media components such as audio, video, text, animation, and graphics into a single presentation.

Network Protocols: The formal standards that govern data management and network communication between two or more devices over a network.

Network Control Program (NCP): The world's first operational packet-switching that allowed users to access and use computers and devices at remote locations and to transmit files between computers.

NGOs (Non-governmental Organizations): Organizations not controlled or affiliated with the government. But such an organization can source funds from the government, individuals, and corporate organizations.

On-demand: Any digital content available whenever the user wants it.

Offline: Not having the ability to access or connect to the Internet and other computer networks at a particular time.

Online Learning: See *Online Education.*

Online Training: Training conducted by organizations on the web, either in-house or through a third-party vendor.

Open-source LMSs: LMSs that education institutions can download online for free. Schools may need computer experts to configure the program before use.

Packet Switching: A digital network transmission technique in which data is broken into small units for fast and efficient transfer through different networks.

Per Capita Income (PCI): The amount of money earned per person in a nation or geographic region.

Personalized learning: The tailoring of pedagogy, curriculum, and learning environments to meet the needs and aspirations of individual learners.

PostgreSQL: A free and open-source relational database management system that allows you to customize different programming languages such as C/C++, and Java.

Private Institution: An institution controlled and funded by an individual or an organization other than the government.

Public Institution: An institution controlled and funded by the local, state, or federal government.

Purchasing Power Parity (PPP): An economic theory that compares different countries' currencies and measures the purchasing power of various world currencies to one another.

Residency: A residency enables a student to complete course activities at the campus and has face-to-face interactions with classmates, faculty, staff, and school administrators.

Shareable Content Object Reference Model (SCORM): A set of technical standards and specifications that allow e-learning content to work and communicate with other learning management systems.

Social learning: The learning facilitated and acquired on social and professional networking sites.

Scholarship: A merit or a need-based award that schools, organizations, or the government give to students for academic purposes. A scholarship could be a monetary award or free tuition.

Self-Hosting: A business model in which an institution manages the server used for its online program internally.

Server: A dedicated computer that controls and manages disk drives, printers, and other network utilities on behalf of other computers.

Simulation: A simplified, dynamic, and precise representation of reality defined as a system.

Social Networking: A practice where people connect on social medial and interact socially or professionally.

Syllabus: A document that provides an overview of what students need to accomplish in a course. A curriculum usually covers course objectives, reading chapters, assignments, course materials, grading policies, assignment due dates, examination dates, and other relevant information.

Synchronous Learning Format: A learning format where students and instructors interact and communicate live in the virtual classroom.

The World Bank: An international banking institution made up of members of the International Monetary Fund (IMF) specialized in granting and advancing loans to member countries for developmental purposes.

Threaded Discussion: A log of messages posted to the discussion board by students and instructors. A discussion becomes threaded when students post messages, and classmates respond to them.

University: A postsecondary institution that offers academic programs that lead to the award of bachelor's, master's, and doctoral degrees. In some cases, a university can offer professional degrees in conjunction with its academic programs.

Upload: A file or information transferred from one computer to another.

US Department of Education: The department in the United States responsible for executing the government's policies on education, such as managing financial aid and gathering data on the state of education in the country.

Wearable Devices: Electronic equipment that people wear or inserted on their bodies to track their health and fitness conditions.

Web-Based Training (WBT): E-learning training delivered by an organization to employees over the Internet or Intranet.

Virtual Reality (VR): A three-dimensional, computer-generated environment that a person can explore in a simulated environment.

Video conferencing: A visual, audio communication tool that people use to communicate on electronic devices on the Internet.

Virtual: The interactions that occur on the Internet without the benefit of participants seeing each other face-to-face.

Web Technologies: The software and hardware tools used for learning and training over the Internet.

Whiteboard: A digital blackboard or chalkboard that instructors use for teaching and exchange of information in the virtual classroom.

Wireless Tablet: A lightweight wireless portable device that has e-mail, video, music, and digital library functionality that you can carry with you anywhere.

World Wide Web (WWW): See *Internet*.

ACRONYMS

A

AAS: Associate in Applied Science

ACE: American Council on Education

ACCA: Association of Chartered Certified Accountants

ACCJC: Accrediting Commission for Community and Junior Colleges

ADL: Advanced Distributed Learning

AHC: At Home in College

AI: Artificial Intelligence

AIR: American Institutes for Research

ALNs: Asynchronous Learning Networks

ALAS: Adaptive Learning and Assessment System

ANQAHE: Arab Network for Quality Assurance in Higher Education

APLUS: Association of Public and Land-Grant Universities

APQN: Asia-Pacific Quality Network

AR: Augmented Reality

ARPA: Advanced Research Projects Agency

ARPANET: Advanced Research Projects Agency Network

ASEP: Automotive Service Educational Program

ASU: Arizona State University

AU: African Union
AVU: African Virtual University

B
BOA: Bank of America
BYOD: Bring Your Own Device
B2B: Business-to-Business
B2G: Business-to-Government

C
CAGR: Compound Annual Growth Rate
CAO: Chief Academic Officer
CAP: College Automotive Program
CAVE: Cave Automatic Virtual Environment
CHEA: Council for Higher Education Accreditation
CDE: Center for Digital Education
CMS: Course Management System
CMSs: Course Management Systems
CNS: Central Nervous System
CUI: Command-line User Interface
CUI: Character User Interface

D
DIY: Do-It-Yourself
DNS: Domain Name System
D2L: Desire2Learn
DOD: United States Department of Defense
DOJ: United States Department of Justice
DSL: Digital Subscriber Line

E
ECAR: EDUCAUSE Center for Applied Research
ECHS: Early College High Schools
EMFs: Electromagnetic Fields
ESA: Entertainment Software Association

F
FCC: Federal Communications Commission
FEDA: Foodservice Equipment Distributors Association
FUN: France Université Numérique

G
GDP: Gross Domestic Product
GMB: Glioblastoma Multiforme
GPA: Grade Point Average
GUI: Graphic User Interface
G2G: Government-to-Government

H
HVAC: Heating, Ventilation, and Air Conditioning
HESA: Higher Education Statistics Agency
HTML: Hypertext Markup Language

I
IAB: Internet Activities Board
ICT: Information and Communication Technologies
ICS: International Correspondence School
ICANN: Internet Corporation for Assigned Names and Numbers
IDC: International Data Corporation
IETF: Internet Engineering Task Force
IIE: Institute of International Education
IT: Information Technology
ILCE: Instituto Latinoamericano de la Comunicacion Educativa
IP: Internet Protocol
IMS: Information Management System
INQAAHE: International Network for Quality Assurance Agencies in Higher Education
IPEDS: Integrated Postsecondary Education Data System
IQs: Intelligence Quotients
ITU: International Telecommunication Union
ITS: Intelligent Tutoring System

K

K-12 (Kindergarten to 12 Grade)

L

LIME: Local Interpretable Model-Agnostic Explanations
LMS: Learning Management System
LMSs: Learning Management Systems
LTE: Long-Term Evolution

M

MIT: Massachusetts Institute of Technology
MOOCs: Massive Open Online Courses
Moodle: Modular Object-Oriented Dynamic Learning Environment
MS-DOS: Microsoft Disk Operating System
MPOE: Metropolitan and Provincial Offices of Education

N

NAFSA: National Association of Foreign Student Advisers
NCP: Network Control Program
NCES: National Center for Education Statistics
NCTE: National Centre for Technology in Education
NILE: National Institute of Lifelong Education
NCREL: The North Central Regional Education Laboratory
NYU: New York University
NUC: National Universities Commission

O

OECD: Organization for Economic Co-operation and Development
OPEC: Organization of the Petroleum Exporting Countries
OU: Open University

P

PCs: Personal Computers
PCI: Per Capita Income
PDAs: Personal Digital Assistants

PII: Personally Identifiable Information
PPP: Purchasing Power Parity

R
RAND: Research and Development
RIACES: Red Iberoamericana Acreditación Calidad Educación Superior
RF: Radiofrequency
ROI: Return on Investment

S
SAT: Scholastic Assessment Test
SAR: Specific Absorption Rate
SCORM: Sharable Content Object Reference Model
SNDMSG: Send Message
SNHU: Southern New Hampshire University
STEM: Science, Technology, Engineering, and Mathematics
SUNY: State University of New York

T
TNE: Transnational education

U
UAE: United Arab Emirates
USDLA: United States Distance Learning Association
USG: University System of Georgia
UCLA: University of California, Los Angeles
UC-Santa Barbara: University of California, Santa Barbara
UIA: University Innovation Alliance
UTEP: University of Texas at El Paso
UPS: United Parcel Service
UMTS: Universal Mobile Telecommunications Service
UN: United Nations
UNESCO: United Nations Educational, Scientific and Cultural Organization
USA: United States of America

V
VR: Virtual Reality

W
WASC: Western Association of Schools and Colleges
WBT: Web-Based Training
WGU: Western Governors University
WWW: World Wide Web
WYSIWYG: What You See Is What You Get

X
XJTLU: Xi'an Jiaotong-Liverpool University

REFERENCES

CHAPTER ONE

1. Doug Lederman (November 7, 2018). Online Education, Ascends. Retrieved 05/31/2019 from https://www.insidehighered.com/digital-learning/
2. John Haplin and Lorna Collier (2015). Effective Instructional Tools for an Evolving Learning Landscape. Center for Digital Education.
3. Docebo (2014). E-Learning Market Trends & Forecast 2014-2016. Retrieved 06/16/2019 from www.docebo.com
4. Docebo (2016). E-learning Market Trends and Forecast 2017-2021. Retrieved 06/16/2019 from www.docebo.com
5. Bhutani, A., and P. Bhardwaj, 2019. E-Learning Market Trends 2019-2025 Industry Size Research Report. Global Market Insights https://www.gminsights.com/industry-analysis/elearning-market-size
6. Pesante, L., 2008. Introduction to Information Security. Retrieved 01/16/2019 from https://www.uscert.gov
7. Congressional Digest (February 2007). Internet History from ARPANET to Broadband. Retrieved 01/07/2017 from http://congressionaldigest.com
8. Ibid.

9. Ibid.

10. History-computer.com (2019). The First E-mail Message of Ray Tomlinson. Retrieved 07/01/2019 from https://history-computer.com/Internet/Maturing/Tomlinson.html

11. Congressional Digest (February 2007). Internet History from ARPANET to Broadband. Retrieved 01/07/2017 from http://congressionaldigest.com

12. Ibid.

13. Ibid.

14. Dahir, A. L. 2018. Half the world is now connected to the internet-driven by a record number of Africans. Retrieved 01/23/2019 from https://qz.com/africa

15. Internet World Stats. Miniwatts Marketing Group (March 31, 2019). Retrieved 07/01/2019 from http://www.internetworldstats.com/stats.htm

16. The population of Countries in Asia 2019. Retrieved 05/26/2019 from http://worldpopulationreview.com/countries/countries-in-asia/

17. Internet World Stats. Miniwatts Marketing Group (June 31, 2019). Retrieved 8/09/2019 from https://www.internetworldstats.com/stats.htm

18. Dahir, A. L. 2018. Half the world is now connected to the internet-driven by a record number of Africans. Retrieved 01/23/2019 from https://qz.com/africa

19. Ibid.

20. Rij, V., and B. Warrington, 2011. Teaching and Learning for an ICT revolutionized society, EC – FAR Horizon project. Manchester: University of Manchester, 2011.

21. BBC News (26 May 2015). Internet used by 3.2 billion people in 2015. Retrieved 9/10/2018 from http://www.bbc.com/news/technology

22. Altbatch, P. H., L. Reisberg, and L. E Rumbley, 2009. Trends in Global Higher Education: Tracking an Academic Revolution UNESCO 2009 World Conference on Higher Education.

23. John Haplin and Lorna Collier (2015). Effective Instructional Tools for an Evolving Learning Landscape. Center for Digital Education.

24. Wise, B., 2010. The online learning imperative: A solution to three looming crises in education. Education Digest Prakken Publications. Retrieved 02/25/2017 from www.eddigest.com

25. Lederman, D., 2018. Online Education Ascends. Retrieved 05/31/2019 from https://www.insidehighered.com/digital-learning

CHAPTER TWO

1. B. Holmberg, *Theory, and Practice of Distance Education* (2nd ed.) (London: Routledge, 1995).

2. R.L. Weaver, "Josiah Holbrook: Feeding the Passion for Self-Help," *Communication Quarterly*, 24(4), 10-18.

3. Triggs, T. D, 2014. Pitman, Isaac (1813–1897). Oxford Dictionary of National Biography, Oxford University Press.

4. Watkins, B. L., 1991. "A Quite Radical Idea: The Invention and Elaboration of Collegiate Correspondence Study," in *The Foundations of American distance education: a century of collegiate correspondence study*, eds. B.L Watkins and S.J. Wright (Dubuque, IA: Kendall/Hunt, 1991), 1-36.

5. History Industrial Revolution. https://www.history.com/topics/industrial-revolution/industrial-revolution

6. http://www.londonexternal.ac.uk. Retrieved March 30, 2009.

7. http://www.uwex.edu/ics/design/disedu2.htm. Retrieved July 30, 2008.

8. Watkins, B. L., 1991. "A Quite Radical Idea: The Invention and Elaboration of Collegiate Correspondence Study," in *The Foundations of American distance education: a century of collegiate correspondence study*, eds. B.L Watkins and S.J. Wright (Dubuque, IA: Kendall/Hunt, 1991), 1-36.

9. Moore, M. G., and G. Kearsley, 1996. *Distance Education: A System View.* (Belmont, CA: Wadsworth Publishing, 1996).

10. Ibid.

11. Ibid.

CHAPTER THREE

1. HigherEducation.com and BestColleges.com (2016). 2016 Online Education Trends. Tracking the Innovations and Issues Changing Higher Education.
2. Holmberg, B. (1986). Growth and structure of distance education. Beckenham, UK: Croom Helm. (1986, p. 26)
3. Holden, J.T., and J. L. Westfall, 2009. An Instructional Media Selection Guide for Distance Learning. United States Distance Learning Association.
4. Sankaran, S. R., and T. Bui, 2001. Impact of learning strategies and motivation on performance: a study in Web-based instruction. *Journal of Instructional Psychology*, 28(3), p. 191-198.
5. NCES National Center for Education (2016) Retrieved 01/25/2017 from https://nces.ed.gov
6. C. Trierweiler and R. Rivera, 2005. "Is online Higher Education Right for Corporate Learning?" American Society of Training and Development, September 2005.
7. Guri-Rosenblit, S., 2009. Digital Technologies in Higher Education: Sweeping Expectations and Actual Effects. New York, Nova Science.
8. U.S. Department of Education (May 2009). Evaluation of Evidence-Based Practices in Online Learning A Meta-Analysis and Review of Online Learning Studies.
9. Saba, F., 2005. "Critical Issues in Distance Education: A Report from the United States Distance Education," Vol. 26, N2, August 2005, 255-272.
10. Poulin, R., and T. Straut. 2016. WCET Distance Education Enrollment Report 2016.
11. Allen, I.E., J. Seaman, and R. Garrett, 2007. "Blending In: The Extent and Promise of Blended Education in the United States," Sloan Consortium, 2007.
12. Digital Learning Collaborative. (2019). Snapshot 2019: A review of K-12 online, blended, and digital learning. Retrieved 08/14/2019 from https://www.digitallearningcollab.com.

13. Betts, K. 2017. The growth of online learning: How universities must adjust to the new norm. Retrieved 08/09/2018 from https://www.educationdive.com

14. Digital Learning Collaborative. (2019). Snapshot 2019: A review of K-12 online, blended, and digital learning. Retrieved from https://www.digitallearningcollab.com.

15. Saba, F., 2005. "Critical Issues in Distance Education: A Report from the United States Distance Education," Vol. 26, N2, August 2005, 255-272.

16. McDonald's Archways to Opportunity. Retrieved 09/13/2017 from http://www.archwaystoopportunity.com/

17. General Motors Program. Retrieved 06/16/2018 from https://www.gccaz.edu/academics/departments/automotive-technology/GM-program

18. Bank of America (2017). Retrieved 01/16/2019 from http://about.bankofamerica.com

19. Allen, I.E., and J.S. Seaman, 2005. "Growing by Degrees. Online Education in the United States, 2005," Sloan Consortium, November 2005.

20. Brown, S. A., and H. A. Lahoud, 2005. An Examination of Innovative Online Lab Technologies. Association for Computing Machinery, 2005.

21. Eaton, J. S., 2001. Distance Learning: Academic and Political Challenges for Higher Education Accreditation. Council for Higher Education Accreditation. 2001. No. 1.

22. Saba, F., 2005. "Critical Issues in Distance Education: A Report from the United States Distance Education," Vol. 26, N2, August 2005, 255-272.

23. Means, B., Toyama, Y., Murphy. R., Bakia, M., and Jones, K. 2009. Evaluation of Evidence-Based Practices in Online Learning: A Meta-Analysis and Review of Online Learning Studies. Washington, D.C.: U.S. Department of Education.

24. HigherEducation.com and BestColleges.com (2016). 2016 Online Education Trends. Tracking the Innovations and Issues Changing Higher Education.

25. Flores, J. G (2009). Distance Learning: Enabling the Race to the Top (USDLA)

26. Hirschheim, R., 2005. "The Internet-Based Education Bandwagon. Look Before You Leap," Communication of the ACM, Vol. 48, No. 7, July 2005.

27. www.elearners.com. Retrieved April 3, 2008.

28. Means, B. T. Yukie, R. Murphy, M. Bakia, and K. Jones, "Evaluation of Evidence-Based Practices in Online Learning: A Meta-Analysis and Review of Online Learning Studies," US Department of Education, Office of Planning, Evaluation, and Policy Development Policy and Program Studies Service, 2009.

29. Allen, I.E., and J. Seaman, 2001. "Going the Distance: Online Education in the United States, 2011," Sloan Consortium, 2011.

30. Allen, E., and J. Seaman, 2017. Online Report Card – Tracking Online Education in the United States. Online Learning Consortium.

31. HigherEducation.com and BestColleges.com (2016). 2016 Online Education Trends. Tracking the Innovations and Issues Changing Higher Education.

32. Merriman, K. 2006. "Employers Warm up to Online Education. Online Degree Programs Offer Flexibility and Cost Advantages that are Becoming Increasingly Popular," Society for Human Resource Management, January 2006.

CHAPTER FOUR

1. Haplin. J., and L. Collier (2015). Effective Instructional Tools for an Evolving Learning Landscape. Center for Digital Education

2. Fishman, T. D., L. Allan, and J. Tutak, 2017. Success by design: Improving outcomes in American higher education. Retrieved 05/02/2018 from https://www2.deloitte.com

3. Ibid.

4. http://www.columbia.edu. Retrieved March 30, 2008.

CHAPTER FIVE

1. F. Saba, "Critical Issues in Distance Education: A Report from the United States Distance Education," Vol. 26, N2, August 2005, 255-272.
2. B.L. Watkins, "A Quite Radical Idea: The Invention and Elaboration of Collegiate Correspondence Study," The Foundations of American Distance Education: A Century of Collegiate Correspondence Study, eds. B.L. Watkins and S.J. Wright (Dubuque, IA: Kendall/Hunt, 1991).
3. B. Nasseh, "Are Higher Education Institutions Ready for Asynchronous Education in the 21st Century?" (1999) [Course web page]. Retrieved July 21, 2011, from www.bsu.edu/classes/nasseh/study/ready.html.
4. M.G. Moore, "From Chautauqua to the Virtual University: A Century of Distance Education in the United States," (2003), Eric Clearinghouse on Adult, Career, and Vocational Education, Columbus, OH. Retrieved February 15, 2011.
5. B. Nasseh, "A Brief History of Distance Education" (1997) Retrieved from http://www.seniornet.org/edu/art/history.html on July 30, 2011.
6. P. Copeland, "The Cavis Systems," Industrial and Commercial Training 1982
7. F. Saba, "Critical Issues in Distance Education: A Report from the United States Distance Education," Vol. 26, N2, August 2005, pp. 255-272.
8. B. Mueller, "Online Education in the Corporate Context," Human Capital, October 2003.
9. E. Allen, and J. Seaman, "Learning on Demand: Online Education in the United States, 2009," The Sloan Consortium, 2010. Retrieved June 25, 2011, from http://sloanconsortium.org/publications/survey/index.asp.

10. Wise, B (2010). The online learning imperative: A solution to three looming crises in education. Education Digest Prakken Publications at www.eddigest.com

11. S. S. Adkins, 2016. The 2016-2021 Worldwide Self-paced eLearning Market: The Global eLearning Market is in Steep Decline. Ambient Insight. Retrieved 04/12/2019 from http://www.ambientinsight.com

12. D. Stalling, "The Virtual University: Organizing to Survive in the Twenty-First Century," The Journal of Academic Librarianship, Vol. 27, No. 1, 3-14.

13. J. G. Flores (2009). Distance Learning: Enabling the Race to the Top. (USDLA). Retrieved 04/23/2017 from https://www.usdla.org

14. British Council (2012). Going Global 2012: The shape of things to come: higher education global trends and emerging opportunities to 2020. Retrieved 07/20/2018 from www.britishcouncil.org/higher-education

15. Philip G. Altbach Liz Reisberg Laura E. Rumbley (2009). Trends in Global Higher Education: Tracking an Academic Revolution. A Report Prepared for the UNESCO 2009 World Conference on Higher Education

16. Ibid.

17. Rij, V., and B. Warrington, 2011. Teaching and Learning for an ICT revolutionized society, EC – FAR Horizon project. Manchester: University of Manchester, 2011.

18. L. Lazar (November 5, 2013) Meeting the Global Demand for Higher Ed Originally published by The Chicago Council on Global Affairs

19. Altbatch, P. H., Reisberg, L., Rumbley, L. E. (2009). Trends in Global Higher Education: Tracking an Academic Revolution. UNESCO 2009 World Conference on Higher Education.

20. ICEF. Information Retrieved 06/09/2016 from http://monitor.icef.com/2013/07/a-closer-look-at-african-student-mobility/ www.uis.unesco.org/Education

21. ICEF Monitor (8 Jan 2020). Africa ascending: Four growth markets to watch. Retrieved 01/13/2020 from https://monitor.icef.com

22. V. Stewart, "Education Goes Digital and Global," Kappanmagizine. org, 2010/2011, Retrieved December 15, 2010.

23. J. G. Flores (2009). Distance Learning: Enabling the Race to the Top. (USDLA). Retrieved 04/23/2017 from https://www.usdla.org

24. The Economics of Higher Education a Report Prepared by the Department of the Treasury with the Department of Education December 2012

25. F. Saba, "Critical Issues in Distance Education: A Report from the United States Distance Education," Vol. 26, N2, August 2005, pp. 255-272.

26. Patterson-Lorenzetti, "Lessons Learned about Student Issues in Online Learning," Distance Education Report, March 15, 2005

27. Council on Higher Education. A Report Prepared for the UNESCO 2009 World Conference on Higher Education. Retrieved 04/13/2017 from www.che.ac.za/sites/default/files/publications/

28. British Council (2012). The shape of things to come: higher education global trends and emerging opportunities to 2020 www.britishcouncil.org/higher-education

29. S. S. Adkins, 2013. The Worldwide Market for Self-paced eLearning Products and Services: 2011-2016. Retrieved 09/04/2019 from http://www.ambientinsight.com

30. V. Stewart, "Education Goes Digital and Global," Kappanmagizine. org, 2010/2011, Retrieved December 15, 2010

31. Ibid.

32. V. Stewart, "Education Goes Digital and Global," Kappanmagizine. org, 2010/2011, Retrieved December 15, 2010

33. Altbach, Reisberg, and Rumbley (2009) Trends in Global Higher Education: Tracking an Academic Revolution. UNESCO 2009 World Conference on Higher Education.

34. ICEF Monitor (28 June 2012), "8 countries leading the way in online education," Retrieved November 3, 2012, from http://monitor.icef. com.

35. Flores, J. G (2009). Distance Learning: Enabling the Race to the Top (USDLA)

36. D. Stalling, "The Virtual University: Organizing to Survive in the Twenty-First Century," The Journal of Academic Librarianship, Vol. 27, No. 1, 3-14.

37. Philip G. Altbach Liz Reisberg Laura E. Rumbley (2009). Trends in Global Higher Education: Tracking an Academic Revolution. UNESCO 2009 World Conference on Higher Education

38. Ibid.

39. F. Saba, "Critical Issues in Distance Education: A Report from the United States Distance Education," Vol. 26, N2, August 2005, pp. 255-272.

40. Wise, B (2010). The online learning imperative: A solution to three looming crises in education. Education Digest Prakken Publications. Retrieved 06/20/2016 from www.eddigest.com

41. Sam, S Adkins (August 2016). The 2016-2021 Worldwide Self-paced eLearning Market: The Global eLearning Market is in Steep Decline. Ambient Insight. Retrieved 7/02/2019 from http://www.ambientinsight.com

42. Belkin, Douglas (2014). Big Issues in Technology (A Special Report) --- What Role Will Large Online Courses Play in the Future of Higher Education? Three experts debate whether MOOCs will create two separate but unequal college experiences. The Wall Street Journal, Eastern edition; New York, N.Y. [New York, N.Y]12 May 2014: R.3

43. The Economics of Higher Education (December 2012): A Report Prepared by the Department of the Treasury with the Department of Education. Based on data from IPEDS and the Delta Cost Project.

44. J. Anderson, J. L. Boyles, and L. Rainie, "The future of higher education," http://pewinternet.org/Reports/2012/Future-of HigherEducation/Overview.aspx#footnote5. Information retrieved 05 December 2012.

45. Poulin, R., and Straut, T. (2016). WCET Distance Education Enrollment Report 2016. Retrieved 9/4/2018 from http://wcet.wiche.edu

46. S. S. Adkins, 2013. The Worldwide Market for Self-paced eLearning Products and Services: 2011-2016. Retrieved 09/04/2019 from http://www.ambientinsight.com

47. Philip G. Altbach Liz Reisberg Laura E. Rumbley (2009). Trends in Global Higher Education: Tracking an Academic Revolution. UNESCO 2009 World Conference on Higher Education.

48. Department of Education and Science (2008). ICT in School. Evaluation Support and Research Unit. Promoting the Quality of Learning. Retrieved 12/09/2018 from https://www.education.ie/en

49. Stewart, "Education Goes Digital and Global," Kappanmagizine .org, 2010/2011. Retrieved December 15, 2010.

50. Flores, J. G (2009). Distance Learning: Enabling the Race to the Top (USDLA)

51. S. S. Adkins, 2013. The Worldwide Market for Self-paced eLearning Products and Services: 2011-2016. Retrieved 09/04/2019 from http://www.ambientinsight.com

52. N. Confessore, "The Virtual University. The New Republic. October 28, 1999.

53. http://www.oraclefoundation.org. Retrieved March 3, 2012

54. http://www.vu.edu.pk. Retrieved March 7, 2010.

55. Ibid.

56. D. Stalling, "The Virtual University: Organizing to Survive in the Twenty-First Century," The Journal of Academic Librarianship, Vol. 27, No. 1, 3-14.

57. Alfred P. Sloan Foundation. Anytime, Anyplace Learning. https:// sloan.org/programs/completed-programs/anytime-anyplace-learning

58. Haplin. J., and L. Collier (2015). Effective Instructional Tools for an Evolving Learning Landscape. Center for Digital Education

59. J.S. Eaton, "Distance Learning: Academic and Political Challenges for Higher Education Accreditation," Council for Higher Education Accreditation, 2001, No. 1.

60. D. Tiene, D. "Addressing the Global Digital Divide and Its Impact on Educational Opportunity," Educational Media International, 2002.

61. J.S. Eaton, "Distance Learning: Academic and Political Challenges for Higher Education Accreditation," Council for Higher Education Accreditation, 2001. No. 1.

62. Poulin, R., and Straut, T. (2016). WCET Distance Education Enrollment Report 2016. Retrieved 9/4/2018 from http://wcet.wiche.edu

63. I. Elaine Allen and Jeff Seaman with Russell Poulin and Terri Taylor Straut (2016). 2015 Online Report Card - Tracking Online Education in the United States. Babson Survey Research Group. Retrieved 04/27/2018 from https://onlinelearningconsortium.org

64. Kristen Betts (2017). The growth of online learning: How universities must adjust to the new norm. https://www.educationdive.com/news/the-growth-of-online-learning-how-universities-must-adjust-to-the-new-norm/433632/

65. I. Elaine Allen and Jeff Seaman (2017). Digital Learning Compass: Distance Education Report 2017. Babson Survey Research Group, e-Literate, and WCET

66. I. Elaine Allen and Jeff Seaman with Russell Poulin and Terri Taylor Straut (2016). 2015 Online Report Card - Tracking Online Education in the United States. Babson Survey Research Group. Retrieved 04/27/2018 from https://onlinelearningconsortium.org

67. E. Allen, and J. Seaman, Class Differences: Online Education in the United States, 2010. The Sloan Consortium. Retrieved June 21, 2011, from http://sloanconsortium.org/publications/survey/index.asp.

68. K. Merriman, "Employers Warm Up to Online Education. Online Degree Programs Offer Flexibility and Cost Advantages that are Becoming Increasingly Popular," Society for Human Resource Management, January 2006.

69. Allen, E., and Seaman, J. (2014). Grade Change: Tracking Online Education in the United States. The Sloan Consortium. Retrieved 01/20/2016 from http://sloanconsortium.org/publications/survey/index.asp

70. Ibid.

71. F. Saba, "Critical Issues in Distance Education: A Report from the United States Distance Education," 26(2), August 2005, 255-272.

72. I.E., Allen, J. Seaman, and R. Garrett. "Blending In: The Extent and Promise of Education in the United States," Sloan Consortium, 2007.

73. Poulin, R., and Straut, T. (2016). WCET Distance Education Enrollment Report 2016. Retrieved 9/4/2018 from http://wcet.wiche.edu

74. Saba, F., 2005. Critical issues in Distance Education: A Report from the United States Distance Education. Vol. 26, N2, August 2005, pp. 255-272

75. e-Learning News, July 22, 2003.

76. Miller, L. (2012). State of the Industry Report: Organizations Continue to Invest in Workplace Learning (ASTD 2012). http://www.astd.org

77. F. Saba, "Critical Issues in Distance Education: A Report from the United States Distance Education," Vol. 26, N2, August 2005, 255-272.

78. J. G. Flores (2009). Distance Learning: Enabling the Race to the Top. (USDLA). Retrieved 04/23/2017 from https://www.usdla.org

79. F. Saba, "Critical Issues in Distance Education: A Report from the United States Distance Education," Vol. 26, N2, August 2005, 255-272.

80. J. G. Flores (2009). Distance Learning: Enabling the Race to the Top. (USDLA). Retrieved 04/23/2017 from https://www.usdla.org

81. Gilmore, G.J., 2003. Distance Learning Technology Brings Instructors to Students. American Forces Press, March 13, 2003.

82. http://www.elearners.com. Retrieved February 20, 2008.

83. http://www.embanet.com/corpsuccess2. Retrieved July 30, 2008.

84. M. Allen, The Corporate University Handbook: Designing, Managing, and Growing a Successful Program (New York: AMACOM, 2002).

CHAPTER SIX

1. John Haplin and Lorna Collier (2015). Effective Instructional Tools for an Evolving Learning Landscape. Center for Digital Education

2. University of Oxford (2015). International Trends in Higher Education, 2015. Retrieved 12/18/2017 from https://www.ox.ac.ukpdf

3. Ibid.

4. http://www.degree.net/schools/100schools.html. Retrieved November 29, 2012

5. David Ferrer (2018). Current Trends in Online Education. Retrieved 4/5/2019 from https://thebestschools.org

6. GetEducated.com (2018). Campus Residency May Improve Online Student Retention and Satisfaction. Retrieved 03/11/2019 from https://www.geteducated.com/onlineresidency

7. Walden University. Retrieved 11/30/2013 from www.waldenu.edu.

8. http://www.degree.net/schools/100schools.html. Retrieved November 29, 2012.

9. GetEducated.com (2018). Campus Residency May Improve Online Student Retention and Satisfaction. Retrieved 03/11/2019 from https://www.geteducated.com/onlineresidency

10. GetEducated.com (2018). Creating an Online or Virtual Campus Community. Retrieved 03/11/2019 from https://www.geteducated.com/onlineresidency

11. Carey, K (2015). The End of College. Creating the Future of Learning and the University of Everywhere. Riverhead Books. N.Y New York

12. Hollands, F. M., and Tirthali, D (2014). MOOCs: Expectations and Reality (Full Report) Center for Benefit-Cost Studies of Education Teachers College, Columbia University.

13. Allen, I. E & Seaman, J. (2014). Grade Change: Tracking Online Education in the United States. Babson Survey Research Group and Quahog Research Group, LLC.

14. Ibid.

15. Hollands, F. M., and Tirthali, D (2014). MOOCs: Expectations and Reality. Center for Benefit-Cost Studies of Education Teachers College, Columbia University.

16. Farr, C., 2013. Online education gets legit: California bill would give college credit. Retrieved 04/09/2019 from https://venturebeat.com

17. Zhu, A., 2012. Massive Open Online Courses: A Threat or Opportunity to Universities? Information retrieved 01/08/2019 from https://www.forbes.com

18. Hollands, F. M., and Tirthali, D (2014). MOOCs: Expectations and Reality. Center for Benefit-Cost Studies of Education Teachers College, Columbia University.

19. Carl Straumsheim (July 26, 2017). MIT Deems MicroMasters a Success. https://www.insidehighered.com/news/2017/07/26/

20. Kamenetz, A. 2013. Exporting Education. Online courses are taking off in developing countries, but there's a major downside. Retrieved 08/20/2018 from https://slate.com/technology

21. College Board (2019). Trends in Higher Education. Retrieved 07/20/2019 from https://trends.collegeboard.org

22. OECD (2014). Education at a Glance 2014: OECD Indicators. OECD Publishing. Retrieved 05/20/2018 from http://www.oecd.org

23. I. Elaine Allen and Jeff Seaman, 2016. Online Report Card. Tracking Online Education in the United States. Babson Survey Research Group and Quahog Research Group, LLC.

24. Wesleyan University. Retrieved 02/20/2016 from http://www.wesleyan.edu/academics/online/index.html

25. Joshua Bolkan (09/05/13). University System of Georgia To Launch For-Credit MOOC Program. Retrieved from https://campustechnology.com

26. USG Begins Next-Generation MOOC Initiative. (Atlanta — September 17, 2013). Press Release. Retrieved 09/20/2018 from https://www.usg.edu

27. Farr, C., 2013. Coursera partners with state universities to bring online education to millions. Retrieved 06/18/2018 from https://venturebeat.com

28. USG Begins Next-Generation MOOC Initiative University System of Georgia Atlanta— September 17, 2013. Retrieved 11/09/2017 from http://www.usg.edu/news

29. Maderer, J., 2013. Georgia Tech Announces Massive Online Master's Degree in Computer Science. Retrieved 12/05/2017 from http://www.news.gatech.edu

30. Lewin, T., 2013. Master's Degree Is New Frontier of Study Online. Retrieved 12/04/2018 from https://www.nytimes.com.

31. Global Freshman Academy (2019). Global Freshman Academy is now Earned Admission. Retrieved 01/07/2019 from https://gfa.asu.edu/

32. Deakin University (2017). 2016 Annual Report. Retrieved 2/25/2018 from https://www.deakin.edu.au

33. Retrieved 2/25/2019 from www.xuetangx.com/

34. Retrieved 2/25/2019 from www.xuetangx.com/

35. Nikhil, S. 2018. 6 New Degrees Coming to Coursera in Computer Science, Data Science, and Public Health. Retrieved 1/1/2019 from https://blog.coursera.org

36. Hollands, F. M., and Tirthali, D (2014). MOOCs: Expectations and Reality. Center for Benefit-Cost Studies of Education Teachers College, Columbia University

37. Anya Kamenetz (2013). Exporting Education. Online courses are taking off in developing countries, but there's a major downside. Retrieved 8/25/2018 from https://slate.com/technology

38. Hollands, F. M., and Tirthali, D (2014). MOOCs: Expectations and Reality. Center for Benefit-Cost Studies of Education Teachers College, Columbia University

39. Ibid.

40. Transifex. Making Education Available Anytime, Anywhere Across Language Barriers. https://www.transifex.com/blog/2013/transifex-coursera-partnership/

41. https://www.coursera.org/about/partners

42. John Haplin and Lorna Collier (2015). Effective Instructional Tools for an Evolving Learning Landscape. Center for Digital Education www.centerdigitaled.com

43. Friedman, Linda Weiser; Friedman, Hershey H. (2013). Using Social Media Technologies to Enhance Online Learning. Journal of Educators Online, v10 n1 Jan 2013.

44. HigherEducation.com and BestColleges.com (2016). 2016 Online Education Trends: Tracking the Innovations and Issues Changing Higher Education

45. Ibid.

46. Retrieved 04/09/2019 from https://about.twitter.com/company

47. Shaban, H., 2019. Twitter reveals its daily active user numbers for the first time. Retrieved 04/09/2019 from https://www.washingtonpost.com/technology

48. Retrieved 03/09/2019 from https://newsroom.fb.com/company-info/

49. Retrieved 03/09/2019 from https://press.linkedin.com

50. Retrieved 03/09/2018 from https://www.lynda.com/

51. Retrieved 03/14/2019 from https://www.youtube.com/channel

52. S.E. Harvey, "Online Videos Invade the Classroom," Retrieved March 28, 2012, from http://www.forbes.com/sites/techonomy/2012/04/23.

53. HigherEducation.com and BestColleges.com (2016). 2016 Online Education Trends: Tracking the Innovations and Issues Changing Higher Education

54. John Haplin and Lorna Collier (2015). Effective Instructional Tools for an Evolving Learning Landscape. Center for Digital Education www.centerdigitaled.com

55. HigherEducation.com and BestColleges.com (2016). 2016 Online Education Trends: Tracking the Innovations and Issues Changing Higher Education

56. Sures, T., 2015. Connecting universities: Future models of higher education. Retrieved 03/14/2019 from https://www.britishcouncil.org

57. Huang, W. & Soman, D. (2013). A Practitioner's Guide to Gamification of Education. (Report, February 2014). Rotman School of Management, University of Toronto

58. Sauvé, L., Renaud, L., Kaufman, D., & Marquis, J. S. (2007). Distinguishing between games and simulations: A systematic review. Educational Technology & Society, 10 (3), 247-256

59. Huang, W. & Soman, D. (2013). A Practitioner's Guide to Gamification of Education. (Report, February 2014). Rotman School of Management, University of Toronto

60. Adkins, S. S., 2016. The 2016-2021 Worldwide Self-paced eLearning Market: The Global eLearning Market is in Steep Decline. Retrieved 03/09/2018 from http://www.ambientinsight.com.

61. John Haplin and Lorna Collier (2015). Effective Instructional Tools for an Evolving Learning Landscape. Center for Digital Education www.centerdigitaled.com

62. Kapp, Karl M. (2012). The Gamification of Learning and Instruction: Game-based Methods and Strategies for Training and Education (p. 11)

63. Sauvé, L., Renaud, L., Kaufman, D., and Marquis, J. S. (2007). Distinguishing between games and simulations: A systematic review. Educational Technology & Society, 10 (3), 247-256

64. Huang, W. & Soman, D. (2013). A Practitioner's Guide to Gamification of Education. (Report, February 2014). Rotman School of Management, University of Toronto

65. Ibid.

66. Ibid.

67. Ibid.

68. John Haplin and Lorna Collier (2015). Effective Instructional Tools for an Evolving Learning Landscape. Center for Digital Education www.centerdigitaled.com

69. Huang, W. & Soman, D. (2013). A Practitioner's Guide to Gamification of Education. (Report, February 2014). Rotman School of Management, University of Toronto

70. Adkins, S. S., 2016. The 2016-2021 Worldwide Self-paced eLearning Market: The Global eLearning Market is in Steep Decline. Retrieved 03/09/2018 from http://www.ambientinsight.com

71. Bates, C., 2009. Scaling new heights: Piano stairway encourages commuters to ditch the escalators. Retrieved from Daily Mail Online: Retrieved 5/10/2017 from http://www.dailymail.co.uk/sciencetech

72. Huang, W. & Soman, D. (2013). A Practitioner's Guide to Gamification of Education. (Report, February 2014). Rotman School of Management, University of Toronto.

73. Robb, D. (2012). Let the games begin. HR Magazine, 57(9), 93-94,96-97. Retrieved 7/8/2018 from http://search.proquest.com/docview/1039492375?ac-countid=14771.

74. Levitz, J., 2010. UPS Thinks Out of the Box on Driver Training. Wall Street Journal. April 6, 2010. Retrieved from www.wsj.com

75. Sauvé, L., Renaud, L., Kaufman, D., & Marquis, J. S. (2007). Distinguishing between games and simulations: A systematic review. *Educational Technology and Society*, 10 (3), 247-256.

76. Prabhat, S. (2017). Difference Between Games and Simulations. Retrieved 4/11/2019 from http://www.differencebetween.net

77. HigherEducation.com and BestColleges.com (2016). 2016 Online Education Trends: Tracking the Innovations and Issues Changing Higher Education.

78. Ibid.

79. Harvard Business Publishing Simulations. Retrieved 02/07/2019 from https://cb.hbsp.harvard.edu/cbmp/pages/content/simulations

80. HigherEducation.com and BestColleges.com (2016). 2016 Online Education Trends. Tracking the Innovations and Issues Changing Higher Education.

81. Personal Communication, (March 8, 2010). Introducing Wiley's "Business Unusual" Facebook stock market simulation. Wiley Higher Education.

82. Sauvé, L., Renaud, L., Kaufman, D., & Marquis, J. S. (2007). Distinguishing between games and simulations: A systematic review. *Educational Technology and Society*, 10 (3), 247-256

83. Great Schools Partnership. Retrieved 09/20/2018 from http://edglossary.org/personalized-learning

84. Ibid.

85. Ibid.

86. John Haplin and Lorna Collier (2015). Effective Instructional Tools for an Evolving Learning Landscape. Center for Digital Education www.centerdigitaled.com

87. Flores, J. G (2009). Distance Learning: Enabling the Race to the Top. (USDLA)

88. HigherEducation.com and BestColleges.com (2016). 2016 Online Education Trends. Tracking the Innovations and Issues Changing Higher Education

89. Great Schools Partnership. Retrieved 09/20/2018 from http://edglossary.org/personalized-learning

90. Tiffany Dovey Fishman, Allan Ludgate, Jen Tutak (March 16, 2017). Success by design: Improving outcomes in American higher education. Retrieved 05/02/2018 from https://www2.deloitte.com

91. Nedungadi, P. & Raman, R (2012). A new approach to personalization: integrating e-learning and m-learning. Association for Educational Communications and Technology

92. HigherEducation.com and BestColleges.com (2016). 2016 Online Education Trends. Tracking the Innovations and Issues Changing Higher Education.

93. Danilova, M., 2017. Can Computer Programs Help Students, Teachers? Retrieved 05/17/2018 from learningenglish.voanews.com

94. http://cardean.edu. Retrieved 30 July 2008.

95. Hart, M., 2015. Students Crave Immediate Feedback in the Classroom. Retrieved 09/20/2018 from https://campustechnology.com

96. Ibid.

97. Fishman, T. D., Ludgate, A., and J. Tutak. 2017. Success by design: Improving outcomes in American higher education. Retrieved 05/02/2018 from https://www2.deloitte.com

98. Ibid.

99. Nedungadi, P. & Raman, R (2012). A new approach to personalization: integrating e-learning and m-learning. Association for Educational Communications and Technology

100. HigherEducation.com and BestColleges.com (2016). 2016 Online Education Trends. Tracking the Innovations and Issues Changing Higher Education.

101. John Haplin and Lorna Collier (2015). Effective Instructional Tools for an Evolving Learning Landscape. Center for Digital Education www.centerdigitaled.com

102. Chee, K. N., Yahaya, N., Ibrahim, N. H., & Noor Hassan, M. (2017). Review of Mobile Learning Trends 2010-2015: A Meta-Analysis. *Educational Technology and Society*, 20 (2), 113–126

103. ABI Research, July 2011. All the Right Conditions for Mobile Learning. Retrieved 05/06/2019 from https://www.upsidelearning.com/custom/mobile-learning.asp

104. Monica Albertini & Monika Gehner (Geneva, 07 December 2018). Press Release. ITU releases 2018 global and regional ICT estimates. Retrieved 05/06/2019 from https://www.itu.int/en/mediacentre

105. Levene, J. & Seabury, H (2015). Evaluation of Mobile Learning: Current Research and Implications for Instructional Designer. Association for Educational Communications and Technology. November/December 2015, Volume 59, Number 6.

106. Nick Floro (October 2011) Mobile Learning: American Society for Training & Development. Retrieved 03/20/2018 from infoline. astd.org

107. Tara Coffin, Henry Lyle & Abigail Evan (2015) Report on the Use of Mobile Devices for Academic Purposes at the University of Washington. Retrieved 01/15/2020 from https://itconnect.uw.edu

108. John Haplin and Lorna Collier (2015). Effective Instructional Tools for an Evolving Learning Landscape. Center for Digital Education www.centerdigitaled.com

109. Chee, K. N., Yahaya, N., Ibrahim, N. H., & Noor Hassan, M. (2017). Review of Mobile Learning Trends 2010-2015: A Meta-Analysis. *Educational Technology and Society*, 20 (2), 113–126

110. Sures, T., 2015. Connecting universities: Future models of higher education. Retrieved 03/14/2019 from https://www.britishcouncil.org

111. Ibid.

112. Sures, T., 2015. Connecting universities: Future models of higher education. Retrieved 03/14/2019 from https://www.britishcouncil.org

113. Hasan Al Zahrani and Kumar Laxman (2016). A Critical Meta-Analysis of Mobile Learning Research in Higher Education. *The Journal of Technology Studies*

114. Ibid.

CHAPTER SEVEN

1. F. Saba, "Critical Issues in Distance Education: A Report from the United States Distance Education," Vol. 26, N2, August 2005, 255-272.

2. John Haplin and Lorna Collier (2015). Effective Instructional Tools for an Evolving Learning Landscape. Center for Digital Education

3. Advanced Distributed Learning. The Advanced Distributed Learning Initiative. Information retrieved 04/03/2019 from http://www.adlnet.gov/

4. Margaret Rouse (2005). Shareable Content Object Reference Model (SCORM). Information retrieved 01/09/2019 from https://searchmicroservices.techtarget.com/definition/Shareable -Content-Object-Reference-Model-SCORM

5. Advanced Distributed Learning. The Advanced Distributed Learning Initiative. Information retrieved 04/03/2019 from http://www.adlnet.gov/

6. Krystle Feathers (2012). The Purpose of an LMS in Quality Online Courses: A Writer's Guide. The Learning House, Inc.

7. Computer Hope (2019). https://www.computerhope.com/jargon/g/gui.htm

8. HigherEducation.com and BestColleges.com (2016). 2016 Online Education Trends: Tracking the Innovations and Issues Changing Higher Education

9. Ibid.

10. W.K. Grollman, and D. Cannon, "E-Learning a Better Chalkboard," *Financial Executive,* November 2003.

11. Robert Tomsho (Jan. 6, 2003). Columbia University to Close Fathom.com E-Learning Service. The Wall Street Journal. Information retrieved 01/09/2019 from https://www.wsj.com/articles/SB104188231770411424

12. F. Saba, "Critical Issues in Distance Education: A Report from the United States Distance Education," Vol. 26, N2, August 2005, 255-272.

13. Robert Tomsho (Jan. 6, 2003). Columbia University to Close Fathom.com E-Learning Service. The Wall Street Journal. Information retrieved 01/09/2019 from https://www.wsj.com/articles/SB104188231770411424

14. John Haplin and Lorna Collier (2015). Effective Instructional Tools for an Evolving Learning Landscape. Center for Digital Education

15. Krystle Feathers (2012). The Purpose of an LMS in Quality Online Courses: A Writer's Guide. The Learning House, Inc.

16. Ibid.

17. John Haplin and Lorna Collier (2015). Effective Instructional Tools for an Evolving Learning Landscape. Center for Digital Education

18. Ibid.

19. Victor van Rij (February 2015). 21st Century Higher Education: Quick Scan of Foresight and Forward Looks on Higher Education in the ICT Age. Information retrieved 4/2/2018 from https://www.researchgate.net/publication/282571437

20. Barbara Means Yukie Toyama Robert Murphy Marianne Bakia Karla Jone (September 2010). Evaluation of Evidence-Based Practices in Online Learning: A Meta-Analysis and Review of Online Learning Studies. U.S. Department of Education Office of Planning, Evaluation, and Policy Development Policy and Program Studies Service. Information retrieved 02/04/2018 from https://www2.ed.gov/rschstat/eval/tech/evidence-based-practices/finalreport.pdf

21. Victor van Rij (February 2015). 21st Century Higher Education: Quick Scan of Foresight and Forward Looks on Higher Education in the ICT Age. Discussion Paper.

22. R. Evans, "The Emerging Role of the Internet in Marketing Education: From Traditional Teaching to Technology-Based Education," Marketing Education Review, Vol. 11, No. 2 (2001).

CHAPTER EIGHT

1. Seaman, J. & Allen, E. I (2016). Online Report Card: Tracking Online Education in the United States. Babson Survey Research Group and Quahog Research Group, LLC. A Report Prepared for the UNESCO 2009 World Conference on Higher Education.

2. HigherEducation.com and BestColleges.com (2016). 2016 Online Education Trends: Tracking the Innovations and Issues Changing Higher Education

3. National Center for Education Statistics (2018). The Condition of Education. Retrieved 07/01/2019 from https://nces.ed.gov/programs/coe/pdf/coe_cha.pdf

4. Tiffany Dovey Fishman, Allan Ludgate, Jen Tutak (March 16, 2017). Success by design: Improving outcomes in American higher education. Retrieved 05/02/2018 from https://www2.deloitte.com/insights

5. Amy Laitinen (2012). Cracking the Credit Hour. New American Foundation

6. Caribbean Business, "The Benefits of Online Education," Thursday, October 26, 2006.

7. National Center for Education Statistics (May 2018). The Condition of Education. Retrieved 05/14/2019 from https://nces.ed.gov/programs/coe/indicator_cha.asp

8. I. Elaine Allen & Jeff Seaman (2017). Digital Learning Compass: Distance Education Report 2017. http://www.digitallearningcompass.org/download-report

9. http://online.northcarolina.edu/sitelist.php. Retrieved December 18, 2009

10. http://www.london.ac.uk/. Retrieved September 30, 2010

11. C. Trierweiler, and R. Rivera, "Is Online Higher Education Right for Corporate Learning?" *American Society of Training and Development.* September 2005.

12. F. Saba, "Critical Issues in Distance Education: A Report from the United States Distance Education," Vol. 26, N2, August 2005, 255-272.

13. H. Judge, "Ready for E-Learning," *Chartered Accountants Journal,* May 2005.

14. J. Anderson, J. L. Boyles, and L. Rainie, "The future of higher education." Retrieved 05 December 2012 from http://pewinternet.org

15. Caribbean Business, "The Benefits of Online Education," Thursday, October 26, 2006.

16. Goodman, J, Melkers, J, Pallais, A. (2016). Can Online Delivery Increase Access to Education? Retrieved 06/28/2019 from https://scholar.harvard.edu/files/pallais/files/online.pdf

17. Caribbean Business, "The Benefits of Online Education," Thursday, October 26, 2006.

18. Wise, B (2010). The online learning imperative: A solution to three looming crises in education. Education Digest Prakken Publications at www.eddigest.com

19. Flores, J. G (2009). Distance Learning: Enabling the Race to the Top (USDLA) (USDLA

20. A. Greenspan, "The Role of Education During Rapid Economic Change," Remarks by Chairman Alan Greenspan at Syracuse University, New York. Retrieved June 7, 2011, from http://www.federalreserve.gov/boarddocs/speeches/1997/19971203.htm.

21. F. Saba, "Critical Issues in Distance Education: A Report from the United States Distance Education," Vol. 26, N2, August 2005, 255-272. (USDLA)***

22. H.M. Hutchins, "Enhancing the Business Communication Course through WebCT," Business Communication Quarterly 64:3, September 2001

23. Jones, K.O and C.A. Kelly, 2003. Teaching Marketing Via the Internet. Lessons Learned and Challenges to Be Met. Marketing Education Review, Vol. 13, November 2003.

24. H.M. Hutchins, "Enhancing the Business Communication Course through WebCT," Business Communication Quarterly 64:3, September 2001

25. Ibid.

26. W.K. Grollman, and D. Cannon, "E-Learning a Better Chalkboard," Financial Executive, November 2003.

27. C.J. Blake, J. W. Gibson, and C. W. Blackwell, "What Do You Know about the Web," Supervision, Vol. 66, Issue 9, September 2005, 3-7.

28. B. Mueller, "Online Education in the Corporate Context," Human Capital, October 2003.

29. L. Doucette, "E-Learning: A New Classroom for Success," Foodservice Equipment and Supplies, July 2002 (www.fesmag.com).

30. R. Ancis, "Cultural Competency Training at a Distance: Challenges and Strategies," *Journal of Counseling and Development*, Spring 1998, Vol. 76.

31. H.H. Brower, "On Emulating Classroom Discussion in a Distance-Delivered OBHR Course: Creating an Online Learning Community," Academy of Management Learning and Education, 2003. Vol. 2, No. 1, 22-3

32. J. Leonard, and S. Guha, "Education at the Crossroads: Online Teaching and Your Perspectives on Distance Learning," Journal of Research on Technology in Education, Fall 2001, Vol. 34, No. 1.

33. Epignosis LLC. eLearning 101concepts, trends, applications. Retrieved 4/4/2019 from https://www.talentlms.com/elearning/

34. Haplin. J. and L. Collier (2015). Effective Instructional Tools for an Evolving Learning Landscape. Center for Digital Education

35. F. Saba, "Critical Issues in Distance Education: A Report from the United States Distance Education," Vol. 26, N2, August 2005, 255-272

36. P.J. Stokes, "Hidden in Plain Sight: Adult Learners Forge a new Tradition in Education." Retrieved April 10, 2009, from www.ed.gov/aus.

37. Flores, J. G (2009). Distance Learning: Enabling the Race to the Top. *USDLA*

38. Ibid.

39. Miller, L. (2012). State of the Industry Report: Organizations Continue to Invest in Workplace Learning. *ASTD*

40. ATD Releases 2016 State of the Industry Report (Thursday, December 8, 2016). Retrieved 4/5/2018 from https://www.td.org

41. Mueller, B., 2003. Online Education in the Corporate Context. Retrieved 9/3/2018 from https://www.chieflearningofficer.com

42. J.F. Milem, (nd), "The Educational Benefits of Diversity: Evidence from Multiple Sectors." Retrieved December 3, 2012, from http://wwwleland.stanford.edu

43. Flores, J. G (2009). Distance Learning: Enabling the Race to the Top. *USDLA*

44. F. Saba, "Critical Issues in Distance Education: A Report from the United States Distance Education," Vol. 26, N2, August 2005, 255-272. *USDLA*

45. Niall Sclater Alice Peasgood Joel Mullan (2016). Learning Analytics in Higher Education. A review of UK and international practice. jisc.ac.uk

46. Anne Boyer and Geoffray Bonnin (2016). Higher Education and the Revolution of Learning Analytics. International Council for Open and Distance Education. Retrieved July 22, 2019, from https://icde.memberclicks.net/assets

47. Hart Michael (November 2, 2015). Students Crave Immediate Feedback in the Classroom https://campustechnology.com/articles/2015/11/02/surveystudents-crave-immediate-feedback-in-the-classroom.aspx

48. Ibid.

CHAPTER NINE

1. Fleming, N., and Baume, D. (2006). Learning styles again: VARKing up the right tree! Educational Developments, 7(4), 4-7.

2. Mokhtar, A., Majid, S., & Foo, S. (2008). Information literacy education: Applications of mediated learning and multiple intelligences. Library & Information Science Research, 30(3), 195-206.

3. B. Silzer, and B. E. Dowell, Strategy-Driven Talent Management: A Leadership Imperative (Hoboken, NJ: Jossey-Bass, 2010).

4. Altbach, P. G., Reisberg, L., and L. E. Rumbley. 2009. Trends in Global Higher Education: Tracking an Academic Revolution. A Report Prepared for the UNESCO 2009 World Conference on Higher Education.

5. Haplin. J. and L. Collier (2015). Effective Instructional Tools for an Evolving Learning Landscape. Center for Digital Education

6. Allen, E. J. Seaman, 2016. Online Report Card: Tracking Online Education in the United States. Babson Survey Research Group and Quahog Research Group, LLC.

7. F. Saba, "Critical Issues in Distance Education: A Report from the United States Distance Education," Vol. 26, N2, August 2005, 255-272.

8. Allen, E. J. Seaman, 2016. Online Report Card: Tracking Online Education in the United States. Babson Survey Research Group and Quahog Research Group, LLC.

9. The Economist Intelligence Unit Limited, "The World at Your Desk: What Companies Should Look at When Considering E-Learning," EIU Business Europe, February 23, 2004.

10. K.O. Jones, and C. A. Kelly, "Teaching Marketing Via Internet: Lessons Learned and Challenges to Be Met," Marketing Education Review, Vol. 13, November 2003. 82.

11. Philip G. Altbach, Liz Reisberg, Laura E. Rumbley (2009). Trends in Global Higher Education: Tracking an Academic Revolution. A Report Prepared for the UNESCO 2009 World Conference on Higher Education.

12. Retrieved May 2, 2018, from http://www.census.gov/compendia/statab/2012/tables

13. Abdi Latif Dahir (December 11, 2018). Half the world is now connected to the internet-driven by a record number of Africans. Retrieved 01/23/2019 from https://qz.com/africa

14. D. Tiene, D. "Addressing the Global Digital Divide and Its Impact on Educational Opportunity," *Educational Media International*, 2002

15. Abdi Latif Dahir (December 11, 2018). Half the world is now connected to the internet-driven by a record number of Africans. Retrieved 01/23/2019 from https://qz.com/africa

16. Peter Lange, Henry Lancaster (July 2014) (9th Edition) 2014 Africa - Mobile Broadband Market. Retrieved 11/12/2016 from https://www.budde.com.au

17. Philip G. Altbach, Liz Reisberg, Laura E. Rumbley (2009). Trends in Global Higher Education: Tracking an Academic Revolution. A Report Prepared for the UNESCO 2009 World Conference on Higher Education.

18. R. Martinez, "Online Education: Designing for the Future in Appraiser Education," Appraisal Journal, Summer 2004.

19. www.elearners.com. Retrieved May 2, 2008.

20. Allen, E., and J. Seaman, 2016. Online Report Card: Tracking Online Education in the United States. Babson Survey Research Group and Quahog Research Group, LLC.

21. Lieberman, M., 2018. Blended Is Best. Retrieved 06/03/2019 from https://www.insidehighered.com

22. D. Hellriegel, and J. W. Slocum, Organizational Behavior (Mason, OH: Cengage Learning, 2011).

23. R. Ancis, "Cultural Competency Training at a Distance: Challenges and Strategies," *Journal of Counseling and Development*, Spring 1998, Vol. 76.

24. Philip G. Altbach, Liz Reisberg, Laura E. Rumbley (2009). Trends in Global Higher Education: Tracking an Academic Revolution. A Report Prepared for the UNESCO 2009 World Conference on Higher Education.

25. Kimani, M., 2008. Red Alert: Accreditation Scam Unearthed. Business Daily. Retrieved 06/09/2016 from http://www.bdafrica.com

26. www.elearners.com. Retrieved May 2, 2008.

27. Ibid.

28. Kimani, M., 2008. Red Alert: Accreditation Scam Unearthed. Business Daily. Retrieved 06/09/2016 from: http://www.bdafrica.com

29. www.elearners.com. Retrieved May 2, 2008.

30. HigherEducation.com and BestColleges.com (2016). 2016 Online Education Trends. Tracking the Innovations and Issues Changing Higher Education.

31. Philip G. Altbach, Liz Reisberg, Laura E. Rumbley (2009). Trends in Global Higher Education: Tracking an Academic Revolution. A Report Prepared for the UNESCO 2009 World Conference on Higher Education.

32. Ibid.

33. http://elearners.com. Retrieved 30 July 2008.

34. R. Martinez, "Online Education: Designing for the Future in Appraiser Education," *Appraisal Journal*, Summer 2004.

35. Maras, D., Flament, M.F., Murray, M., Buchholz, A., Henderson, K.A., Obeid, N., Goldfield G.S. (2015 April). Screen time is associated with depression and anxiety in Canadian youth. *Preventive Medicine*, Volume 73, pp. 133–138

36. Yanchun Zhang, Zhihui Li, Yan Gao, and Chenggang Zhang (2014). Effects of fetal microwave radiation exposure on offspring behavior in mice. *Journal of Radiation Research*. Retrieved 05/29/2019 from https://www.ncbi.nlm.nih.gov

37. Adams J., G. T. (2014 September). Effect of mobile telephones on sperm quality: A systematic review and meta-analysis. *Environment International*, Volume 70, pp. 106–112.

38. Yanchun Zhang, Zhihui Li, Yan Gao, and Chenggang Zhang (2014). Effects of fetal microwave radiation exposure on offspring behavior in mice. Journal of Radiation Research. Retrieved 05/29/2019 from https://www.ncbi.nlm.nih.gov

39. Henry Bodkin (2 May 2018). Mobile phone cancer warning as malignant brain tumors double. Retrieved 5/07/2019 from https://www.telegraph.co.uk

40. Adams, J., G. T., 2014. Effect of mobile telephones on sperm quality: A systematic review and meta-analysis. *Environment International*, Volume 70, pp. 106–112.

41. Brissenden, M. (Aug 30, 2016) AM - Australian Broadcasting Corporation; Sydney: Australian Broadcasting Corporation.

42. Identity Theft Resource Center (2016) Retrieved 03/15/2019 from https://www.cslawreport.com

43. Identity Theft Resource Center (2018). Data Breaches, the New Normal, and a call to action for industry. Retrieved 06/01/2019 from https://www.idtheftcenter.org

44. Zalaznic, M., 2013. Cyberattacks on the rise. Retrieved 01/14/2019 from www.universitybusiness.com.

45. Identity Theft Resource Center (2016) Retrieved 03/15/2019 from https://www.cslawreport.com

46. Lily Hay Newman (07.09.18). The Worst Cybersecurity Breaches of 2018 So Far. Retrieved 01/14/2019 from https://www.wired.com

47. Zalaznic, M., 2013. Cyberattacks on the rise. Retrieved 01/14/2019 from www.universitybusiness.com

48. Ibid.

49. Haplin. J. and L. Collier (2015). Effective Instructional Tools for an Evolving Learning Landscape. Center for Digital Education

50. I. Elaine Allen; Jeff Seaman (January 2014). Grade Change. Tracking Online Education in the United States. Babson Survey Research Group and Quahog Research Group, LLC. Retrieved 01/04/2019 from https://www.onlinelearningsurvey.com

51. Lieberman, M., 2018. Blended Is Best. Retrieved 06/03/2019 from https://www.insidehighered.com

52. Anderson M. S., 2008. Scientific inquiry: Maintaining the legitimacy of the research enterprise. Proceedings of the 4th International Barcelona Conference on Higher Education, Vol 1. Ethics and relevance of scientific knowledge: what knowledge for society? Global University Network for Innovation. Available: www.guni-rmies.net. Accessed 6 April 2011.

53. Bretag T, Walker R, Green M, Wallace M, East J, et al., 2010. Academic integrity standards: aligning policy and practice in Australian universities. Successful Priority Projects proposal to the Australian Learning and Teaching Council. From http://www.apfei.edu.au/altc-priority-project.html.

54. The University of Iowa. Plagiarism. Retrieved 06/03/2019 from https://clas.uiowa.edu

55. Tips to Avoid Plagiarism. Harvard University. Retrieved 01/14/2019 from https://www.extension.harvard.edu

CHAPTER TEN

1. Haplin. J. and L. Collier (2015). Effective Instructional Tools for an Evolving Learning Landscape. Center for Digital Education

2. M. Vivoda, "Distance Learning. The Online "Classroom" is a Convenient Way to Increase Knowledge," RDH, August 2005.

3. Haplin. J., and L. Collier (2015). Effective Instructional Tools for an Evolving Learning Landscape. Center for Digital Education

4. J.R. Evans, "The Emerging Role of the Internet in Marketing Education: From Traditional Teaching to Technology-Based Education," Marketing Education Review, Vol. 11, No. 2, 2001.

5. Ibid.

6. D. Tsichritzis, D "Reengineering the University," Communication of the ACM, Vol. 42, No. 6 June 1999.

7. R. Martinez, R. "Online Education: Designing for the Future in Appraiser Education," Appraisal Journal, Summer 2004.

8. L. Doucette, "E-Learning: A new Classroom for Success," Foodservice Equipment and Supplies, July 2002 (www.fesmag.com).

9. Rudy Hirschheim (2005). The Internet-Based Education Bandwagon: Look Before You Leap. Communications of the ACM July 2005/Vol. 48, No. 7

10. http://www.ion.illinois.edu/resources/tutorials/pedagogy/StudentProfile.asp. Retrieved June 15, 2008.

11. I.E., Allen, and J. S. Seaman, "Growing by Degrees. Online Education in the United States, 2005," Sloan Consortium, November 2005.

12. I.E., Allen, J. Seaman, and R. Garrett, 2007, "Blending In: The Extent and Promise of Blended Education in the United States," Sloan Consortium, 2007.

13. B. Mueller, "Online Education in the Corporate Context," Human Capital, October 2003.

14. Knowles, M.S. (1980). The Modern Practice of Adult Education: From Pedagogy to Andragogy (2nd cd.). New York: Cambridge Books.

15. B. Mueller, "Online Education in the Corporate Context," Human Capital, October 2003.

16. https://www.starbucks.com/careers/college-plan. Retrieved August 16, 2018.

17. E-learners. Accreditation from www.elearners.com. Retrieved July 10, 2011.

18. http://elearners.com. Retrieved 30 July 2008.

19. E-learners. Accreditation from www.elearners.com. Retrieved July 10, 2011.

CHAPTER ELEVEN

1. Haplin. J., and L. Collier (2015). Effective Instructional Tools for an Evolving Learning Landscape. Center for Digital Education

2. H.H. Brower, "On Emulating Classroom Discussion in a Distance-Delivered OBHR Course: Creating an Online Learning Community," Academy of Management Learning and Education, 2003. Vol. 2, No. 1, 22-36.

3. N. Mercer, The Guided Construction of Knowledge: Talk amongst Teachers and Learners Clevedon, UK: Multilingual Matters, 1995), 25.

4. Rudy Hirschheim (2005). The Internet-Based Education Bandwagon: Look Before You Leap. Communications of the ACM July 2005/Vol. 48, No. 7

5. M.G. Moore, and G. Kearsley, 2005. Distance Education: A Systems View, (Belmont, CA: Wadsworth. 2005), 33-36.
6. Ibid.

CHAPTER TWELVE

1. C. Hamilton-Pennell, "Getting Ahead by Getting Online," *Library Journal*, November 15, 2002.
2. W. K. Grollman, and D. Cannon, "E-Learning a Better Chalkboard," *Financial Executive,* November 2003.
3. Monica Albertini & Monika Gehner (Geneva, 07 December 2018). Press Release. ITU releases 2018 global and regional ICT estimates. From https://www.itu.int/en/mediacentre
4. W. K. Grollman, and D. Cannon, "E-Learning a Better Chalkboard," Financial Executive, November 2003.
5. E-Learning Market Trends & Forecast 2014 - 2016 Report A report by Docebo. March 2014.
6. Anthony Scarsella and William Stofega (2019). Worldwide Smartphone Forecast Update, 2019–2023. Retrieved 01/29/2020 from https://www.idc.com
7. http://www.apple.com/ipad/. Retrieved May 1, 2010.
8. C. Nemey, "Tablet Sales Expected to Grow Fivefold by 2017," from www.itworld.com/mobile-wireless. Retrieved January 31, 2012.
9. *USA Today*, "iPads Take Place Next to Crayons in Kindergarten," April 13, 2011, http://www.usatoday.com/tech/news/2011-04-13-ipads-kindergarten.htm. Retrieved September 19, 2011.
10. Ibid.
11. Ibid.
12. John Haplin and Lorna Collier (2015). Effective Instructional Tools for an Evolving Learning Landscape. Center for Digital Education.
13. http://jmc.stanford.edu/artificial-intelligence/what-is-ai/index.html. Retrieved 02/05/2019
14. J. Anderson, L.Rainie, and A. Luchsinger. 2018. Artificial Intelligence and the Future of Humans. Retrieved 01/05/2019 from http://www.pewinternet.org

15. IBM (2018). IBM Watson Education. Retrieved 00/20/2019 from https://www.ibm.com/watson/education

16. Miller, K. (2015). Disruption, Innovation, and Change: The Future of the Legal Profession. Law Institute Victoria. From https://www.liv.asn.aue

17. John Haplin and Lorna Collier (2015). Effective Instructional Tools for an Evolving Learning Landscape. Center for Digital Education.

18. B. Unglesbee. 2019. Higher ed Trends to Watch in 2019. Received 07/20/2019 from https://www.educationdive.com

19. John Haplin and Lorna Collier (2015). Effective Instructional Tools for an Evolving Learning Landscape. Center for Digital Education.

20. Ibid.

21. W.W. Conhaim, "Education ain't what it used to be," Information Today, 2003

22. Altbach. P. G., Reisberg, L. & Rumbley, L. E (2009). Trends in Global Higher Education: Tracking an Academic Revolution. A Report Prepared for the UNESCO 2009 World Conference on Higher Education

23. British Council (2016). The Scale and Scope of UK Higher Education Transnational Education. Retrieved 06/22/2019 from https://www.britishcouncil.org

24. Altbach. P. G., Reisberg, L. & Rumbley, L. E (2009). Trends in Global Higher Education: Tracking an Academic Revolution. A Report Prepared for the UNESCO 2009 World Conference on Higher Education.

25. ICEF Monitor (11 Dec 2019). Africa ascending: The demographic juggernaut driving student mobility in the 21st century. https://monitor.icef.com

26. British Council (2012). Going Global 2012. The shape of things to come: higher education global trends and emerging opportunities to 2020. Retrieved 06/21/2019 from http://www.britishcouncil.org/ihe/educationintelligence

27. Ibid.

28. ICEF Monitor (23 Dec 2015). Goal-oriented: International enrolment targets around the world. Retrieved 01/13/2020 from https://monitor.icef.com/

29. British Council (2012). Going Global 2012. The shape of things to come: higher education global trends and emerging opportunities to 2020. Retrieved 06/21/2019 from http://www.britishcouncil.org/ihe/educationintelligence

30. Ibid.

31. Ibid.

32. Elaine Allen, Jeff Seaman, (2016) Online Report Card: Tracking Online Education in the United States. Babson Survey Research Group and Quahog Research Group, LLC.

33. Poulin, R. and Straut, T. (2016). WCET Distance Education Enrollment Report 2016. Retrieved from WICHE Cooperative for Educational Technologies website: http://wcet.wiche.edu

34. British Council (2012). Going Global 2012: The shape of things to come: higher education global trends and emerging opportunities to 2020. Retrieved 06/21/2019 from www.britishcouncil.org/higher-education.

35. Lange, P., and H. Lancaster. 2014. (9th Edition) 2014 Africa - Mobile Broadband Market. Retrieved 01/17/19 from https://www.budde.com.au

36. Altbach. P. G., Reisberg, L., and L.E. Rumbley, 2009. Trends in Global Higher Education: Tracking an Academic Revolution. A Report Prepared for the UNESCO 2009 World Conference on Higher Education.

37. Ibid.

38. HigherEducation.com and BestColleges.com (2016). 2016 Online Education Trends: Tracking the Innovations and Issues Changing Higher Education.

39. Laureate International Universities, "Walden University Partners with Hospitals and Healthcare Systems Nationwide" Retrieved January 26, 2012, from http://laureate.net/en/OurNetwork

40. http://cardean.edu. Retrieved 30 July 2008.

41. Laureate International Universities Network, April 2012, www. laureate.net. Retrieved April 28, 2012.

42. C. Trierweiler and R. Rivera, "Is Online Higher Education Right for Corporate Learning?" American Society of Training and Development, September 2005.

43. Fishman, T. D., L. Allan, and J. Tutak, 2017. Success by design: Improving outcomes in American higher education. Retrieved 05/02/19 from https://www2.deloitte.com

44. Ibid.

45. Ibid.

46. Flores, J. G., 2009. Distance Learning: Enabling the Race to the Top. *USDLA*

47. http://www.avu.org/avuweb/en. Retrieved December 2, 2018.

48. Ibid.

49. Flores, J. G., 2009. Distance Learning: Enabling the Race to the Top. *USDLA*

50. Eaton, J. S., 2001. Distance Learning. Academic and Political Challenges for Higher Education Accreditation. Council of Higher Education Accreditation, 2001.

51. British Council (2016). The Scale and Scope of UK Higher Education Transnational Education. Retrieved 06/22/2019 from https://www.britishcouncil.org

52. Ibid.

53. Ibid.

54. Ibid.

55. British Council (2012). The shape of things to come: higher education global trends and emerging opportunities to 2020. Retrieved 06/21/2019 from http://www.britishcouncil.org/ihe/educationintelligence

56. British Council (2016). The Scale and Scope of UK Higher Education Transnational Education. Retrieved 06/22/2019 from https://www.britishcouncil.org

57. British Council (2012). The shape of things to come: higher education global trends and emerging opportunities to 2020. Retrieved 06/21/2019 from http://www.britishcouncil.org/ihe/educationintelligence

INDEX

Note: Page numbers followed by *t* indicate tables and *f* indicate figures.

United States Department of
Justice (DOJ), 144
United States Distance Learning
Association (USDLA), 57
United States Military, 64
Unitel, 57
Universal Mobile
Telecommunications Service
(UMTS), 142, 143
Universidad Internacional de La
Rioja, Spain, 128–129
University Innovation Alliance
(UIA), 194
University of Colorado, Boulder, 84
University of Hawaii, 87
University of Illinois, 67
University of Iowa, 147
University of Kent, 69
University of Liverpool, 80, 198
University of London, 14, 69, 119
University of Montana, 195
University of North Carolina, 119
University of Nottingham, 198
University of Phoenix, 119, 161
University of Phoenix Online,
123–124
University of Texas, Austin, 194
University of Texas, El Paso
(UTEP), 195–196
University of Washington, Seattle, 92
University of Wisconsin, 14
University System of Georgia
(USG), 74
University System of Maryland, 50
Unix, 103

U.S. Department of Education, 31,
39, 56, 163
U.S. News, 32
User-activity reports, 109

V

Values, assumptions, beliefs, and
expectations (VABEs), 139
Van Hise, Charles, 14
Video content management system,
110
Video games, 81, 82, 83
Villanova University, 187
Virtual reality (VR), 3, 187–188
Visual learning, 133*t*
Volkswagen, 82

W

Wake Forest University, 168
Walden University, 69, 194
WallStreetSurvivor.com, 84
Walmart, 193
Wearable devices, 3
Web 2.0, 93
Web-based training (WBT), 63
WebCT, 100
Wesleyan University, 14, 74;
independent-study program, 44
Western Association of Schools
and Colleges (WASC), 72
Western Governors University
(WGU), 127, 194
Westminster University, 198
Wharton School, University of
Pennsylvania, 84

ABOUT THE AUTHOR

Bola Bayode earned a Ph.D. in Applied Management from Walden University, Master of Jurisprudence from Emory University School of Law, Master of Business Administration from Strayer University, and Bachelor of Science in Political Science from Ogun State University. He is president at Bright Education and an Adjunct Professor of Management and Employment Law at Montreat College. He previously served as Dean and Associate Program Dean at Strayer University and taught humanities at Axia College of the University of Phoenix. Before transitioning to academics, Dr. Bayode had over ten years of experience in the private sector that traversed telecommunications, retail business, and banking industries and delivered several career-oriented and leadership seminars for employees and managers at Verizon Communications, Inc.

Dr. Bayode belongs to several academic and professional organizations including but not limited to Association for Talent Development (ATD), Council of Adult & Experiential Learning (CAEL), Harvard Business Review, Higher Education Administration, Higher Education Management, Higher Education Teaching and Learning, Online College Executives & Professionals, Academic Executive Network, and the United States Distance Learning Association (USDLA). He is also a visiting professor at Crawford University in Nigeria.